Never

RICK ASTLEY

Never

THE AUTOBIOGRAPHY

MACMILLAN

First published 2024 by Macmillan
an imprint of Pan Macmillan
The Smithson, 6 Briset Street, London EC1M 5NR
EU representative: Macmillan Publishers Ireland Ltd, 1st Floor,
The Liffey Trust Centre, 117–126 Sheriff Street Upper,
Dublin 1, D01 YC43
Associated companies throughout the world
www.panmacmillan.com

ISBN 978-1-0350-4939-4 HB
ISBN 978-1-0350-4940-0 TPB

1 3 5 7 9 8 6 4 2

A CIP catalogue record for this book is available from the British Library.

Typeset by JCS Publishing Services Ltd
Printed by IVE

Visit **www.panmacmillan.com** to read more about all our books
and to buy them. You will also find features, author interviews and
news of any author events, and you can sign up for e-newsletters
so that you're always first to hear about our new releases.

This book is dedicated to Lene and Emilie.
Jeg elsker jer x

Jayne, John and Mike.
Love you x

Thank you to Alexis Petridis, my partner on
this book.
Never again . . . x

Contents

Preface

I've been asked to write an autobiography before, and I always said no. Why did I say yes this time?

I was wondering that this evening. It's a Thursday in July 2024 and I'm in a hotel in York, between two gigs. It's summer, which means festivals and outdoor shows. Last night I was at the Eden Project in Cornwall; tomorrow I'm in Scarborough; tonight I have a night off. I've just had dinner, and a glass of wine. Then I had a second glass of wine: two things I find it very difficult to say no to are nice wine – a Chilean Chardonnay or a buttery white Burgundy for preference – and good coffee. And I started thinking about this book. I said no in the past because I thought autobiographies were for Keith Richards or Elton John – people who've had careers that stretch back to the 1960s, people who've made hundreds of albums. I didn't think I'd done enough. So, what changed my mind?

I think it had something to do with Glastonbury. I was watching this year's festival on TV the other night. Coldplay were headlining, they were amazing, and I thought: *God, it gets no better than that.* Then I thought: *You played there, last year. You played Glastonbury. You. Rick Astley.*

You went to Glastonbury, you played a set on the Pyramid Stage, it went down really well, people said lovely things about you. Then you played again, the same day, doing Smiths songs with Blossoms. And instead of getting slated and destroyed and people tearing the tent down in disgust at some eighties pop star desecrating the catalogue of Morrissey and Marr, it went down a storm.

That's insane.

If you want evidence that people think of you differently from the way they once did, there it is: thousands of people were singing along to you covering 'There Is a Light That Never Goes Out' so loudly that you could barely hear your own voice. If someone had told you that would happen even three or four years ago, you would have laughed at them and told them to stop talking rubbish.

But it did happen. I'd somehow gone from being Rick Astley, manufactured pop star, a puppet of the evil empire of Stock Aitken Waterman, who people that liked The Smiths thought was a total twat, to Rick Astley, who had a No. 1 album on which he wrote and produced every song and played every instrument himself and who's welcomed at Glastonbury.

How? Well, it's quite complicated.

It involves a weird childhood and a time when I was one of the biggest artists in the world, and another time when I hated being a pop star so much that I gave it up entirely, and randomly meeting a girl who worked for a record company in Denmark and falling in love with her, and inadvertently becoming an internet sensation for reasons I don't entirely understand and ... actually, there is a unique story there, isn't there? I knew it would be good for me to tell it myself, and I realized it was the right time to do it.

It was harder work than I'd thought. I've had to delve quite deep and there are times when I've found it really upsetting. But it's also been a bit like therapy. You end up addressing things, reliving parts of your life, looking at yourself, putting stuff into context. You end up talking about things that you haven't really talked about before. It makes you conscious of trying to live better for however many years you've got left – because you revisit times when you could have been better, you could have done things differently.

And you see how much luck and chance is involved in your life and career. You can have drive and ambition and talent, but there's a huge amount of luck involved too: you know, someone wrote a three-and-a-half-minute pop song in 1987, and my life completely changed as a result of that. It's ridiculous, really.

But the main thing it's left me feeling is unbelievably grateful. When I think about what could have happened to me, what might have been, there's a massive feeling of thankfulness that I am where I am now, thirty-seven years after that song.

It's almost as if there are two Rick Astleys – the professional Rick Astley and the private Rick Astley, but they're both incredibly happy. The professional Rick Astley gets to play live in big venues and see the effect that his music has had on people over the years. He gets to make exactly the music that he wants to make – which definitely wasn't always the case – and moreover, people seem to like it. He got a second chance at fame, which is rare enough in itself. But, more than that, he got a second chance at fame *on his own terms*, which means it's completely different from his first burst of fame, which largely felt as if he was just doing what he was told to, whether he wanted to do it or not.

And the private Rick Astley has, by anyone's standards, a fantastic life. I've got an incredible, stable, loving family. I've been with my wife, Lene, for thirty-six years. Our daughter Emilie just got married, a couple of weeks back, to her partner, Paul, in a ceremony by a loch in Scotland, an hour and half outside of Glasgow. They live in Denmark, and they're happy in exactly the way you would wish your children to be happy. We live in a beautiful house. We have fantastic friends. We enjoy travel and good food and – as I've already mentioned – nice Chilean Chardonnays and posh white Burgundies.

The thing is, it really didn't have to turn out like that. In fact, I would say that the chances were stacked against it ever turning out like that.

As you'll see when you turn the page.

Introduction

It's not long after sunrise one morning in the early 1980s. I'm seventeen years old, and my older brother Mike and I are walking from the outskirts of Newton-le-Willows, where we live with my dad, to our gran's council house on Dixon Avenue, near the centre of town, where our mum has lived since the divorce. It's a route we must have taken hundreds of times in the years since my parents split up: past the Bull's Head pub, down Southworth Road through Naylor's Wood and up the High Street, then past another pub, the Blue Lion, where the band I'm in, FBI, sometimes plays.

But this morning is different.

We're trying to look as inconspicuous as possible, which is easier for me than it is for Mike. Mike is walking the couple of miles to my gran's in a pair of carpet slippers, carrying an eight-inch kitchen knife.

I can't really remember what we were talking about as we

walked, but presumably we must have touched on what we were going to say if anyone asked us, not unreasonably, why Mike was carrying an eight-inch knife through the centre of Newton first thing on a Wednesday morning.

I've no idea what excuse we came up with – walking around with a kitchen knife anywhere outside of a kitchen is a difficult thing to explain away at the best of times – but, clearly, we couldn't tell them the truth. Because Mike was walking through Newton with the knife that moments ago he'd held to my dad's throat and threatened to murder him with.

Life in the Astley household was rarely normal. For one thing, the Astley household didn't in fact live in a house; we lived in a Portakabin in the middle of a field, next to my dad's garden centre: it's a long story, which I'll come to in a bit. But even by our standards, it had been quite a morning.

I don't know what had started the argument with my dad, but it was almost definitely nothing. That was the thing about Dad's rages. You never knew what was going to set one off; there was no rhyme or reason to them at all. One morning he'd wake me and my brothers up with a cup of tea – 'Oh, it's cold outside, lads, you're going to need this' – the next, he'd wake us up by screaming at us, calling us lazy bastards, demanding to know why we weren't out of bed yet: nothing had changed in the interim except my dad's mood.

He wasn't a caricature horrible parent, always in a filthy mood. Dad could be generous, funny and encouraging. He wasn't a big drinker – the occasional nip of whisky in front of the telly at night, the odd night out with his mates at the Conservative Club in town – and even when he did drink, it seemed to put him in a good mood: you'd hear him before he arrived home, singing old Frank Sinatra songs. The kinds of things parents get angry about – bad school reports, stuff like that – didn't seem to bother him at all. Not long before, I'd inadvertently ripped the door off his brand-new van. I'd been helping him out at the garden centre, loading stuff into the back of it for a delivery, and reversed off with the passenger door still open, straight into a forklift truck: I think I was paying more attention to what was on the radio than what I was supposed to be doing. When he found out, I held my breath, waiting for the eruption, but it never came. Dad wasn't exactly overjoyed, but he was basically all right about it.

But then the explosion would come because he couldn't find the right drill bit he needed, or something daft like that. There would be shouting, stuff would go flying, things would get smashed until they were completely obliterated. It had been going on all my life. It was terrifying when I was young-er, but you sort of got used to it as you got older. We didn't ignore it exactly – it's hard to ignore someone who's smash-ing up a load of terracotta pots with a hammer because he can't find a part for his drill – but we just got out of his way and left him to it. It had almost become a joke between me and Mike and my eldest brother, John: 'Bloody hell, Dad's at it again.'

This morning, though, it wasn't a joke. He'd completely lost it. I was standing outside our front door when he came up to me, ranting and raving and screaming his head off about something I'd supposedly done. Then he pushed me over and started trying to kick me. The rages I was used to, but this was different. I'd seen him be violent towards my mum, once, years ago, but I'd never known him to hit any of his kids. Instead, he used to take his anger out on inanimate objects. Until now. Suddenly, I was on the floor, and he was trying to kick me. That was when Mike appeared from inside, with the knife in his hand.

I should say at this point that Mike was definitely not the kind of older brother that you would have expected to spring valiantly to your rescue. He was more the kind of older brother who seemed actively to enjoy tormenting his youngest sibling. When the Astley brothers went to the local airshow and got taken up in a plane as a special treat, Mike was the one who'd turn to me mid-flight and quietly announce the plane was definitely going to crash: 'I don't think the pilot knows what he's doing, Rick. I think he's turned the engine off. I think we're going to die.' It was also Mike who was responsible for my lifelong phobia of snakes. I'm terrified of them, to the extent that at one point, when we checked into a hotel room, my wife would go through any magazines that were there when we arrived, and tear out any pages that had photos of snakes before I saw them. It all started with Mike, terrorizing me with one of those jointed toy plastic snakes. He'd hide behind the bedroom door with it, waiting for me to come in.

And when I went to secondary school, Mike was the reason teachers always frowned when they heard my surname. 'You're not . . . Mike Astley's brother, are you?' When I said I was, they'd roll their eyes: *Oh God, there's another one.* In a way, I couldn't blame them. Mike had barely bothered going to secondary school at all. He'd get up every morning, put his snorkel parka on, go in for registration and then immediately leave. I suppose they had complained to my dad about it, but not turning up for school was also on the list of things that my dad wasn't particularly bothered about. Still, it seemed a bit much. I had barely started school, and my card was already marked. Great. Mike strikes again.

This morning was different. When Mike appeared with the knife, he somehow didn't even look like Mike. Mike was the classic surly, monosyllabic teenage boy. If they'd had hoodies in the early eighties, his would have been permanently up. But this morning, his eyes were dead, like a shark's. He looked like someone who'd finally had enough: of living in a Portakabin instead of a proper house, of my dad's rages, of all the stuff he'd quietly ignored or put up with. He walked straight up to my dad, put the knife to his throat and said, calmly but very clearly, 'If you fucking move, I will kill you, here and now. I will kill you stone dead, right now, if you move an inch.'

I got up off the ground and stared at them both. It suddenly felt as if the world had contracted, as if there was only the three of us in it. For a moment, I genuinely thought he was going to do it. It definitely wasn't beyond him. Mike wasn't a scrapper, but he was physically tough. We all were: that's what came of spending hours after school and at weekends working for my dad, lifting concrete posts and panels for fencing, loading the van, taking stuff out for delivery. And Mike had spent his teenage years giving the distinct impression that he didn't give a shit about anything, with the possible exception of his motorbike, and he even rode that in a way that suggested he didn't think much about the possible consequences of his actions. Plus, he had a knife and he looked like he'd snapped. *Shit. This is actually happening*, I thought. *He's going to murder our dad.*

The silence could only have been a few seconds, but it seemed to go on for ever. Then my dad spoke, breaking the spell. He was still boiling red, but he told us we should leave, which sounded like a better idea than any of the other possible outcomes. Mike lowered the knife. And we left. Mike didn't even put his shoes on. We just went.

We somehow managed to arrive at my gran's without anyone noticing us. When we told Mum what had happened, she didn't seem as shocked or horrified as you might expect. For one thing, Mum knew what my dad was like – she'd been married to him. And, for another, my mum was as weird as my dad was, in her own way. After the divorce, she did all the things a mum was supposed to do – we went to stay with her for the weekend and she took us out to the shops, bought us treats, even took us on holiday with her to Blackpool or wherever. But there was something missing, some sort of emotional connection. It's hard to explain exactly what it was, but you knew it wasn't there. It was as if she was behind a pane of glass or something, and it was noticeable even when I was a kid. My parents had split up when I was four, and I'd stopped going to stay with her at weekends years ago. Still, there was a spare room at my gran's that me and Mike could share, and she said we could stay there as long as we needed to.

That still left a question that I didn't have an answer for: what the hell do I do now? I was seventeen and, as far as I could see, I had no prospects. Living up to the stellar academic standards set by Mike, I'd left school without a single qualification. I didn't bother writing anything at all in any of my O-Level exams: I'd simply sat there eating Polo mints and staring into space until they said we could leave. There didn't seem to be any point, because my future was already mapped out. I was going to go and work for my dad at the garden centre, like Mike and John had done. But that was suddenly off the cards, so now what? I had no idea.

There was the band, FBI. I'd started out as the drummer and ended up as the singer. People said I had a good voice. We had management and were big locally, as they say: we could pack them in at the Blue Lion and the Legh Arms. But what did that mean? It wasn't as if London record labels were sending platoons of talent scouts out, with firm instructions not to come back until they'd found out what was big in Newton-le-Willows and signed it: *Get me that band with the lad from the garden centre on lead vocals, or don't bother coming to work on Monday.*

Even if they had, I wasn't sure that FBI was going to work. I'd started to sense the other members of the band weren't as committed as I was. It was me that wrote the songs, me that spent hours in front of the telly analysing and memorizing what the bands on *The Tube* were doing – everything from what instruments they used to how their songs were structured. It was me that drove the band to every gig (until a couple of the dads helped out), me that made sure they were out of bed at lunchtime to practise, me that insisted we didn't need a fag break every ten minutes at rehearsals, that our time might be better spent writing and learning material.

In fairness, I could see why they weren't as dedicated as I

was – none of them were living in a Portakabin in the middle of a garden centre with a certifiable nutcase who smashed things when he couldn't find the right drill bit. But it was still niggling at me. A few weeks back, I'd tried laying down the law to them. We were standing in the kitchen of our bass player Pep's house – his parents let us rehearse in a back room – on another bloody fag break. I'd suddenly announced that I was going to be as famous as David Bowie and that the rest of them could either come with me or sod off. I suppose the idea was to spur them into action, but it didn't work. They merely looked at me, like you might look at a teenager who worked in his dad's garden centre and had just announced he was going to be Newton-le-Willows' answer to David Bowie. I'd stormed out. I walked home to the garden centre feeling like a complete twat.

So where did that leave me? Not a clue. You try thinking straight when you've watched your brother threaten to murder your dad before you've even had breakfast. As far as I could gather, Mike's big idea for the future involved signing on the dole and waiting to see if anything came up. Perhaps I should join him. I didn't have any better plans.

Chapter One

The story about my dad was that he'd had a bump on his head when he was younger, and that he was never the same afterwards. I don't know whether that's true or not. I mean, I know that he did have a serious accident in his van when he was younger, because he talked about it. The brakes failed while he was driving down a hill, and he basically threw himself out of the van onto the road, which accounted for his lifelong refusal to wear a seatbelt: he always said that if he'd been wearing one that day, he would never have got out of the van alive. The family legend was that he hit his head on the road when he threw himself out and refused to have proper treatment. He took himself off to the hospital, and they wanted him to go for tests to a place called Winwick, but he wouldn't. Winwick was a mental health hospital – its original name was Lancashire County Asylum, and some people still believed there was a stigma around places like that. Certainly, my dad didn't like the idea of it at all. He apparently said, 'If I go in there, I'll never come out,' and that was that.

I suppose that could be true – it sounds like the kind of thing my dad would have said – but whether that accounts for his behaviour when I was a kid, the weird sudden changes of mood and the rages, I don't know.

But I do know that he never wanted to marry my mum. She was already pregnant with my elder sister Jayne, it was the 1950s, and it was a matter of doing the decent thing. It wasn't the best grounding for a marriage, and if they'd ever had a chance of happiness, that probably ended when my older brother David died. It happened in 1962, before I was born. He was their second child, between Jayne and my brother John. He was five when he got sick with what turned out to be meningitis. By all accounts, my dad blamed my mother for his death. I've no idea why, because no one ever spoke about David in our house. The first time I ever heard his name mentioned was when I saw an old picture in a photo album and asked Jayne who it was. The minute I asked, I knew I'd done something wrong, that this was some-thing that had happened that wasn't meant to be discussed. Maybe his death explained the way my mum was, the way she always felt slightly distant, even from her children: the shock of what happened to David, the fact that her husband blamed her for their son's death, could have caused some-thing in her to shut down.

Whatever the reason, by the time I arrived – in 1966, three years after my brother Mike – my parents' marriage was in real trouble. I don't have any memory of my mum and dad ever being affectionate towards each other. Quite the opposite. My vague recollections of the whole family being together involve a lot of shouting and things being thrown. Or worse. One of my earliest memories is of walking into the kitchen and seeing my dad physically attacking my mum. In my memory, he had her up against the work surface in the kitchen with his hands around her throat – I don't know for certain that's right, but I do distinctly remember running out of the kitchen in tears, really frightened.

My parents, Cynthia and Horace – although Dad hated the name Horace, so everyone called him Ozzy – had moved from Warrington to Newton-le-Willows before I was born. We lived on Park Road North. It was a big three-storey house, which meant Jayne and my older brothers could amuse themselves by hanging a wallet with a fiver in it on a piece of fishing line and lower it out of a top-floor window onto the street below; when a passer-by stopped to investigate, they'd suddenly yank it away.

The whole place was like a monument to my dad's skills as a handyman. He was the kind of person who always had the right tools for any job, who could turn his hand to anything practical. It was in his blood. His dad had been a builder. He was rumoured to have built the top of the chimney at the Burtonwood Brewery in the middle of a gale, when no other builders dared go up there, although by the time I knew him, Granddad Astley seemed to spend most of his time in the less challenging environment of the pub. Dad had also trained as a mechanic in the army, so he was good with engines as well, but his official job was making fencing – he had his own business building big concrete base panels in huge fibreglass moulds at a place we called the Yard. I really loved it at the Yard. For one thing, there was loads of sand for mixing the concrete, which could also function as a massive sandpit if you were a small boy, and there was a forklift truck that, incredibly, we were allowed to play on: health and safety regulations were presumably not enforced quite as strictly as they are today. And for another, there was Ralph, an old guy who worked there with my dad. Ralph was fascinating. He seemed to arrive at work every morning direct from the nineteenth century: he actually wore clogs. He didn't say much, but what he did say had a habit of sticking in your head for ever. 'Life's a good 'un if you don't weaken' was one of his sayings, which I suppose is the Northern equivalent of 'keep calm and carry on'.

So we had a lot of things in our house that you wouldn't expect in a working-class family in the late sixties and early seventies, all of which my dad had built himself. We had central heating, which really wasn't that common. There was a fully fitted kitchen with a massive fridge. There was a tiled shower room downstairs, at a time when most people's idea of a shower was a plastic thing you attached to the taps in the bath to rinse your hair. We had a wood-panelled dining room with a half-sized billiard table in it that my dad had bought off a wealthy couple in Yorkshire. It could be lowered and, with the aid of the fitted wooden boards that came with it, it doubled as a dining table. Looking back now, it was a bit twee, but at the time it felt quite luxurious to me.

The house was also a kind of monument to my dad's eccentricity. In the front garden he built a pond which was pretty big in relation to the plot it was in. To get to our front door, you had to cross a bridge over the pond. There was a waterfall that he'd built as well. Instead of a back garden there was a kind of yard which was mostly filled by a fishing boat that never, as far as I know, went anywhere near the water. My dad's friend had built it from scratch, and I have no idea how it ended up outside our house, but there it was. I used to play in it all the time when I was little. I've owned five different motorboats over the years, so maybe that's what gave me the bug for boating. And he had a safe hidden in the little cloakroom next to the kitchen. I didn't know anyone else who had a safe in their house, but we did; it was under the carpet, buried in concrete. There was money in there – hundreds of pounds in cash. My dad paid for everything in cash, I suppose because the kind of business he was in dealt in cash. He always had a big roll of banknotes in his back pocket, maybe a grand and a half. I don't remember people in Newton being poor when I was a kid – it was a working-class town, but everyone seemed to have a job – but I don't remember anyone else walking around with a roll of money the way my dad did.

*

My mum had a little gig on Saturday evenings, playing the piano in a local pub. She used to perform in the snug, away from the main bar. I think people went there more for a sing-song than they did for a drink; in a way, it was like the karaoke of its day. She was an amazing pianist – she could sight-read classical music and she could simply pick up any tune: if you started singing her something, she'd come up with an accompaniment. Maybe the job in the pub was where she had an affair, if she in fact did have one. My dad, who'd never liked the idea of her playing piano in a pub, was convinced she had, but I don't know if it was true or not. My mum was pretty, but she wasn't a particularly flirtatious person, so it seems a bit unlikely to me. But that didn't matter. Dad decided she had, and when my dad got an idea into his head, there was no budging him: it became gospel truth, and there was no point in trying to convince him otherwise.

In any case, my mum didn't have a chance to convince him otherwise. Dad just threw her out. She went out one day, he put all her clothes in plastic bags and left them on the door-step and changed the locks. John remembers him calling a solicitor: 'I believe my wife's been associating with another man and I've thrown her out of the house – what do I do?' And he remembers her coming home that night and banging on the kitchen window, asking to be let in, and Jayne telling him not to, for fear of how my dad would react.

I was too young to remember any of this, but I remember the aftermath. My mum moved in with a friend of my gran's for a little while, then to my gran and granddad's house. It turned out that the house we lived in was in my dad's name, so she thought there was no way of getting half of it off him. There never seemed to have been any question of her taking us with her, even though she knew first-hand how unpredictable and violent my dad could be. She couldn't have moved us into our gran's – there wasn't the room – but the idea that she could put her name down for her own council house and get us to join her there didn't seem to occur to her, or us. It's something I've only really thought about recently: she could have gone to the council, and explained her situation – a mother of four children, two of them under ten, a violent husband – and tried to sort something out, but, for whatever reason, she didn't.

To be honest, I think my mum might have had some kind of breakdown when her marriage fell apart. She never said she had, she never sought treatment, but looking back, it would make sense. She'd lived with four kids and a mad husband who'd made it clear that he didn't want to marry her, one of her children had died and her husband had blamed her for it, then she'd been thrown out of the family home overnight over an affair that might not have even happened. That's got to have had some kind of psychological impact on you. I suppose I'm trying to work out reasons Mum was the way she was, for the rest of her life. There was a kind of vagueness to her, an unpredictability that was different from my dad's: Mum would do and say things and you'd just think, *Wow, where did that come from?*

There are people who get divorced and stay friends – they have their ex-partners round for Sunday lunch, or they all get together to go on holiday, or for Christmas. My parents' divorce wasn't like that at all. My dad literally never spoke to my mum again. At first, she would come back to the house to see us, and, of course, he was there. He would completely ignore her, not even a 'hello'. She would sit in the dining room and ask us about school, and he would go and sit in another room until she left. Mum stopped coming to the house after a little while, but if she rang up to speak to us, Dad would pick up and not say a word, then place the receiver on the table next to the phone. It became a sort of signal – if Dad did that, we would know it was Mum on the other end of the line. If he came and got us on a Sunday evening, after we'd spent the weekend with Mum at our gran's, he would wait outside. It was bizarre: if my gran or granddad came out and walked us down the garden path to the car, he'd talk to them and pass the time of day perfectly happily. But, as far as I know, he never said another word to my mum for the rest of their lives.

I didn't understand why it had happened, but I knew it marked the Astleys out as different from everybody else. I started primary school the year after my mum and dad split up, and I think there was only one other kid in the entire school, a girl, whose parents weren't together. It felt weird, my mum coming to meet me after school, because that was the only way she could see us during the week. My dad employed a housekeeper after he threw my mum out, which marked us out as different as well. It makes us sound quite posh, but it wasn't really like that: he simply couldn't cope with four kids and a full-time job, so Mrs Hill used to come every morning before we woke up and get us ready for school, and she'd be there in the evening when we got home, to make us our tea. She was nice, but it was still strange, having someone who wasn't your mum and wasn't your aunty getting you dressed – no one else I knew had an arrangement like that.

Mrs Hill wasn't prepared to deal with my dad's moods. One day, Mike was mucking about with a mate in the living room, pretending to play cricket with a table tennis bat and some ball bearings. He hit a ball bearing straight through the living-room window: it didn't shatter, but it left a hole, almost like a bullet hole. Mrs Hill came into the room, saw what had happened, took her pinny off and went straight home rather than be around when my dad found out what had happened and erupted. I met Mrs Hill – her name was June – many years later. It was just by chance at my sister Jayne's house; it was very emotional. We hugged and I thanked her and told her that it had meant a lot to me that she had been there for us. It was something I probably really only grasped after becoming a dad myself.

At the time, we just got on with it, spending weeknights at the house, and weekends at my gran's with Mum, playing cards or watching *Match of the Day* with my granddad, a huge Liverpool supporter. I sometimes got the feeling that the atmosphere at Gran's was slightly strained – that my gran and grandad had felt they were done with raising children and the day-to-day business of family life, and then were suddenly plunged back into it when my mum moved in, bringing their grandkids with her, at least at weekends. Meanwhile, sometimes life at home could seem almost normal. My dad would come home with sweets – Crème Eggs or, his favourite, Raspberry Ruffles – and he'd sit in front of the TV with us: I'd watch *The Clangers*, sitting on his knee, or we'd all settle down in the evening for *The Dick Emery Show*. He'd make you laugh, singing daft songs; he'd sing Frank Sinatra's 'You Make Me Feel So Young', but change the words so it was 'you make me feel so old'. Or we'd visit my dad's sister, Aunty Barbara, and her husband Don, who moved in with Granny Astley after Grandad Astley died. They had a daughter, Lorraine, and a son called Bryce, who was my age and who I got on with really well. I used to spend a lot of weekends with them. Aunty Barbara was like a substitute mum to me, a really warm, kind woman who seemed to have the maternal instincts my own mum didn't. I'd sleep on a mattress on the floor next to Lorraine and Bryce's bunk beds, and we'd play in the ancient car that sat in the garage, an old 1950s Ford Popular. Everything would seem fine, and then the next day, Dad would be in an absolutely foul mood, and he couldn't, or wouldn't, curb that mood around us. As I said, you got used to it in a way, but it was a strange, unsettling way to live – you never knew when his mood would change, or what would cause it.

I think the divorce affected us all in different ways. Jayne moved out a couple of years later and got on with her own life. By the time she was eighteen, she was living with her boyfriend, Barry, a lovely guy who later became her husband. They're still together today. John became quite quiet and seemed the best able to simply absorb our dad's outbursts when they happened. Mike, as I said, became . . . well, delinquent's a bit strong, but he definitely developed a certain couldn't-care-less aura.

I remember being frightened all the time as a kid. Your mum's suddenly gone, your dad flies into rages for no reason – it's going to make you quite wary. I didn't like the dark. My dad kept a couple of horses in a field he rented near our house, and I hated going with him to feed them at night. I'd sit in the cab of his van in the pitch dark, rigid with terror. At home, if it was my bedtime, and John and Mike were out at Sea Cadets or whatever, I wouldn't go to bed. I'd simply sit at the top of the stairs where my dad couldn't see me, waiting for them to come home: I didn't want to be up there alone in the dark. I was a bit nervous around water, although that had something to do with being taken to see *Jaws* when I was nine – no, I don't know why anyone thought it was a good idea to take a nine-year-old to see *Jaws* either – and a bit cagey around bikes, after I fell off mine up by the private road at the edge of Newton where the posh houses were. I landed face-first, tore a load of skin off my face and concussed myself and ended up in hospital for a few days. That had its upside – they put me in a men's ward and all the old guys used to buy me crisps and sweets when the food trolley came round – but I have always since been the kind of cyclist that keeps his hands on the brakes.

*

I enjoyed primary school, St Peter's C of E. It was literally round the corner from our house. The teachers were nice. We did nativity plays and performances. Thinking back, being distracted by anything outside our house just made me feel better. I was the Pharaoh in *Joseph and the Amazing Technicolor Dreamcoat*, in a silver suit, with orange tassels under the arms that my sister sewed on, and my school shoes. The Pharoah's character is based on Elvis Presley. Maybe that's why I got the role, because I already had a quiff. I was born with it. It must be a genetic thing, because my daughter, Emilie, came out of the womb with her hair like that too. When she was a baby, her godmother, Heidi, was walking with her in Tivoli Gardens in Copenhagen, and a woman came over and said 'I hope you don't think I'm being rude, but that child looks exactly like that singer, Rick Astley.'

Quiff or not, I had no idea who Elvis was. I might have seen some of his films on the TV, but that wasn't the Elvis the role required: they were after the feral, sexy 1950s Elvis, whoever he was. My main memory of the performance was that I sang through a microphone. I've no idea where they got one from, but my voice was definitely amplified. I was amazed: you held this thing and you sang into it and your voice came out of some speakers in the school hall. I thought that was the coolest thing in the world.

The first record I owned was 'I Feel Love' by Donna Summer. That sounds like evidence of early good taste; it is, after all, the song that Brian Eno famously told David Bowie was the future of music. But I got it completely at random. There was a shop near where we lived that sold clothes – it was where you went and got your school uniform from – that had a little record shop adjoining it. My dad took me there to get a pair of jeans. I didn't realize there was a deal on, where if you bought a certain brand, you got a free single. I bought the right brand, but only because they were the same ones my brother Mike wore. When the shop assistant told me I could pick anything from the Top 20, I panicked: I was the youngest person in the shop, it was all a bit intimidating. So I said, 'I'll have No. 1 please', and that was 'I Feel Love'. I got lucky: if I'd gone in a couple of weeks later, I'd have been stuck with 'Angelo' by Brotherhood of Man, which no one ever claimed was the future of anything.

I didn't buy records much, because I didn't need to. There was a lot of music already in our house. Not so much from my dad, who hated pop – he was fond of colliery brass-band music and Frank Sinatra – but from my brothers and, especially, my sister Jayne. I remember the sound of Motown and Northern soul and the smell of cigarettes wafting from her bedroom on her sixteenth birthday. My dad had let her throw a party, he'd even bought them a keg of beer, and whatever was going on up there seemed quite otherworldly to me. Later, Jayne's real love was progressive rock. She loved Pink Floyd and Genesis, Rick Wakeman and Camel, who were the first band I ever saw live. Jayne took me along to see them at Manchester Free Trade Hall, when I was ten: I can still remember the smell of patchouli oil, and the screen behind them, which showed a film loop of geese flying across the sky while they played their most recent album, *The Snow Goose*. She loved a more obscure band called Egg, and a French band called Magma who invented a whole apocalyptic science-fiction universe and – get this – their own language, which they sang in. I used to listen to them and make up my own words, which were a bit more down to earth: 'Dad's a boss mechanic, Dad's a boss mechanic at Ford's, he makes Escorts and Ford Cortinas.'

I used to sneak into Jayne's room and play her records when she wasn't there: 'Big Yellow Taxi' by Joni Mitchell, 'What's Going On' by Marvin Gaye. I used to stare and stare at the sleeve of *What's Going On*, Marvin Gaye standing in the rain in a suit and a raincoat, with his collar up. I didn't think he looked the kind of person who'd make an album like *What's Going On*, which was gorgeous and melodic, or sing the way the guy on *What's Going On* sang, with a beautiful, sad, pleading voice. He didn't even look like a pop star to me; he looked more like a movie star, a Black version of Steve McQueen or Paul Newman; he seemed serious, powerful, a bit dangerous, like someone you wouldn't mess with. He looked as if he didn't care whether you liked his album or not. That was interesting – that you could look a certain way, but sound completely different.

My brother John loved Queen. No danger of sneaking into his room when he was out to enjoy his copy of *A Night at the Opera* – it had been made very clear to me what would happen if I so much as breathed near his records – but he graciously used to let me stand outside his bedroom door and listen while he played it. And I remember him listening to The Beatles while he painted the banisters of our staircase. He'd broken his ankle and Dad, being Dad, had decided that was no impediment to him doing odd jobs around the house while he recovered. So he painted the bannisters with his foot in a cast, playing one Beatles album after another. They were intriguing to me too – some of the songs on *Sgt Pepper* sounded as if they were meant for kids. What was that all about?

It all seeped in. Because of the music I've made, people are always astonished at how much I know about prog rock, but I could probably sing every word of every track of every 1970s Genesis album to you today. I still enjoy it: a couple of years back, we all went on an Astley siblings-and-partners outing to see Rick Wakeman perform *The Six Wives of Henry VIII* at Hampton Court Palace – it's down the road from where I live now, so I got on the computer as soon as it was announced and bought twelve tickets. I even wrote a song about all this stuff a few years ago, called 'The Good Old Days': 'the place of my birth was the music that my brothers and my sister played to me, and how I believed in the stories they told me'. It was music that transported you somewhere else, like science fiction or historical fantasy novels do, which was a useful thing, given the strange situation at home. There was something about that music that I wholeheartedly wanted to jump into and absorb myself in.

The first band I remember really loving myself, and which didn't have anything to do with my brothers or sister, where I actually bought the record, rather than absorbing it as it was played around the house, or being given it free with a pair of jeans, was The Police. Then I heard AC/DC's *Highway to Hell*. I remember listening to it on the radio, sitting completely transfixed in the cab of my dad's van, thinking, 'What is this?' I'd never heard anything like it before. In my memory, DJ Tommy Vance played the whole album from start to finish during the *Friday Rock Show* on Radio 1, but I'm not sure if that really happened; I might be embroidering it in my mind. I would have been twelve or thirteen. I rushed out and bought it, played it over and over again. But I didn't become a heavy-metaller. I didn't become anything. I'd just started secondary school, and standing out in any way seemed like a very bad idea.

Primary school had been as cute as you could imagine. Selwyn Jones High School was anything but. It had been a grammar school when Jayne went there, but it had merged with the local secondary modern while John was a pupil and become a comprehensive. John was smart, the kind of kid who should have gone to university, but Selwyn Jones now wasn't the sort of school that sent pupils to university and, frankly, going to university wasn't something that people from where I'm from really did. So John left school and went to work with my dad. His job was making the fibreglass moulds for the concrete fencing. He worked in a shed on the Yard, coating layers and layers of fibreglass with resin. The smell of the resin in the shed used to make you woozy when you breathed it in: being in that shed is probably the closest I've ever been to taking drugs.

The atmosphere at school seemed to change the minute I left primary school and stepped through the gates of Selwyn Jones. Suddenly, it was tough, it was judgemental, and it was violent: I'd never seen fistfights at St Peter's, but you saw some horrible scraps at Selwyn Jones. Once you got out, there was the rivalry with the local Catholic school, St Aelred's, to contend with. It was serious. I'm not making this up, there used to be 150 kids in different uniforms, girls as well as boys, pitching against each other in Newton High Street, over absolutely nothing: someone had said something to someone else in the queue for the chippy and it had turned into this mass fight. It was ludicrous and horrible at the same time.

In fact, it was simply horrible. You didn't realize how ludicrous it all was until years later – at the time, it was all deadly serious. I remember hanging out with some friends in a cul-de-sac where my friend Phil Taylor lived when Selwyn Jones were on holiday and St Aelred's weren't. We were with a girl called Catherine Higgins, who lived there too. She was a couple of years below us, one of those younger kids who used to tag along and get teased, and then one day she bought herself a pair of those skintight spray-on Spandex jeans – like Olivia Newton-John wore at the end of *Grease*, when she's transformed herself into a bad girl – and suddenly Catherine Higgins didn't look like a younger kid you'd tease any more. Catherine Higgins started attracting a lot of attention. I don't know if our proximity to Catherine was what started the trouble with someone from St Aelred's, but the word went round that they were looking for her, or us. We ran into someone's house and hid, peering out from behind the net curtains. I'm not joking, a gang of about fifty kids in Aelred's uniform appeared across the field at the back of the house, looking for us. And, to use gangster film phraseology, some of them were tooled up: they had bits of wood and stuff like that in their hands, things they'd picked up to use as weapons. They didn't find us; nothing happened and eventually they went back to school. That was what my adolescence was like. It was bloody stupid.

When we were in school, I think everyone who went to Selwyn Jones was slightly frightened by the experience of being there, and as a result the atmosphere was brutal: there was a lot of piss-taking, a degree of bullying, you'd see other kids getting annihilated by their classmates for one minor reason or another. I decided the best course of action was to become as inconspicuous and ordinary as possible. I wasn't particularly great academically – so no one could call me a nerd or a swot – and I wasn't bottom of the class either. I wasn't wildly popular, but neither was I a loner. I merely wanted to pass under the radar. But that was a lot easier said than done, thanks to my dad's unconventional attitude to housing arrangements.

Chapter Two

My dad had bought a cottage near Clitheroe, a town about an hour north of Newton. The place was an absolute wreck – you couldn't live in it as it was – so he moved a caravan outside, where we stayed over quite a few different weekends. As far as I remember, the idea was for him to move into the caravan while he was doing the house up. I don't recall there being any suggestion that we would be going to live with him in Clitheroe, even when the house was finished. Dad was going to hand his business at the Yard over to my eldest brother John; he would run it and Mike and I would work there when we'd finished school. And Dad was also going to buy a terraced house in Newton, where me and my brothers would live. Because I was the youngest, Mrs Hill would come and keep an eye on me, and my mum was only down the road. I think Dad simply wanted to get away from the responsibility of being a parent. It was a job he hadn't wanted, and a job he patently wasn't cut out to do. There was a thing he used to say a lot when I was kid: 'Open the gates and let me out.' It was kind of a joke, but I think he genuinely meant it; I really think he felt caged by being a parent. He wanted to be free of the responsibility, just to be on his own, living his own life.

I know that sounds bad – I was twelve years old, in a single-parent family, and the single parent had decided to leave – but, honestly, I thought it was a pretty good idea. For one thing, what twelve-year-old boy wouldn't jump at the chance of living without parental supervision? And for another, it felt as if we'd be happier like that than we were living with my dad – it sounds incredible to say it, but I thought life would be less erratic if it was only the three of us, without Dad around.

But then the plan came unstuck. It turned out that Dad leased the land that the Yard was on from the local council, and they wanted it back, to build houses on. They offered him a choice of land around Newton in exchange for him giving up the lease, and he picked a big field on the outskirts of town, close to the colliery and the border with Lowton. It was a good deal – Dad would actually own the new land – but it meant that there wasn't really a business to hand on to John. Dad would have to start a new business and build it up himself before he could do that. He clearly wasn't going to be moving to Clitheroe for the foreseeable future.

There was another issue. Dad had found a buyer for our house. He didn't want to pull out of the sale, so we effectively had nowhere to live. When we first moved out, I shuttled around between a few different locations. I stayed with my mum at Gran's for a bit, but that was a bit of a squeeze. At one point, Mike and I moved in with Jayne and her husband, Barry, in their little terraced house for a few months, which really couldn't have been great for them. They hadn't been married that long, they were setting up home together, and her two younger brothers suddenly turned up in the spare room because they had nowhere else to go. Then all of us – me, Mike, John and Dad – moved into a building on the Yard. It had been an office, but it had a shower and toilets, so it could just about function as a bungalow. But it obviously wasn't a permanent solution, because Dad had given up the lease on the Yard.

I know that all of this sounds nuts: Dad wanting to leave his kids in Newton and move to Clitheroe, Dad selling the house without finding anywhere for him or his children to live. But it would make perfect sense if you knew my dad – he was impulsive, he seemed to do things without fully considering what the consequences might be. Whatever it is in someone's character that tethers them to the normal, accepted way of behaving, my dad didn't possess it. In some ways, that was a positive. Dad threw himself into things, and I think I've got a bit of that: this sounds like a great idea, it's fun and exciting, let's do it. That said, I've behaved that way about stuff like booking the Royal Albert Hall to sing Frank Sinatra songs. My dad did it with things like where we lived. There's quite a big difference.

I occasionally got the impression that he didn't really know what he was doing, especially when it came to bringing up kids. Sometimes, I wonder if his impulsiveness was down to fear. He couldn't really cope with being a father, and he'd ended up with three boys to look after by himself. He didn't know what he was doing and he acted rashly because he was frightened by the whole thing, then he regretted his decisions afterwards. He was like that with everything. If we went on holiday, he simply hooked a caravan up to the back of the truck and then set out in the general direction of Scotland – I don't think he really knew where he was going.

Which brings us to his solution to the Astley family's housing crisis. It was the school holidays when he took us over to the new field, which now had a Portakabin in the middle of it, with a Portaloo next to it. I don't think it registered with me at first that this was supposed to be our permanent new home. I thought it was almost like a camping trip, that we'd go back to living in a house once the holidays were over. It didn't seem particularly habitable. There was one big room and a smaller room, which I suppose could have been an office, if the Portakabin had been used for the purpose that a Portakabin is supposed to be used for. We slept in the big room, all four of us, in beds that were lined up as if they were in a barracks. It gradually dawned on me that we were staying permanently. Dad quickly dug trenches and got services put in, so we had water and electricity. In time, he got central heating and installed a kind of toilet block next to the Portakabin. He put up more walls, partitioned rooms off – Mike and I shared one bedroom, Dad and John shared another – and had them decorated, so it looked a bit more like a home. Still, there was no getting around the fact that it wasn't a home – it was a fucking Portakabin in the middle of a field. But it was where we lived.

Mum didn't seem to have anything to say about it – you

might have thought she would, given that her ex-husband had announced he was moving three of her kids into a Portakabin in the middle of a field, but that was Mum for you. To be honest, I wasn't really seeing that much of her by now. I'd stopped going round to see her at my gran's every weekend, partly because I was at that age where you'd rather be out with friends, and partly because it always felt a bit awkward when I went there, as if I was almost pestering her to be my mum.

In time, a garden centre of sorts sprang up around the Portakabin. All sorts of stuff sprang up around that Portakabin. My dad moved the horses he kept on the rented field onto the new land. We got chickens and a couple of goats. There was a lot of heavy machinery around and a couple of train wagons with rounded roofs that Dad got from somewhere, put massive locks on and used for storage. He kept cement in one of them, put a huge safe in the other. It was the kind of safe you'd have in a bank – the thing was about four feet high; it had to be moved with a forklift. There was an enormous greenhouse, a tractor, vans, trucks, a couple of cars that Dad was supposed to be fixing, but never got around to, so they sat there, with weeds growing up through them. All sorts of things. It kept changing. One time, he did a deal with some guy who worked for Mr Kipling, trading him some knackered fence panels for boxes and boxes of cakes that had been damaged in transit. So, for a while, we lived surrounded by these industrial-sized boxes of slightly battered Fondant Fancies. We used to have competitions to see how many of them we could eat, or how many of them we could get in our mouths at once.

When word got around about the Astleys' new living arrangements, my plan to keep a low profile at school took a considerable battering. Remember, the idea was not to do anything, or say anything, or appear in any way out of the ordinary, thus not attracting attention and not giving people any ammunition to use against me in the piss-taking environment of Selwyn Jones High School. It was all going pretty well until the day when, in the middle of an English lesson, someone put their hand up and blurted out, 'Miss! Miss! Rick Astley lives in a tin hut!'

Oh, for fuck's sake. It's just . . . not something you can really explain away, particularly when you yourself don't fully understand what you're doing living in a Portakabin in the middle of a field. Or, rather, you can explain it, but only in a way that's going to make matters worse: 'That's quite right, Miss, I do live in a tin hut. But there's a very good reason I live in a tin hut. It's because my dad's a lunatic. Did I ever tell you all about the time I caught him trying to strangle my mother? He also smashes things with a hammer when he's angry and I'm terrified of him. Now, if you'd all go back to the business of ignoring me – because, I assure you, there's nothing out of the ordinary here, I've a perfectly unremarkable, thoroughly boring everyday life, like everyone else, except in, as we've established, a tin hut, with the odd bit of strangling and the occasional item smashed with a hammer – that would be fantastic, thanks.'

The weird thing was that the reactions to the revelation about our new home were surprisingly mixed. There were definitely people who thought it was hilarious. But there were also people who thought it was genuinely amazing.

Hang on, you live in the middle of a field, and get to drive around in a tractor and a van after school and your brothers burn around the place on trial bikes and you're allowed to set fire to stuff and there doesn't appear to be any actual rules? There are power tools everywhere and horses and heavy machinery and rusting vehicles? Your dad never reads your school reports or comes to parents' evenings? And you've got industrial-sized boxes of Fondant Fancies that you can eat whenever you want? Cool!

*

People thought my dad was amazing. Everyone knew him, because you couldn't really miss him. He used to exercise the horses by taking them through the town, running behind them, dressed like something out of *Huckleberry Finn* – a big straw hat, massive baggy jeans and scruffy boots. Or he'd ride through the town on a two-wheeled trap pulled by a beautiful dapple-grey horse, still dressed like something out of *Huckleberry Finn*. And – the piece de resistance – he'd have a boombox next to him blaring out brass-band music. I got used to people coming up to me at school: 'Saw your dad the other day – he's fucking mad, him.' They weren't taking the piss – they meant it in a really positive way. Outside of home, Dad was always really friendly, always singing: a complete eccentric, but a complete eccentric people loved. He made everyone else's dad look boring: *God, we have to live in a three-bedroom semi and the most interesting thing my dad does is go to the pub with his mates.*

I could see what they meant, I always agreed with them and I suppose there was a little part of me that thought, *Yeah, we're different*, in a positive way. But they had no idea what living with my dad was really like. The constant uncertainty, the temper, never knowing what was going to happen next. It was exhausting. The people who thought my life was great didn't live the way I did on a daily basis. They didn't know the sense of impending doom you used to feel when you heard Dad's truck arriving home. It was a Volkswagen and the engine made a very distinctive sound; you could pick it out a mile away. That was the signal for the music to go off, whatever we were doing to stop and a state of high anxiety to descend, because you didn't know what mood he was going to be in when he came through the door. Sometimes it would be fine, and the music would go back on – if he was in a good mood, Dad would even sing along – and other times it wouldn't. In fact, I used to go to my friends' boring three-bedroom semis, with their supposedly boring parents and their very noticeable lack of trial bikes or tractors or horses and think, *This is what I want.* I would have swapped our lives for a house on the White's Estate, with a normal family, in a heartbeat. Instead, I was living in a state of constant uncertainty and fear – fear of my dad's temper, fear of what was going to happen next, fear that life was out of my control. Worse, I felt ashamed – I was ashamed of how we lived, ashamed of my dad.

It had an impact and I don't think it's ever stopped affecting me. It's determined how I behave, my reaction to things, all sorts. I've always craved stability. Both my brothers and my sister must have done, because they've ended up with really stable lives: they're all still with their partners after years and years, happily married, kids. Mike, of all people, is a chartered accountant – I don't think any of us saw that coming. In a sense, the way we grew up made me quite driven – if your alternative is a Portakabin in the middle of a field, you're going to jump at opportunities and work really hard to make sure you achieve something else. Even when I was really famous, if someone had come along with a contract and a cheque and told me that if I signed it, they'd give me enough money to live an ordinary, secure life for the rest of my days, but I would never be allowed to set foot on a stage or in a recording studio and I'd be banned from singing again, I'd have signed it straight away. Especially when I was really famous, because there's nothing stable or normal about being a pop star, so I felt I'd jumped out of the proverbial frying pan. I feel bad about saying that, because obviously it's a privilege to be a pop star – most people's jobs aren't like that. But that's how I felt: I was more interested in feeling secure and safe than I was in being famous, or anything that comes with it. And there are times when I've thought that I would happily trade everything I've done in music, the money I made, the lot, to have grown up the way my friends did, in a 'normal' house on an estate, with a mum and dad who loved them, or at least expressed their love in a normal way.

But we didn't, so we got on with it as best we could. A lot of my friends had to be home, get a snack then get on with homework before they were allowed to do anything else. It wasn't like that at ours. I don't remember anyone ever mentioning homework – I don't think it crossed my dad's mind. There was always work to be done at the garden centre. It's not that Dad was a slavedriver, but there was an understanding that that was what we did, that was where our future lay, and you just did what Dad told you to. If he said, 'See that old trailer, it's blue – I want it green,' you'd simply go and do it, no questions asked. There wasn't any point in going, 'Tell me why we're repainting it again?', so you never bothered saying anything; you got the brushes out and set to.

Looking back, I feel that had a really big effect on me too, in terms of being driven. I think one of the reasons I wanted to be successful, to earn money, was to answer my dad back: it would give me the ability to say 'no' when he told me what to do. I wanted to make enough money so that I wouldn't have to go along with it if he said, 'You've got to do this' or 'You've got to live here.' It's weird – I still sometimes feel like that now, like I'm answering him back, and my dad's been dead for a few years. I'm incredibly grateful for my career, but the thing I'm most grateful for is that I've earned the freedom to make my own choices.

Actually, there's another thing about my upbringing that's stayed with me. If I have downtime, I don't tend to sit and relax; I find manual jobs for myself to do around the house. It's as if I can't allow myself to sit down. I've got a day off and I end up on a ladder, cleaning out the gutters along the garage, because my dad instilled in me the idea that you should do everything yourself. And then I realize I've taken on more than I can handle and think: *What are you doing? Is Ronan Keating doing this? Is Gary Barlow up a ladder cleaning out his own gutters?* But it's just the way I am: if I don't have stuff to do, I find my mood can slip into a bit of a dark place. I've always been prone to that kind of thing: I've never been suicidal, but I find it quite easy to get into a depressed state. Even when I was younger, there were periods when I sank into the kind of mood where I never went out: I stayed at home, I couldn't be bothered. I think I was a bit more sensitive than my environment – either at school, or at home – catered for.

At the garden centre, you worked at weekends and after school. You got home, got changed out of your uniform and then bagged up 20 hundredweight of gravel and 20 hundredweight of cement. The bags weighed 112 pounds, and by the time I was fifteen I could lift them over my head, I was that strong from moving heavy stuff around. I would load up concrete fencing onto the truck for John, then we'd go out and deliver it: 2x3-foot flagstones, concrete posts, whatever, twelve or sixteen of them at each address. It's hard to describe it without making it sound a bit Dickensian, but it didn't feel like that at the time. It wasn't 'boo-hoo, poor us, made to work', it was simply how it was. Dad worked really hard too; it was all physical graft. I never saw him sitting at a desk unless he was typing out an invoice.

Dad would vanish off for hours and hours in his flatbed truck while we were working at the garden centre. We would have no idea where he was going, or when he was coming back. You might have thought he was going to see a woman, or going off to the pub and drinking, but he wasn't. He certainly wasn't at the pub because he wasn't pissed when he got back: you could tell the rare occasions when my dad was pissed, because he used to sing, and sing so loudly you'd hear him coming quite a long time before he arrived at the house. And if my dad was ever involved with a woman after my mum, I didn't know about it, but it doesn't seem terribly likely. You know, the guy drove a pony and trap around Newton-le-Willows playing brass-band music and he lived in a Portakabin in the middle of a field with his three children, and he was also a cantankerous old git. He wasn't exactly a catch. And besides, no one would go in a flatbed truck to visit their secret lover looking the way my dad did. He could scrub up when he wanted to – once a year, he'd put on a suit and go to York races with his brother, and he occasionally dressed up a bit to go to a brass-band concert – but he did it so rarely that you were always a bit shocked when he did: you'd look at him and think, *Who is this?* Most of the time he was in his baggy jeans and boots, and, frankly, he looked a bit like a tramp. I couldn't imagine any self-respecting woman falling head over heels for that.

I think he was drifting around, doing anything he wanted: temporarily opening the gates and letting himself out, as he would have put it. If he saw something that was interesting, he would stop and stick his oar in. He'd usually end up buying something. He'd see something he was interested in, or thought we could use at the garden centre, and get his roll of money out: 'How much do you want for that, then?'

Once, he arrived back home with 25,000 strawberry plants that we had to repot. He'd got it into his head that strawberry patches were going to be the next big thing in gardening. Anyone else would have thought that and bought 500, but no: 25,000. He would do these things without warning. There would be no prior discussion, no suggestion of what he was going to do, no 'I think I might buy another horse, what do you think?' He'd arrive home randomly with another horse. If he'd turned up saying, 'I've bought a helicopter' or 'I've bought a submarine', none of us would have been surprised. There might be a few shared glances and rolled eyes between me and my brothers, but that was it as far as reactions went: it was just another stupid idea that we had to get along with. It was another form of uncertainty, I suppose, like his moods.

Dad was capable of incredible acts of generosity and kindness, but they were as random as anything else. He'd forget your birthday, then suddenly announce he was buying you a new twelve-speed racer bike, because yours was looking a bit shabby. He wasn't keen on John and Mike riding motorbikes. They both had pretty bad crashes, then a friend of Mike's was actually killed on his motorbike right outside the garden centre. He was hit by a car going over the crossroads. We literally heard the accident happen, went racing across the field to see what it was. My dad got there first and yelled at us not to come any closer. After that, he bribed John to give up his motorbike by buying him a car, a brand-new Honda Accord. He let Mike go on riding his trial bike – I think he thought he would get it out of his system, then settle down and want a car too. He didn't, and John didn't grow out of biking either, free car or not. They both still ride today, a couple of weekend warriors.

Being the youngest, I thought my older brothers were a pain in the arse, but I must have looked up to them. I'd had a go on Mike's trial bike, and I'd ridden round the field on a knackered old moped that had mysteriously turned up at the garden centre. I wanted my own bike, but my dad wouldn't let me have one after John's and Mike's accidents: 'I can't go to the hospital again in the middle of the night, wondering if one of you is alive or dead, or has to have a leg amputated.' I got a motorbike jacket instead. That was about as close as

I came to having an identity at school: my brothers are both bikers, I'm going to get a bike one day. They weren't Hell's Angels or greasers or anything like that, they were just into bikes. John kind of modelled himself on Kenny Roberts, the first American to win the Grand Prix world championships, and a bit of a controversial rebel figure: he had a Yamaha with the same paint job as Kenny Roberts, and a helmet that looked like his too.

*

Owning a jacket was as far as my motorbiking career went, and the jacket didn't last that long. I swapped it for a drum kit from another lad at school. You may wonder precisely what kind of a drum kit you can get by swapping your biker jacket. The answer is: a terrible one. It was ancient, made by a company called Ajax, and the heads on the drums were made of pigskin. It didn't matter; it was mine. I'd always fancied playing the drums. I don't know why – maybe it was something to do with getting your aggression out. I remember the year ABBA won the Eurovision Song Contest, watching it on TV at my gran's with my cousin Janet, and playing the drums along to it, with a pair of knitting needles and some cushions. There was a drum kit in the music room at school, but, for some reason, you weren't allowed to touch it. Then, one dinnertime – that's lunchtime for any Southerners reading this – me and a few other lads were allowed to have a go. The rest of them got bored pretty quickly, but I loved it. I was in there all dinnertime, bashing away. I could play a bit too; all that practice with the knitting needles must have stood me in good enough stead that I could grasp the basics straight off.

Most parents would react with a certain degree of horror if their kid came home saying they'd swapped their leather jacket for a drum kit. The drums are a really noisy instrument to practise on, or at least they were in those days, before you could get electronic kits that you plug headphones into. But, unpredictable as ever, my dad didn't bat an eyelid – he told me I could set them up in the greenhouse and play them, as long as the garden centre was closed. He was the same later, when I got a saxophone from a small ad in the local paper: the sound of someone learning the sax when they've got no idea what they're doing is a fairly nerve-shredding experience for anyone in earshot, but my dad never minded.

I practised all the time, playing along with The Police and especially *Highway to Hell* by AC/DC. They were good to learn to: the drumming on Police records is very intricate and subtle – Stewart Copeland's an amazing player – and AC/DC is more straightforward, rock and roll, really powerful. I can't remember my dad ever complaining about the noise, or asking me to give it a rest – I think if it ever got too much for him in the evening, he'd nip out to the local Conservative Club for a couple of hours. That was the other side of life with my dad, the side my friends saw and loved: he let you get away with things that other parents would be horrified by.

So I had a drum kit and somewhere to play it. It turns out that that makes you a very appealing prospect to anyone who wants to form a band, because the two things that are always hardest to find are someone with drums – because, as I said, most people's parents weren't very keen on having someone playing them in the house – and somewhere to practise, because . . . well, for the same reason: no one wants a load of teenagers round disturbing the peace with a cack-handed version of 'Wild Thing' while they're trying to watch the telly.

At school, I was in a class called HU, with an art teacher called Mrs Hubbard – I think the idea of the class was to round up all the kids who were quite bright, but couldn't get it together to study – because, say, they were busy bagging up gravel and shifting concrete posts – and try to inspire them into working harder. It didn't really pan out, at least as far as I was concerned, but it was a better approach to education than some of the other teachers came up with. My maths teacher, who seemed to have thrown in the towel entirely, took me aside and told me that if I was quiet and didn't be-have disruptively, I could go and sit at the back of the class and not do any work.

A couple of my mates in HU were into music: Geoff played the bass, and Phil had a guitar. Phil was a bit like me – one of those kids who was trying his best to pass through the school unnoticed – but he was pretty good on the guitar. His stepdad was a nurse and had a band at weekends, playing the local working men's club circuit, and he'd taught Phil a bit. My dad didn't mind them coming to the greenhouse either. So we were a band, of sorts. Geoff, who was a bit cooler than the rest of us, volunteered to be the lead singer, which was good news: neither Phil nor I wanted to do it, because it would have interfered with our plan of attracting as little attention as possible. We played 'Mr Tambourine Man', because that was one of the songs Phil's stepdad had taught him on the guitar. We did 'Transmission' by Joy Division, because Geoff loved Joy Division. And we did 'So Lonely' by The Police, which I sang, hidden behind my drum kit. We called ourselves Give Way, because Geoff had stolen a 'give way' road sign off its post on his journey home one night. We put it in front of the drum kit.

It was fun, and we might have stayed where we were, jamming in the greenhouse of Parkside Garden Centre once or twice a week, had the school not announced that there was going to be a Valentine's Day disco and a band made up of pupils would be playing at it. There was a kind of audition involved. We applied, and so did another couple of bands. The other bands consisted of the school's cool kids – the captain of football and rugby, the guys who always got picked first for teams, the guys with the right shoes and the right haircuts, the ones the girls liked. They weren't bad lads, they didn't look down on anybody, but in the social ranking of the school they were right at the top, and it was pretty obvious who was going to get the Valentine's disco gig.

Until we all played at the audition. I'm not really one for blowing my own trumpet, but we absolutely wiped the floor with them. They were all right, but we were loads better. Even the teachers looked surprised – 'What's happening? The cool kids have just been in and then these three have come on and they're better by a country mile – that can't be right.' Then again, we'd kept such a low profile since we started at Selwyn Jones, maybe the teachers looked confused because in fact they didn't recognize us: 'Who are this lot? Are they at this school? Hang on a minute – is the drummer that lad that's supposed to live in a tin hut?' They were so startled, none of them seemed to notice that we had a clearly stolen road sign propped up in front of the bass drum. We got to be on last at the gig. Headliners!

I was sitting at my drum kit in the greenhouse, practising, when Jayne told my dad. 'You know Rick's band's won a competition and they're playing at the school dance?'

He looked as confused as the teachers. 'You what? That bloody racket they make – someone's actually asked them to play?'

Then he looked at me, or rather at my ancient drum kit. 'You're going to go and play a show with that?'

I nodded.

'It's a right mess, that.' Dad frowned.

I agreed.

'Right,' he said. 'Come on, we're going to get you a proper drum kit.'

And that was that. The roll of notes came out of his back pocket and he bought me a brand-new Pearl Maxim drum kit, in silver. Cue astonishment from my bandmates: 'Your dad's amazing!'

They were right. Sometimes he really was.

The gig at the school disco went incredibly well. When I say it went incredibly well, it wasn't The Beatles at Shea Stadium: we only did five songs and it was pretty shambolic. But for a band our age, who'd never played live before, it wasn't bad at all. Far from it. People liked us; we went down great. And simply being seen on stage, in a band, seemed to shift my position at school a little. It was as if I'd found a kind of niche, something I could be known for that wasn't the Astleys' peculiar living arrangements, or my dad's eccentricity, or my brother Mike's reputation preceding me – something

I didn't mind being known for. Maybe it planted an idea in my head that playing music could change things for me, and change them for the better. I also couldn't help noticing that in the aftermath of the gig, I got five Valentine's cards, which was five more than I'd ever received before.

I think one of them was from Debbie Smith, a girl in my year who I fancied. That's not her real name; I've changed it to respect her privacy. In fact, I'm sure it was from Debbie, because not long after, she asked me out. It happened at Newton Cricket Club, which provided the only real source of entertainment in the town if you weren't old enough to go to the pub. Everybody went – weirdly, the rivalry between Selwyn Jones and Aelred's didn't seem to matter if you were there, and, more weirdly still, I didn't mind standing out there. I didn't mind being the first lad on the dancefloor. All the others were hanging back in the shadows, but me and my mate Mark Berry would get up and dance. And I dressed up: really tight jeans that I'd taken in myself on my sister's sewing machine, little black suede boots and legwarmers, which were quite a daring thing for a boy to wear at the time, as they were seen as more for girls. I've never been at the forefront of developments in the world of fashion, but I think I can safely say that I was the first boy to wear legwarmers at the Newton-le-Willows Cricket Club disco in 1982. There was, I seem to remember, quite a lot of piss-taking as a result, and then an influx of boys wearing legwarmers over the next few weeks.

They did two discos a week, one for under-18s and one for over-18s, where they sold alcohol. The music at the first one was more poppy, but the over-18s' disco was proper

American soul and funk. The North-West has always taken dance music very, very seriously indeed, whether it was the Northern Soul scene in the seventies, or acid house later in the eighties. So, even though it was only a disco at a cricket club for teenagers, they had really good DJs, guys who worked at local record stores and knew their stuff, who played the latest imports from the States. Even the under-18s' pop night didn't mean naff pop music like 'Birdie Song' or 'Agadoo' or whatever – the music was good. The cricket club had quite an effect on my brothers' and sister's music taste, then on mine. The first band I went to see without a sibling in attendance was Shalamar, who somehow fetched up at the Spectrum Arena in Warrington: I was down the front with Mark Berry again, transfixed as much by the sight of Jody Watley – because she was gorgeous, and what's more I don't think I'd ever been that close to a woman with that few clothes on before – as I was by the music. I started liking soul singers like Luther Vandross, who's still the best vocalist I've ever heard in my life.

Anyway, I'm getting off the point. That particular week at the cricket club, the music wasn't as important as being approached by Debbie Smith's sister's boyfriend, bearing the news that she wanted to go out with me. That was apparently the way you did it: you didn't ask yourself; you got a mutual acquaintance to ask for you. I was very pleased. Debbie was pretty cool. She was a bit edgy by the standards of girls at Selwyn Jones and came into school one day with her hair cropped short and bleached white: she looked incredible. She had great taste in music – a bit left field, but she really knew what she liked and didn't like. She loved Siouxsie and the Banshees, Japan and a band called Fashion, who no one really remembers now, but were very much of their time. They wore a lot of make-up and had experimental-looking haircuts and enigmatic stage names: Lûke, Mulligán, Dïk. We spent a lot of time at her house – obviously, no bloody way was I taking her back to the Portakabin – listening to music. If you played me 'Love Shadow' by Fashion today, I'd still be transported back to Debbie's bedroom. She lived in a town a few miles away, in a little bungalow on a housing estate with her mum and dad – precisely the kind of normal life that I always craved. Her town was a bit of a trek from Newton. I used to borrow my mate's moped and helmet and ride over there: I didn't have a licence, but I'd had enough practice around the garden centre not to kill myself en route.

I really fell in love with Debbie. I was probably partly in love with the idea of having a girlfriend – I'd never had one before, and it had a bit of 'this is where life begins' attached to it. Having this attractive, cool girl who wanted to go out with me made me feel normal, for once, like I finally fitted in somewhere – not some oddball who lived in the middle of a garden centre, getting by trying to be as invisible as possible. Perhaps there was also some psychological stuff tied up in it about wanting a female presence in my life because my mum had left when I was so young, and we'd never really had a proper mother–son relationship; there was always that strange distance with her. But I mostly simply fell for her, enough that when she broke off the relationship after a few months – her sister's boyfriend did that on her behalf as well, I seem to remember – I was genuinely devastated. It's completely commonplace when you're in your teens – lots of relationships only go on for a few months, you're meant to move on to the next one – but I couldn't deal with it at all. It really felt like my life was over. I suppose a psychiatrist would say that the extremity of my reaction was all bound up in what had happened with my mum – she had left me, and now *another* woman was leaving me – although I definitely wouldn't have thought that at the time. I just felt completely devastated. I walked back from the cricket club to the garden centre on my own, feeling very sorry for myself, and moped around for the next week. The following Monday, I went back to the cricket club, somehow convinced it was all a temporary blip and we were getting back together. But apparently we weren't: she'd already asked someone else out, and – to make matters worse – it was Peter Dale, who everyone called Pep, who was also in a band, a band from Aelred's, called FBI. Once again, it was a long, miserable walk back to the garden centre. I think that precipitated one of my periods of not going out for weeks.

When I finally decided to go back to having some kind of social life, I met Phil from Give Way at the cricket club. He said he had something he wanted to talk to me about. It turned out that Debbie had decided she wanted to go out with me again. He looked a bit surprised at my reaction: I think he expected me to be delighted, but I was more confused than anything else. We did start going out together again, and we were a couple for a really long time, but I think part of me realized then that this wasn't necessarily for ever. I'd been really hurt, and from then on, there was always a bit of me that I held back in that relationship: I wasn't going to make myself that vulnerable again.

*

I wasn't crazy about the idea of going to work with my dad at the garden centre when I left school, largely because it meant dealing with my dad all day every day, without a break, but with plenty of opportunities for him to lose his temper thrown in. But it just seemed inevitable, and in a way it was welcome – at least I had an idea what was going to happen, unlike a lot of people. The early eighties were not a great time to be an unskilled, not particularly academic, working-class teenager in the North of England. There was massive unemployment in Britain at the time and it hit young people in places like Newton hard. The days when the school opened their gates to let you out and the local factories opened theirs to let you in, and people went straight from one to the other, were over. A lot of local industry was shutting down – you'd hear it on the news all the time, this business or that business was closing, 1,800 jobs out of the window – and there was a kind of pessimism about the future in my generation there, an overwhelming sense of 'What are we going to do?'

Maybe that pessimism spilled over into everyday life. I remember it being quite a bleak time and teenage life being pretty violent. There were stupid rivalries between kids from Newton and kids from other towns. Lads seemed to want to fight, regardless – they'd go on a coach trip to a club in another town and if they hadn't managed to start trouble with the locals while they were there, they'd start a fight on the coach home. I was always on red alert for that kind of thing, probably because of my dad. I was used to people's moods suddenly changing and becoming ugly, and I wanted to avoid it as much as possible. You couldn't always. I went to a party in Haydock when I was still at school – my mate Elly lived there – and it suddenly all kicked off: everyone who was there from Newton was getting beaten up. It turned out that some guy from Newton had tried it on with a girl, and her boyfriend was at the party, and it all turned pretty ugly. I had quite long hair at the time, and so, apparently, did the bloke who'd started the trouble. So they're looking for a lad from Newton with long red hair to give him a kicking. Elly had to tell them I was his cousin and had nothing to do with what had happened to get me out of there in one piece.

About a week later, I was walking past the chip shop on the high street in Newton. There were three older guys in there I didn't recognize, but they started staring at me as I went past. I kept walking, and the next thing I know a blue Vauxhall Viva pulls up alongside me with the windows down. It's the three guys from the chippy, and they do not like me. They think I'm the one from the party in Haydock. I just keep walking. The car speeds past me, into a car park. It stops, they get out and follow me. I start running, convinced I'm going to get beaten up. Eventually, I get to some houses and there's a guy outside one of them, locking his car up. I rush up to him: 'Please, pretend you know me – there's three lads following me, they're going to beat the crap out of me.' Thankfully, he totally played along: 'Where have you been? Come on, get in the house.' We watched them walk past, laughing and pointing at me, then he drove me back to the garden centre. When I told Elly about it at school, he made some enquiries and I found out how lucky I'd been to get away. Those guys were looking to murder someone; one of them was apparently a trainee policeman who liked violence and carried his truncheon with him when he was off duty. It's odd – that incident has never really left me. I'm not keen on people following me, which is hardly a major problem in everyday life. Unless, of course, you become an internationally famous pop star, because people have a tendency to follow you then: not in a bad way; they simply spot you and think, 'Is that him?', then trail you for a bit to make sure. But whatever the reason, they're still following you. Great.

So it was a strange time to be a school leaver, but at least I knew there was something waiting for me beyond applying for work at the Job Centre and seeing what came up. For a time, I thought I'd make a go of it. I got the idea in my head that I should go to agricultural college, really learn how to make the garden centre work – the way my dad ran it was pretty chaotic, as I'm sure you can imagine. Dad thought it was a good idea, but my school wasn't really the right environment for someone like me to learn in. I loved technical drawing, but I was in a class where the main objective among the pupils was to destroy each other's work as perfectly as you could. You'd sneak someone's drawing away from them, guillotine it down the middle, then put it back together so neatly they couldn't tell, until they lifted it up and it fell into two pieces. I was as bad as anyone else for doing things like that. It was a bit of a shambles, really. You couldn't avoid the sense that you weren't going to get out of the school with anything worthwhile.

I ended up simply thinking, *What's the point? I could sit*

here for weeks on end really trying in lessons like biology, but, agriculture college or not, I am still going to end up working for my dad. There was no guarantee that Dad was going to listen to anything I learned at college. He was in charge, the buck stopped with him and you weren't really encouraged to question him or come up with ideas of your own. I was just going to be doing what I was already doing at weekends and after school, but with the advantage that I was going to get a wage packet at the end of the week. When I started thinking like that, I couldn't see any reason to be at school. I wanted to get out of there as soon as possible and get earning. I couldn't see the point of revising for my O-Levels – what difference was it going to make if I passed or failed them? You didn't need qualifications where I was headed.

The only reason I bothered turning up to the exams at all was because I thought they'd contact my dad if I didn't show. I couldn't imagine he'd blow up if they did – he really wasn't that interested in education – but you never knew, and it didn't seem worth taking the risk. But I didn't write a word once I was there, except my name. I went to work at the garden centre. Everything turned out exactly as I expected. Until the morning my dad attacked me, and Mike threatened to kill him, and we both left. I didn't see that coming at all. And it ultimately changed everything.

Chapter Three

When I left school, Give Way petered out. We'd never done much other than rehearse anyway, and Phil, the guitarist, had decided he wanted to stay on at school and go into sixth form. That was quite rare among my friends, but Phil was really smart and his plans didn't end there. He wanted to go to university to study computing, much to everyone else's confusion: 'You're going *where* to do *what*?' In Newton-le-Willows in 1982, you might as well have announced that your career plans involved building your own spaceship and flying it to Jupiter, but Phil had somehow worked out where the future lay.

Phil going to sixth form meant the end of Give Way, so when I was asked to join FBI – the band from St Aelred's whose bass player, Pep, Debbie had asked out after she dumped me – I said yes. Not surprisingly, the whole school rivalry thing had stopped once we'd left school – it would have been a bit pathetic if it hadn't – and I must have got over the business with Pep and my girlfriend. Perhaps I had decided it was less important than finding a band who not only needed a drummer, but actually had some gigs lined up, even if the gigs were only playing for younger kids at a school in St Helens where Pep's dad was a teacher. I think he used to put FBI's name forward whenever there was a school disco.

FBI's repertoire was even weirder than Give Way's. The guitarist, Neddy – Kevin Needham – was obsessed with, of all people, The Shadows: his dad was a bit of an old rock-and-roller and he must have got it off him. Another guy in the band liked gothier stuff, so we did Shadows covers *and* 'Bela Lugosi's Dead' by Bauhaus, which was a bit of an odd combination to start off with. Then there were a couple of early Beatles tracks – 'I Wanna Hold Your Hand' and things like that – mixed up with songs that had recently been in the charts: stuff by Big Country, 'Rip It Up' by Orange Juice. It was a peculiar cocktail, but it seemed to go down pretty well at the school discos and the cricket club.

The thing was, I didn't really want to be in a covers band. There were dozens of them around the North-West at the time, playing the pubs and working men's clubs, which was fine – good for them – but that wasn't where my ambitions lay. I wondered if those bands had once had dreams of really making it but had reached a point where they'd just given up and settled for simply making a living instead. The way I saw it, you could make a pragmatic decision that you wanted to earn some money straight away, so you learned covers and got on the club circuit. Or you could be brave or daft enough to say, 'No, we've got our own thing: we're going to write songs and do what we want to do,' and set your sights a bit higher. I was definitely in this second group.

So I got Will, who played rhythm guitar, to show me a few chords, and I somehow put things together to write a couple of songs. At rehearsals, I sang them from the drum kit, but we decided that wasn't really working, so we bought a drum machine and used that when my turn came to sing. It was only second-hand – a Roland Dr Rhythm 55, the same model Depeche Mode used when they were first starting out – but still: a drum machine! It felt like something out of science fiction, as if we should have got Phil, with his mysterious computing expertise, to program it.

We unveiled the drum machine at a Battle of the Bands competition in St Helens. When we arrived, we discovered that not only did we have a dressing room, but that there was music playing in it. There was a little speaker in the corner, which seemed to be blaring out Radio 1. They were playing 'Give It Up' by KC and the Sunshine Band. Then we realized it wasn't the radio and it wasn't KC and the Sunshine Band. The speaker was part of a kind of internal tannoy system in the venue and the version of 'Give It Up' was being played by one of our fellow competitors, up on stage. They were a covers band, but they sounded amazing: as good as the real thing and therefore far better than us. So much for the low musical horizons of the working men's club bands.

We consoled ourselves with the thought that we had original songs – clearly no one was going to win a Battle of the Bands contest playing covers, however good they were – and more importantly, we had a drum machine. Then the next contestants came on. They were a bit older than us, but they had their own songs and *they* sounded far better than us too. Plus they had an image. They were wearing matching outfits, but not the kind of naff matching outfits you associate with a working men's club band. They weren't in bow ties and red ruffled dinner shirts. They had baggy black trousers and their shirts were pretty funky. They looked a bit like Haircut 100. They looked as if they could have been in *Smash Hits*, or at least more like they could have been in *Smash Hits* than we did. *Shit*. Mind you, they didn't have a drum machine.

We did, and that turned out to be the problem. When it came to our turn, things started out OK, until I got down from the drum kit and prepared to dazzle the audience with the songs I'd written. I started the drum machine, at which point it became apparent that someone had fiddled with it and cranked the speed setting up to full. Perhaps it was sabotage, but it was more likely an honest mistake; besides, how it had happened was nothing like as important as what was happening: the noise that came out sounded less like music than a particularly violent machine-gun shoot-out. We should have said something to the audience to make a joke out of it – that was the other thing about those working men's club bands: they always had a bit of patter because they were experienced at winning over audiences. We just looked at each other – what the fuck is going on? – while I pressed every button the drum machine had, trying to fix it. At least it got an audience reaction, albeit not the audience reaction we were after. They were in hysterics. Back to Newton we went.

But the Battle of the Bands competition ultimately had some positive effects. We got rid of the drum machine and got a guy called Chris Brown in to play drums, which meant I was now, officially, the lead singer. We took a few hints and tips from our competitors and bought our own matching outfits from Afflecks Palace in Manchester: black trousers and shirts with a design of a hand painted on them. I wrote more songs. My big number was called, I'm sorry to say, 'Shake Your Arse'. I had the idea that you should come up with something that people could sing along to straight away, so the chorus was a kind of duet between the vocals and the drums: 'Shake your arse!' – thump-thump-thump – 'Shake your arse!' Leonard Cohen obviously wasn't going to be losing any sleep over my lyrical abilities, but I thought it was catchy as hell.

Just how catchy it was became clear when we started playing gigs at the Legh Arms in Newton, a big pub in front of McCorquodale's, where my mum worked. It didn't usually host live bands, but we'd plucked up the courage to ask the landlord if we could play. He agreed on the condition that he only paid us in beer – fine by us – and that we played on his quietest night of the week, a Tuesday. The first week, our friends turned up, but I have to say, we killed it. Word must have got around after that, because by the second or third time we played, the place was rammed. It was fantastic. Well, I'm not sure *we* were fantastic exactly, but it *felt* fantastic: it was a pub full of people, all our age, singing along to songs I'd written. 'Shake Your Arse' went down a storm.

We started getting more gigs in different pubs around Newton. I wrote more songs, including one called 'The Taming of the Shrew', which I'd love to tell you was influenced by my deep love of Shakespeare, and my desire to write songs with the profound power of great literature, but I can't, because I'd never read *The Taming of the Shrew*. I didn't know what it was about and I didn't even know what 'The Taming of the Shrew' meant.

I think this was probably all Morrissey's fault. I'd loved The Smiths from the moment I heard my brother Mike playing them. The first time I listened to 'This Charming Man', I was completely hooked – the sound, the lyrics, the fact that they came from a place down the road to me, everything about them. I'd never come across anything like it before. I heard that line about 'a jumped-up pantry boy who never knew his place' and thought: *What?* The weird thing was, I recognized it straight away. My mum had taken me to see a stage production of *Sleuth* in Morecombe when I was ten or eleven years old, with Michael Williams playing the role that Michael Caine played in the film, and that was a line from it – 'You're a jumped-up pantry boy who doesn't know his place.' It had always stayed with me, probably because I was far too young to be watching *Sleuth* in the first place. And there it was, in a song. What the fuck? It was the kind of songwriting that was too original to copy, but I gave it a go anyway. After spotting the reference to *Sleuth*, I realized that Morrissey's lyrics were often inspired by plays and books. And I must have decided to try that myself, without understanding that you were supposed to actually read some books first before incorporating their influence into your songs. Hence 'The Taming of the Shrew'.

Never mind: it wasn't as if anyone in FBI was stopping rehearsals to quiz me about the deeper meaning of the imagery in the third verse – 'Hang on, Rick, do you not feel that Shakespeare's attitude to women in *The Taming of the Shrew* has been rendered obsolete, even offensive, by the rise of feminism?' And there was always 'Shake Your Arse', which by now we'd turned into a bit of a showstopper, or at least our idea of a showstopper. Chris had got a second set of drums, so we set the tom-toms from his old drum kit at the side of the stage, and I battered them as I sang, thump-thump-thumping to my heart's content.

*

By the time we played another Battle of the Bands competition in Warrington, we even had management. Someone in FBI had approached the club band we'd heard playing 'Give It Up' in St Helens – they were called American Buzz – and had been pointed in the direction of their managers, Dave Warwick and Tony Graham. We didn't think anything more about it – after the great drum-machine disaster, it seemed unlikely anyone would be in a tearing hurry to work with us – but one week Dave and Tony turned up at the Legh Arms. I'm not sure if they even particularly liked FBI's music, but they saw a pub packed with kids going nuts to a local band, and they definitely liked that. They realized something was going on and offered their services.

Dave and Tony's management company was a funny set-up. They had an office above a wool shop in a suburb of Warrington – I seem to remember they owned the wool shop as well, so they were nothing if not diverse in their business interests. As managers, their big client was Gordon Burns, who presented *The Krypton Factor* and the local news on Granada TV. But Dave had been a DJ in the 1960s, and they had a few bands too, mostly working men's club acts. The jewel in their musical crown was a sextet called Poacher, who weren't exactly a household name but had done a lot better than you might have expected a country and western band from Warrington to do. Poacher had been on the telly and put records out; they'd even had a minor hit in America.

Dave and Tony's management company definitely made things happen for FBI. Poacher let us tape some demos in their studio, which sounds a bit grander than it was. It was only some equipment in a barn at the back of the Old Crow, a pub in Newton that the bass player's dad owned, but it was still a chance to record. The drummer from another one of their club bands gave us advice on writing songs: simple, useful stuff, like making sure you had a way to get from the verse into the chorus that really announced that the chorus had arrived. We got asked to go to Granada TV and record a couple of songs; they used to have a little spot at the end of the local news, where they'd sometimes show a clip of a new band from the North-West. Our performance never did get broadcast, but we spotted Tony Wilson, who ran Factory Records when he wasn't reading the news on Granada, in the corridor of the studio. I chased after him, telling him I was in a band and asking him to take a look at the TV performance we'd recently recorded. He said he'd try, but something about the way he said it suggested he doubted we were the next New Order. Dave and Tony even got a talent scout from Warner Brothers to come up and see us, although he went back to London unconvinced that the world was about to be set on fire by 'Shake Your Arse', or a singer who'd never read *The Taming of the Shrew* singing about 'The Taming of the Shrew'.

Still, things were definitely moving in the right direction. The only problem I could see was FBI themselves, or rather everyone else in FBI but me. I was either conceited or stupid enough genuinely to believe that we were going to make it. I really had a fire in me. I thought we had a tiny window of opportunity to make it happen: *We've got to do this now, because the next thing you know, we'll be twenty-five and that'll be it, over.* I wasn't sure the others felt that way. Chris was still at school, and he was really into sport, so he sometimes didn't turn up for rehearsals because he was playing rugby. Some of the band were on the dole and seemed more interested in doing nothing than being in a band: there were times I literally had to get them out of bed to practise. All of which led up to my cringe-inducing lecture on how I was going to be as famous as David Bowie.

Maybe I was getting a bit full of myself. It's hard to say it without sounding twattish, but I had realized that when I sang, it attracted attention. You'd see other singers in pubs and clubs and the audience wouldn't even look up from their pints, but that didn't seem to happen to me: people took notice. Maybe it was because my voice didn't really match my appearance. Even in my painted shirt from Afflecks Palace, I looked about twelve years old, but I didn't sound that different to the way I do now. My voice was a bit more affected and stylized – it was the 1980s, the era of David Sylvian from Japan and Edwyn Collins from Orange Juice, and singing in a slightly affected voice was definitely a thing – but if you heard a recording of me then you'd definitely recognize it as me. In the unlikely event that you do want to hear a recording of me from that era, you can. Someone – I think it was my cousin – made a video of FBI playing at another Battle of the Bands in Warrington, and it's been uploaded to YouTube. I find it mortifying today, but at least they didn't film the one with the drum machine. If you want to go and play it now, I can wait here with my eyes shut and my fingers in my ears until you're done.

*

My voice attracted attention, but I don't really think it was arrogance about my talent that was driving me. It was that I saw music as a way out – not out of Newton exactly, but out of my situation in Newton – and I was desperate to succeed. What I really wanted, more than anything, was that safety and stability in my life. Obviously, a career in music probably wasn't the *ideal* choice if safety and stability were what I was looking for – as I would learn in due course, the music industry is as mad as a box of frogs – but it seemed more likely to provide it than life with either of my parents.

Even before the incident with Mike and the kitchen knife, working at the garden centre didn't seem like a particularly solid opportunity. My dad was so unpredictable and so irrational, there was every chance he'd just turn around one morning and decide he was selling the whole thing and that would be that. None of that mattered now. I hadn't been back to the Portakabin since the business with the knife. Mike had moved his big Nissan saloon car off the garden centre land and round to his mate's house, which seemed to draw a line under our time living there, although I did start working there again, on and off, whenever John said he wanted help: I needed the money. Mike had started taking an Open University course in accountancy, which was amazing in every sense: Mike was the last person you would have thought would get into something like that, but he really stuck with it. I was unbelievably proud of him for doing it.

But if I'd thought that moving in with my mum would make my life a bit more stable, a bit less erratic, I was wrong. True, Mum didn't fly into violent rages, or unexpectedly turn up at the front door with a horse or 25,000 strawberry plants, but she was still perfectly capable of springing the kind of surprise that pulled the rug out from under your feet. This was underlined when, not long after Mike and I moved in, she suddenly announced that she was getting married again.

What's more, she was getting married to a bloke all her children didn't like. She'd had boyfriends before who had seemed great. There was a guy called Trevor whom she knew from work, and we all really liked him – he was into motorbikes, which was a definite point in his favour as far as Mike and John were concerned – but that fizzled out: he was ten years younger than my mum, and his parents weren't very happy about him being involved with an older woman. And then she met Bob. Bob was a bus driver – they'd met when she got on his bus. Bob was already married, although he now seemed to be getting divorced. It would have seemed romantic, had Bob not given every impression of being a total idiot. He was a slob. He seemed incredibly selfish and thoroughly unpleasant.

In a sense, it was unfair of me to make judgements about Bob, because I didn't really know him. None of us had ever socialized with him at all, never sat down and eaten a meal with him, never said more than two words to him. Maybe he had hidden depths, but if he did, none of us were aware of them, because we didn't know him. That was what was weird about it: a bloke I didn't know was now apparently going to be my stepdad. He was coming to live in my gran's house with us. Mum didn't seem to think this was odd at all. There wasn't any discussion about it, no sense of breaking the news gently. It was, as they say, a fait accompli, which seems even stranger to me now than it did then: I'm a parent, I have a daughter, and the idea of making a decision like that without even mentioning it to her feels crazy. I got the feeling she simply wanted to get on with her life, regardless of her kids. Even if she had been deeply in love with Bob, you might have thought she would have said something about the fact that two of her kids had recently come to live with her after running away from a violent altercation with their dad – 'It's a difficult situation, can you just bear with me for a bit?' – but she obviously didn't think like that. So we headed off to the registry office in St Helens, completely bewildered. The whole thing seemed miserable and wrong, but, if nothing else, it underlined that I was definitely going to have to fend for myself in the future.

And I didn't fancy my chances of fending for myself in Newton. The town had always been a certain way when I was growing up – it was working class, we made things, we built stuff, and all the factories and the noise around it was evidence of that – but you only had to drive down the road where my dad lived to see that everything was changing. Just past Parkside Garden Centre was Parkside Colliery. It had employed 1,600 men in the 1970s, but now there was a small army of police in riot gear. The miners were on strike against a wave of pit closures, and Parkside was a flashpoint because some men wanted to strike, and others wanted to keep working. There were other miners who'd arrived from Yorkshire to strengthen the picket, and there were police trying to get the miners they called scabs into work past the picket line. It was genuinely frightening. I didn't pay much attention to what was happening on the news when I was younger, and I wasn't particularly interested in politics, but it was hard to ignore when something that you'd seen on the telly was also happening on your street, right in front of you. It was real, and you could somehow tell things in town were never going to be quite the same again, however it ended.

*

In early 1985, Dave, one of our managers, told us that someone called Pete Waterman wanted to come and see us live. I don't know how Dave got him interested in FBI. He might have known him from when he was a DJ, or it might have had something to do with the fact that Pete Waterman had unexpectedly fallen in love with Newton-le-Willows, or rather, had fallen in love with a hairdresser from Newton called Gaynor. She had a salon in town above a record shop called the Home of Tunes, which was owned by Kev Edwards, the DJ who used to play at the cricket club on a Friday.

To be honest, I didn't spend much time wondering how they got him to come, because I had absolutely no idea who Pete Waterman was. Dave explained that he was a record producer, part of a team called Stock Aitken Waterman – or SAW, as they were known in the music industry – who'd had a couple of hits with Hazell Dean and Divine. Years later, I ended up touring Japan with Hazell and discovered she lived around the corner from me – she and her family are lovely – but at the time her name, and indeed that of Divine, didn't provoke much more than a blank stare from me. I might have heard them in a club or seen them on *Top of the Pops*, but if I had, they hadn't resonated with me, certainly not enough to find out who'd produced them.

The thing was, in 1985, no one outside the music business really knew who Pete Waterman was. SAW weren't exactly chancers – Pete had been in the industry for years, working as an A&R and a manager – but they were definitely still scuffling around, trying anything to get something going: attempting to launch a female version of Frankie Goes to Hollywood (it didn't work), writing Cyprus's entry in the 1984 Eurovision Song Contest (it came seventh), whatever. The few hits they'd had were aimed squarely at clubs, based on the hi-NRG sound that was big on the 1980s gay scene.

But even if I'd never heard of him, this guy was apparently a producer, with an office in London, both of which sounded promising – it wasn't as if FBI were inundated with offers. A showcase gig was set up, in the suitably glamorous surroundings of a Warrington social club called Monks. There were other bands on, and an audience made up of a few people we and the other bands knew – it wasn't like an audition – but it was obvious the whole point was for Pete Waterman to see FBI.

Pete helpfully cleared up any lingering doubts about who or what he was by arriving at the gig dressed exactly like an eighties music business mogul. He was driving a Jag and wearing a pair of bright red leather trousers. We were suitably impressed. We did our show, suggested the audience shake their collective arse – thump-thump-thump! – and that seemed to be that. Pete Waterman certainly didn't rush backstage, pull a contract and a pen out of his red leather trousers and demand we sign. He just disappeared into the night in his Jag. *Oh well*, I thought, *we gave it a shot*.

A couple of weeks later, I got a phone call from Dave. Could I come and meet him and Tony at their office? No need to bring the rest of the band over to Warrington – they only wanted to see me. That sounded odd: what was going on? When I arrived, they told me that Pete Waterman was interested, not in signing FBI, just in signing me. Truthfully, I don't think it was any reflection on the rest of the band. I think the problem Pete Waterman had with FBI was that we *were* a band and, as history has shown us, SAW really weren't interested in signing bands: they only wanted singers they could mould to their sound.

Even so, my initial reaction was a flat 'no'. For one thing, I didn't particularly want to be a solo singer, and for another I didn't want to let the rest of the band down; it seemed wrong. But I kept thinking about the offer, turning it over and over in my mind. I suppose it was a first opportunity for me to have the kind of security I wanted. Because of how things were growing up with my dad and my mum, I've always felt there was . . . a wolf at the door, if you like, and that it was down to me to keep the wolf at bay – to make my life more stable, to make enough money so that I wasn't reliant on other people. If I earned a bit of cash, I didn't have to do what my dad told me to, I could make my own way. If I earned a bit of cash, I'd feel less frightened. And what if it wasn't my first opportunity, but my only opportunity? It wasn't like anyone else was exactly beating down FBI's door looking to sign us. What if I was right, that I really was a lot more committed to music than the rest of the band? What if I was throwing away my chance for a band who weren't that bothered? And even if it wasn't my big break, my one great opportunity, surely I might as well give it a go? I would hardly be signing my life away here. It was just a contract with some producers I'd never heard of. It might be a toe in the water, a bit of experience. Even if it didn't work out, I could come back to FBI having learned something.

Eventually, I phoned Dave and told him I'd changed my mind and I wanted to sign after all. He and Tony called a meeting with the whole band to let them know what was going on. It was as awkward as you might imagine. Dave and Tony tried to spin the situation in a positive way to the rest of the band. This didn't mean the end of FBI. It probably wouldn't work out with me and Pete Waterman, and if it didn't, we'd be back together again. And if it did work out with SAW, they'd need a backing band for me, and they'd surely call on FBI's services if they did. It was a valiant effort on Dave and Tony's part, but from the atmosphere in the room, I got the feeling Pep and the others didn't believe a word of it. I felt awful, but I still felt I was doing the right thing.

Not long afterwards, Pete and Gaynor turned up in the Jag and drove me down to SAW's studio. When we got to London, he took a detour and drove me around the sights – Big Ben and Buckingham Palace – then took me to dinner at an Italian restaurant on Brewer Street called Topo Gigio.

It was a sweet thing to do. I'd never seen Buckingham Palace or Soho before: the only time I'd been to London had been with my dad, to the Motor Show at Earl's Court.

But, then, the trip around London and the meal in Soho had the added benefit of giving Pete more time to talk, something he hadn't stopped doing since I got in the car. It wasn't a conversation; it was a monologue that had been going on for three hours and showed no signs of drawing to a close any time soon, and it was almost entirely about SAW. If I hadn't known anything about them when Dave and Tony first mentioned their names, I certainly did now. They were the best in the business. They were the success story of the year. They were the talk of the music industry, which they were apparently in the process of turning on its head. They were going to do this, they were going to do that, they were going to do the other. It was extraordinary. The way he was going on, you would have thought SAW had been personally responsible for the careers of The Beatles, Michael Jackson and Madonna, rather than two hi-NRG singles and Cyprus's entry in the Eurovision Song Contest. I'd never met anyone so unshakeably convinced of their own brilliance, so certain about their own tastes, so confident they knew exactly what the public wanted. You couldn't help liking him, but if there had been a salt shaker in the car, I would have taken several pinches from it. Instead, I simply kept nodding and making positive noises. It was hard to work out whether I was in the presence of a genius – the kind of person who was so self-assured they were almost guaranteed to be a success – or someone who belonged in a straitjacket.

My heart sank a little when we finally arrived at their studio. It was behind Borough tube station in south London and in the 1980s, Borough really wasn't the most salubrious area. You could tell it was a bit rough by the studio's huge metal doors and the keypad you had to use to get in. It certainly didn't seem like the part of London where The Biggest Producers in Britain would be based.

But when we got inside, things looked up. It was definitely a proper recording studio, although I knew enough about studios by then to notice that it didn't seem to have a live room, where you could record musicians playing guitar or drums. That seemed to say something about how SAW made records, and confirmed what I'd thought all along: they weren't interested in bands, and never had any intention of signing FBI.

What's more, it was a studio that had gold discs on the wall. Not as many gold discs as you might have expected on the basis of Pete's lecture – if Pete was as successful and important as he was claiming to be, the place would have been wallpapered with them – but enough to impress me. Whatever SAW were, they were still way further up the ladder than I was.

Pete said they were currently working on a track by a band called Dead or Alive, whose lead singer was like Boy George, only a Scouser, and more outrageous. It was going to be a huge hit. *Yeah, of course it is*, I thought. *God, does this guy ever stop telling you how great he is?* Then he played it to me. Bloody *hell*. You could see the link between 'You Spin Me Round (Like a Record)' and the singles SAW had made previously – it was definitely based on that hi-NRG sound, and it had a bit of a Frankie Goes to Hollywood feel – but it was in a different league altogether. It sounded *fantastic*. It was total pop music, aimed directly at the charts, but it was incredibly exciting. There was no intro, no build-up. The thing just leapt out of the speakers the second it started and grabbed you by the throat. It sounded like the best night out of your life condensed into three minutes. Now I was really impressed. Perhaps Pete's lecture in the car wasn't a load of bollocks after all, or at least not complete bollocks: on the evidence of 'You Spin Me Round', SAW really were very good at what they did.

He said he needed to get my voice on tape, so that Mike Stock and Matt Aitken could hear me. Pete wanted me to do a version of 'Wherever I Lay My Hat', the Marvin Gaye song Paul Young had had a huge hit with a couple of years back, accompanied by a keyboard player who happened to be in the studio at the time. The choice of song made sense: I was a white guy with a voice that people seemed to think was soulful, and Paul Young was the biggest singer like that in pop at the time. I've never heard the recording I made that night, and I don't really want to. It's probably awful.

The next morning, I went back to Newton and waited for the verdict on my efforts. A week or so later, I got a phone call from Dave: Pete Waterman Limited wanted to sign me, to something called a production deal. In truth, I had no idea what a production deal was, but the general gist seemed to be that I would be going back to Borough to do some more recording. I figured it might at least result in me making a single and that was good enough for me. I didn't bother consulting a lawyer. No one suggested it to me, and there hardly seemed to be any point. The money involved was buttons anyway; it was only about enough to cover my train fares from Newton to London.

I signed the contract in Dave and Tony's office, and then . . . nothing happened. The weeks rolled by without any word. The Dead or Alive single that I'd heard in SAW's studio came out, and it was deservedly a huge hit, which impressed some people I knew – 'You've signed a deal with the guys who did *this*?' – but made things even more awkward when I ran into the other members of FBI: if the producers I'd signed with were making more hits, it was increasingly clear that I wasn't coming back to the band. And I kept running into the other members of FBI because I was still in bloody Newton. There was no sign of the phone call inviting me back to London to record.

Eventually, Dave and Tony contacted Pete and asked him what he was doing: 'You've signed this kid and he's just sitting around at home. He's not doing anything; he's not earning any money. Even if you don't think he's ready to record yet, he's not developing anything, so he'll never be ready to record.'

So Pete came up with a solution. I could go to London and work in the studio in Borough. My job would mostly in- volve making tea and fetching sandwiches, but it would also mean learning the ropes when it came to making records. I said I couldn't afford to travel up and down to London all the time, but Pete had a solution for that too. He had a place in Crouch End, and I could live there with him during the week. Making tea and fetching sandwiches, being Pete Waterman's flatmate: it wasn't exactly what I thought would happen, but it was a definite improvement on living at Gran's with my mum and Bob.

Chapter Four

People always say that when I went to work at PWL – Pete Waterman Limited – I was quiet. They're right. It was partly because I was there to learn, and I took that seriously. I wanted to soak it all up, not stick my oar in. And it was partly out of shyness, because I felt a bit out of place, particularly around some of the other juniors who worked at the studio. They were really nice people, but they were definitely different from me. They were quite cocky, and I got the feeling that some of them came from wealthy families and simply fancied working at a recording studio for something to do. In reality, they might have just been middle-class Southerners – I hadn't met many of those before – who I automatically assumed were posh. Whatever they were, they didn't seem to be people who'd spent much of their youth humping concrete posts and fencing panels around Merseyside and Cheshire.

But I was quiet mostly because I was gobsmacked at what was going on at PWL. If it's an exaggeration to say that everything Pete Waterman had said on the way down from Newton had come true, it certainly seemed to be in the process of coming true. It was as if his endless speech in the car was some mad act of manifesting, decades before anybody talked about manifesting. 'You Spin Me Round' had turned Stock Aitken Waterman from a marginal concern into a very hot property indeed. Big pop stars wanted to work with them. So did a succession of new acts, whose record companies had sent them to PWL looking for a hit-making boost. There were even rock bands: they had seen what had happened to Dead or Alive – who, after all, had started life as a goth band – and decided they wanted some of that too. On top of that, SAW were constantly trying to develop artists of their own. They had a singer called Princess who they'd discovered working as a backing vocalist. The song they came up with for her, 'Say I'm Your Number One', was fantastic. It sounded nothing like anything else SAW had done: it wasn't a dance-floor track, it was more like a super-cool American electronic soul record, with a distinctly British flavour sprinkled on top. There was O'Chi Brown, who Pete had met when she was singing reggae, and he was now intent on turning her into a disco diva.

They were only the tip of the iceberg. The traffic through the studio was incredible.

People would turn up, record some songs, then – a little worryingly, given my own position – never be heard of again. I remember a ridiculously handsome Black guy called Austin Howard who they were trying to market as a sophisticated soul singer – he looked a bit like Marvin Gaye – and a band called Splash, who sounded like a poppier version of Go West. One day, we were told Mandy Smith was coming in to make a single. Hang on, *Mandy Smith*? She was all over the tabloids because she was in a relationship with Bill Wyman from the Rolling Stones, a relationship that had begun when she was thirteen. She turned up in a big, black car but I wasn't really sure what she was doing there. Could she sing? I didn't know and I don't think SAW cared. It was as if it didn't matter whether she had any musical talent or not, because she had notoriety. They thought they could knock out a song for her, and her tabloid fame would get it in the charts. Pete was convinced her single was going to be a hit. I thought it was a bit of a tacky idea. I couldn't work out why they were doing it – it seemed like a novelty record, and why did they need to bother with them when they were already having huge chart singles? – but of course, I didn't say that. I just made Mandy Smith a cup of tea – she seemed nice enough – and let them get on with it.

Afterwards, early on in my own pop career, I ended up spending a bit of time with Mandy: there was a period where we always seemed to be on the same TV shows in Europe. We would both be with people from PWL who I knew, so we hung out together. She turned out to be lovely. God knows what was going on in her personal life – it's not for me to judge, anyway – but she was a really decent human being, nothing at all like the Jezebel Lolita she was painted as in the tabloids.

Her single wasn't a hit, at least not in Britain, but it hardly mattered. They had so much work coming in that they were building two more recording studios in the basement. One was supposed to be for recording drums in, which seemed a bit unnecessary, given that none of SAW's records actually had live drums on them, but perhaps they had plans to diversify. There was talk of developing a second production team and of keeping the studio open twenty-four hours a day: SAW would work there during the daytime, then the reserve squad would come in and work all night. Was that normal? I had no idea, but I thought probably not, because nothing about PWL seemed very normal.

For one thing, it quickly became clear that, despite being one-third of a production partnership and getting a credit on the songs they came up with, Pete didn't produce anything or write songs at all. He might come up with song titles or make occasional suggestions – 'Those chords are a bit jazzy,' 'It's too dark and muso; you can't dance to that.' Sometimes his comments were pretty abstract – 'It's too red, you need to make it more blue' – but somehow they'd always get interpreted to the point where Pete would decide the song was a hit. So he was important, but he wasn't a musician and he didn't technically know his way around a studio. That work was done by Mike Stock and Matt Aitken. The studio was very much their domain. You had to go through two separate sets of doors to get to it, and you certainly weren't encouraged to disturb them while they were working. They were a kind of study in opposites. Mike was blond and quite bubbly – I remember thinking that in another life, he could have been a member of Bucks Fizz – while Matt was dark and Northern and a bit dour; he came from a village near Wigan. The thing they had in common was that they were brilliant musicians and writers. Matt was an amazing guitarist. Sometimes I would watch them working together, going over and over a new melody on a keyboard, changing the chords underneath. It was a real education, seeing how substituting a couple of notes could completely alter the mood of the song, watching how they applied certain rules to pop. You might think it's a great idea for your song to have a big, long atmospheric intro, but the radio won't – tell them what the bleeding song is, right from the start.

There's a myth that SAW records were just mass-produced, carelessly banged out without any thought or effort. But it simply wasn't true. You might not have liked what they did, but Mike and Matt worked incredibly hard at doing it – everything had to be exactly the way they wanted it, every note in a song was there for a reason. I think that in fact they played up to the 'production line' image sometimes, because they knew it riled music journalists. And they *hated* rock critics and the music press; they thought they were snobby and condescending and irrelevant. And all the bad reviews in the world didn't stop their records from selling.

Under the circumstances, you could say that Pete being credited as a writer and producer was a bit of a con, but I've heard about credits on songs going to people who had far less to do with them than Pete Waterman did. And besides, Pete was absolutely integral to the whole operation. I think Mike and Matt would tell you that it would never have been anywhere near as successful without him. He dealt with the business side of things, talking to record labels, sorting out the contracts and the deals. He handled A&R, looking for artists, working out how to promote them. He came up with ideas for cover versions, usually old soul and pop songs he liked that dated back to when he was a DJ in the sixties and seventies. He kept his ear to the ground about what was happening in clubs – what records were big, what the new musical trends on the dancefloors were – and he either tried to incorporate it into the sound of SAW records, or he got remixes done for the B-sides that fitted with what was going on, whether it was acid house or rare groove or Balearic beat. He acted as SAW's public face. It was Pete who gave the interviews. He was always turning up at the office with an Italian film crew or something in tow. I was going to say that Pete took care of the interviews because Matt and Mike weren't as forthcoming as him, but then no one was as forthcoming as Pete; he made an over-excited cocker spaniel look retiring.

Which brings us to Pete's other role at PWL. He was a kind of agent of chaos. Mike and Matt were both quietly eccentric in their own way. Even after the money started rolling in, they insisted on eating lunch from a greasy spoon around the corner from the studio, John's. No matter what they were working on, how big a deal it was, or how pressing the deadline, they knocked off every day at 10 p.m. and went to a pub round the corner from the studio, the Gladstone. It's still there, and like everything else in Borough, it's gone up in the world since the eighties – it's all craft beer and Anglo-Indian fusion food now – but back then it was a really rough south London boozer. One time, the studio got broken into and some gold discs were stolen. Pete had a quiet word at the bar of the Gladstone, and the next day, the gold discs were discreetly returned. It was that kind of a pub, and they went there every night, without fail. You would have thought they might be sipping cocktails in a trendy wine bar in Soho and eating at Langan's Brasserie, but no: it was shepherd's pie or lasagne and chips from John's caff and the Gladstone at ten on the dot.

I thought that was a bit odd, but their little eccentricities were absolutely nothing compared to Pete's. He kept doing completely mad things. It was Pete who decided that the studio needed some striking decoration, so he bought a decommissioned missile – no, I have no idea where he went to buy a decommissioned missile – and hung it off the ceiling. When the space in the offices became a bit tight, Pete's solution was to buy a wooden shed from a garden centre, get the rest of us to carry it up the stairs, erect it on the flat roof of the building and use that as an extra office. One day, he told me he had something he needed me to do urgently and sent me to Cardiff to pick up two model trains he'd had specially made. When I say model trains, I don't mean the little ones you see on model railways. These things were about a metre long, handmade, and cost thousands of pounds. They were in glass cases and they were a fucking nightmare to get back to London on the train. But that was Pete. You had absolutely no idea what he was going to do next. And before you say it: yes, he did remind me a bit of my dad, albeit without the temper tantrums. He was only fifteen years older than me but he had a paternal air about him, not least because he called everyone who wasn't Matt or Mike 'kid'.

Instead of the temper tantrums, Pete seemed to specialize in saying the first thing that came into his head, without much consideration as to whether saying it was a good idea or not, or whether what he'd said made any sense. As it turned out, Pete's impulsivity was to cause me quite a lot of problems later on, but, for the time being, it was incredibly entertaining. He would tell these great stories about his career in the music business, packed with starry names: 'Now listen, kid, I remember when Stevie Wonder said to me . . .' You could never work out if they were really true or not; it didn't take long for you to realize that Pete was not one to let facts get in the way of a good yarn.

Sometimes, Pete's more far-fetched stories made a kind of sense. He had this kit car that looked like a Ferrari GTO. It was an absolutely beautiful-looking thing, as long as you didn't look under the bonnet. It only had a Nissan engine in it. One day, I was standing outside the studio with a guy called Mike Duffy. He did a lot of engineering at PWL, and we'd become really good friends. He's still one of my closest friends today. We were admiring the kit car, when Pete suddenly appeared. He was expecting a visit from a guy who worked at a bank that was somehow involved with the financing of the studio. When he arrived, Pete showed him the car and told him it was a real Ferrari – one of the most expensive cars in the world – looking at us for confirmation: 'Isn't that right, lads?' We nodded, knowing it was nothing of the sort. But you could see the logic there – the guy was from the bank, and Pete wanted him to think he was more successful than he actually was.

At other times, Pete's stories just defied all rational explanation. One year, the company hosted a Christmas dinner in a huge aircraft hangar full of old planes. Pete got up to make a speech, standing next to a Vulcan bomber. He tapped the bottom of the plane and said: 'This takes me back. One of my first jobs when I was a kid was at the factory that made these, outside of Coventry.' That seemed credible enough; Pete was from Coventry and there were definitely factories there that made aircraft. Certainly, it was more plausible than what he said next: 'They used to strap me to the bomb doors, the plane would take off and they'd open the bomb doors and I'd have to check they were working.'

The reaction was great. Everyone who had been invited to the dinner – all these heads of major record labels – looked really confused: *What the fuck is this guy talking about? He used to check the bomb doors were working while the plane was in mid-air? Is this a joke? Is he serious?* Everyone there who worked for PWL looked at each other and raised their eyebrows: *Uh-oh, Pete's off again . . .*

I loved working there. I'd drive to the studio in the morning, listening to Pete talking. He usually wasn't talking to me, he was talking to people from record labels on his mobile phone – the first mobile phone I think I'd ever seen in real life, one of those early ones that was the size of a house. Sometimes he'd be shouting and screaming at them over some deal he wasn't happy about; sometimes he was having a discussion about a new track or where an artist's career was going. Either way, I listened and tried to learn. Pete seemed to have his fingers in a lot of different pies. He had the studio. He had an interest in a record label called Supreme. He had his own publishing company, All Boys Music. Right, what *is* a publishing company? What's a publishing deal? How does that work?

I did the same thing in the Gladstone every evening. Because I was signed as an artist, I was allowed to drink my pint at SAW's table – they'd buy all the other juniors a drink and tell them to sit somewhere else. I didn't say much, I simply sat there, absorbing what they were saying: whose single was doing well and why, which labels were really on fire at the moment and which ones were struggling to get a hit, the new club records that Pete had got hold of, how they sounded, whether they could use that sound in their own productions. They were always very clear about who they were making records for. It was Tracey and Sharon and Dave, who wanted to go out to Cinderella Rockefeller's or Ritzy's on Friday and Saturday night and dance to pop tunes; they weren't interested in anyone else, or what anyone else thought. There was a part of me – the part that liked The Smiths and other bands – that wasn't 100 per cent comfortable with that line of thinking. That part thought maybe it was a bit limited. Then again, I knew that, if I was going to make records myself, I wanted them to reach as big an audience as possible, and you couldn't argue with SAW's chart positions.

And in between the car journey there and the Gladstone, I worked as what was called a tape op. They hadn't been joking; a lot of the job did involve fetching sandwiches and making tea and coffee, but at least I was fetching sandwiches and making tea for pop stars. I played table tennis with Dead or Alive. Pete Burns was quite intimidating; he had an aura and carried himself like a star, but the complexities of his private life were a bit beyond me. He was married to a woman called Lynne, but he also seemed to have a full-time boyfriend, Steve, who was the drummer in Dead or Alive, not that anyone was doing much actual drumming in the PWL studios. The rest of the band were really nice: they were from Liverpool, and I think they just liked running into a lad who knew where St Helens was.

I made tea for Bananarama when they came in to write and record, which always changed the atmosphere in the studio. Bananarama insisted on co-writing their songs with Mike and Matt, which I don't think went down very well. Mike and Matt liked to write songs themselves; they didn't want artists interfering. Like I said, everything had to be exactly so. And Bananarama always turned up in a little gang of their friends and boyfriends. All of them seemed quite hip and edgy. They were people who worked for style magazines, people who actually went to hip bars in Soho while we were sitting in the Gladstone. And all of them made it clear they thought SAW were deeply uncool, which, by their standards, they were. You know, in their early days, Bananarama had hung around with the Sex Pistols and at the Blitz, the club where the New Romantic movement was born. Mike and Matt had played in function bands, doing covers in Park Lane hotels, and they still dressed like a couple of suburban dads who shopped at Marks & Spencer, in polo shirts and stonewashed jeans. Pete made a bit more of an effort with clothes, but I suppose Mike and Matt thought there wasn't any point wearing a designer suit if you were sitting working in a studio all day. It was a real clash of cultures, and I don't think Pete helped matters much, at least if his story about trying to get Bananarama to record an album of ABBA covers called 'ABBA Banana' is true. Then again, it wasn't as if Bananarama were forced to be there. They loved 'You Spin Me Round' and they'd sought SAW out because they needed hits. And they got them with 'Venus', 'I Heard a Rumour' and 'Love in the First Degree'.

When I wasn't making tea or picking up metre-long model trains for Pete, there were dozens of other jobs to do. You changed the tape reels, unpacked new synthesizers and other bits of equipment – Pete was always keen for SAW to have the most cutting-edge gear; he didn't care how much it cost. You were at the bottom of the pecking order, but it didn't matter. Everyone who worked there was great, from the girls in the office to David Howells, who was MD of the whole business. There was a guy called Tops – his real name was Tony Henderson, but everyone called him Tops – who occupied the office in the shed on the roof. He was Pete's assistant, a job title which seemed to cover everything from looking after artists when they went on tour – he went around America with Bananarama – to picking up the latest addition to Pete's classic car collection from somewhere up North.

Tops came from Liverpool and when he found out I was going back to Newton every weekend, his ears pricked up. He loved the meat pies from a Lancashire bakery called Holland's – they were massive in fish-and-chip shops and football grounds around the North-West – and he wondered if I could bring him some down. So every Monday I'd turn up at PWL with Tops' Holland's pies, and I'd sit in his shed, listening to him telling tales about his career in the music business. He'd worked with all sorts of people. He had been around the world with Ian Gillan from Deep Purple. He had accompanied Musical Youth round America when they had become the first Black artists to get their video played on MTV, and every soul legend had wanted to meet them, from Diana Ross to Michael Jackson to Stevie Wonder. He told me Pete had been with him when they met Stevie Wonder, so apparently that story was true after all. He was really funny and entertaining. I enjoyed his company so much that sometimes I would bunk off from the studio for half an hour to go and sit in Tops' shed.

But most of the time, I worked really hard. The best part of the job was that everyone was so encouraging of your own musical efforts. If there was any downtime, they were happy to let you use the studios and the equipment – the best drum machines and keyboards in the world! – to work on your own material. Mike Duffy used to help me out a lot, and all the juniors used to muck in together. All of us were working on writing, all keen to get into Pete's good books by coming up with something that might impress him. So whoever was great on keyboards used to play them on my stuff and, in return, I'd sing on the demos of his songs. Sometimes we used to hang out together at weekends – three of the girls who worked at PWL shared a house not far from the studio and they used to throw fantastic parties. One of them was so fantastic, I woke up in their hallway the next morning with people stepping over me on their way to leave the house: I'd had an unfortunate experience with some ouzo the night before.

Usually, though, I went back to Newton, saw Debbie and kept out of the way of my mum and Bob. Sometimes, John would ring up and ask me to help him out at the garden centre, so I'd spend an afternoon with him, travelling around in the truck, putting sheds up. Things had thawed out between me and my dad. There wasn't any big reconciliation; we didn't sit down and talk things through. We just never mentioned the incident with the knife again – we put it behind us and got on with things. And if there weren't sheds that wanted putting up, I'd head over to Phil from Give Way's house. His stepdad had a little studio in his basement where he let me work on songs. I'd play everything: drums first, then bass, guitar and keyboards.

I was getting better, and Pete made encouraging noises whenever I played him something. Sometimes he used to send me downstairs to the second studio, to write with Phil Harding and Ian Curnow, the guys who were becoming PWL's reserve squad producers: the B team, as everyone started calling them. A couple of those songs even got released. One turned up as the opening track on Mandy Smith's album, which probably tells you more about how desperate they were for material for Mandy Smith's album than it does about the song's quality. Another, 'Modern Girl', was on the soundtrack of a film called *Knights & Emeralds*, which was, if you can believe this, a teen romance set against a story of two rival marching bands in Birmingham. The film bombed so badly that, for years, I didn't think either it or the soundtrack album had come out, but they did, and there I am on it, singing 'Modern Girl'. It sounds absolutely nothing like anything else I ever released, a sort of choppy mid-eighties pop-rock thing: no one's ever heard it, and they're not missing much. I really wasn't coming up with anything that was going to set the world on fire. Encouraging noises or not, I didn't truly think SAW were ever going to let me write my own songs, even if they did get round to making a record with me.

I'd slowly started to wonder whether that was ever going to happen. Everyone in the studio knew that I was supposed to be an artist, that I was theoretically there to record something with them, but they had so much going on. They'd found Mel and Kim, or rather Mel and Kim had found them. They'd spotted Pete at an event at the Hippodrome on Leicester Square, rushed up to him and demanded an audition. They were perfect SAW artists – a more glamorous version of the kids in the Ritzys and Cinderella Rockefellers that SAW aimed their music at – and their career took off big time. Their first single, 'Showing Out', was a Top 3 hit.

I thought that with all that happening, the chances of me getting a look-in were pretty slim. But I was wrong. SAW's success made Pete more keen to throw his weight around in the music business. In a way, you can see why. When they delivered Mel and Kim's second single, 'Respectable', the label told them they had to take out the part that featured sampled vocals – 'tay-tay-tay-tay' – because they thought it was gimmicky. SAW refused. The single went to No. 1: the 'tay-tay-tay' turned out to be the hook, the bit everyone remembered. If you wanted evidence that SAW knew more about what the public wanted than the music industry did, there it was, at the top of the charts.

*

One day in 1986, Pete told me he and I were going to a meeting at the headquarters of RCA Records in Bedford Square. This was something different. All the artists that SAW had found themselves had been signed to small club labels, or places where Pete had an in, like Magnet, a company he had worked for back in the seventies. When they signed Mandy Smith, they'd had to start their own independent label, PWL, because not even the club labels or Pete's old mates would release it. But RCA was big time. RCA had invented the 7" 45 rpm single. It was the label that had signed Elvis Presley and David Bowie. There were enough gold and platinum discs on the walls at Bedford Square to remind me that SAW were still a relatively small set-up, No. 1 singles or not.

You wouldn't have thought so, though, from the way Pete carried on when we got into the meeting with Peter Robinson, who was head of RCA's A&R department. He gave him a monologue that made the one he'd given me in the car down from Newton sound self-effacing. And this time it wasn't all about him (although quite a lot of it was); it was about me. I was incredible. I had the best voice Pete had ever heard. Peter Robinson should trust him – RCA needed to be in on this. It went on and on and on. It might even have been the first time Pete let fly with the story about how I was a teaboy at the studio they'd unexpectedly discovered could sing. That was absolute crap, but I didn't really mind. It was a better story than the truth. I don't remember anybody else speaking, certainly not me: even if I'd had anything to say for myself, no one could get a word in edgeways.

Pete was a brilliant salesman, but there was one tiny flaw in his pitch: he didn't have a note of music to play – something Peter Robinson seemed to have noticed. The first thing he said when Pete finally stopped talking was, 'Pete, I trust you, and I'm sure Rick's great, but I am going to have to hear him sing.'

That seemed to me to be an insurmountable problem. The only song I'd really recorded was 'Modern Girl', and we couldn't possibly play him that. It wasn't representative of the music I wanted to make and it certainly didn't match the spiel Pete had just given him: it was crap. But there was nothing else. Pete was, as they say, busted: his bluff had been thoroughly called.

He didn't seem to think so. He didn't even bat an eye-lid. 'No problem. We'll do a showcase for you at the studio. When can you come?'

When we left Bedford Square, I asked Pete, very politely, what he thought he was doing, and, more importantly, what the hell we were going to do now. He seemed completely un-fazed. His idea was that Mike and Matt would knock some-thing together and accompany me on keyboards and guitar. After all, they were great musicians and they had plenty of live experience from playing in covers bands at the Park Lane hotels; it would be a breeze for them.

It seemed like a plan, until he floated it to Matt and Mike and they told him, in no uncertain terms, to fuck off. They were busy, in the studio, making hit records, actually; they didn't have any time to spare, and even if they had, they didn't intend to spend it playing keyboards and guitar for me. Once again, Pete didn't seem discouraged at all. He nodded and then turned to me.

'Right, kid. You know those demos you've got?'

I did – the ones he'd made encouraging noises about, but clearly had no intention of releasing.

'You can wipe your voice off them and sing over the back-ing tracks.'

Hang on a minute. This is the big idea you've got to get me signed to a major label? I'm going to sing my own songs – songs you don't even seem to like particularly – over a crappy demo tape I've made in my mate's stepdad's basement in Newton?

Apparently it was. I went back to Newton and wiped my vocal off the demos. I didn't have any better ideas.

My main memory of the audition was how cobbled-together and seat-of-the-pants it was, how unlikely it seemed that anything good could possibly come out of it. There was a vocal microphone borrowed from the studio and someone had managed to find a shitty old amplifier from somewhere. I sang four songs through that, no reverb or echo, nothing to make my voice sound more professional, to a cassette. I wore a jacket I'd got from Next and I didn't really know what to do with myself. Should I dance while I was singing? Maybe put on a bit of a show? But it was two o' clock in the afternoon, and I wasn't on stage, I was standing in the reception of PWL in front of four people – Pete, Peter Robinson, David Howells from PWL and my manager Tony, who'd come down from Warrington for the audition – singing a load of songs that didn't sound *anything* like SAW productions. They were only rough demos and I'd played everything on them, including the drums. I felt like a bloody idiot, and dancing was only going to make me feel more of a bloody idiot. I settled for a compromise, sort of half-heartedly dancing about a bit, trying to ward off the feeling that however RCA had discovered Elvis Presley and David Bowie, it probably wasn't like this.

When I'd finished, the silence was broken by Peter Robinson asking who wrote the songs. Pete said I did, then totally brazened it out, as if this was all part of a cunning plan to suddenly reveal another side to my talents. 'Oh yeah,' he shrugged, 'that's the other thing about Rick – the kid's a great songwriter.'

I can't imagine it was any good. But I must have done something right. Or Pete's patter was incredibly convincing. Or perhaps Peter Robinson had just turned up to check I could at least sing vaguely in tune, and trusted that the power of SAW's hit-making abilities would do the rest. Whichever it was, RCA offered me a deal.

Pete negotiated a percentage and I got half and he got half. I thought that was fine. I should probably have consulted a lawyer, but I really wasn't bothered. I didn't even think about it for a split second. For one thing, Pete had negotiated a bigger percentage out of RCA than a new artist's manager would have done. Rather than RCA simply signing an artist, Pete was essentially proposing that he handle everything and present them with finished records: no need for an A&R, no need to search for a producer or a studio; it was all in hand. And for another thing, I was aware both that RCA were a huge global company that had the power to break artists around the world – this wasn't signing to some little UK dance label or one of Pete's old mates' outfits – and that it was highly unlikely they would have looked at me twice were it not for Pete and the fact I had SAW behind me. They weren't buying Rick Astley; they were buying a much bigger package than that.

Should I have consulted a lawyer? Yeah, probably. Should it have been weighted a bit more in my favour, given the amount of work I was about to do? Yeah, probably. Would I advise a young artist today to do what I did? No, probably not. But do I regret signing it? I've got to be honest: not for a minute.

I've had a few conversations with other artists who've complained about deals they did in the past, and I've always ended up thinking: *Yeah, that doesn't sound 100 per cent right, but you are complaining about a deal you did years ago, complaining now from the comfort of your very nice house. Sorry: one of a number of very nice houses you own.* It's like that with me. Sometimes you are confronted with a sliding-doors moment, an opportunity that might not be absolutely perfect, but that you know you have to grab regardless. I might not think that way if things had worked out differently, but as it is, I'm in the privileged position of having had a very nice life. Since my early twenties I haven't had to spend much time lying awake at night, wondering how I am going to pay the bills or make ends meet. And that's ultimately because of one record deal, which it would be crazy to regret. And because of one song, which I'll get to in a minute.

Chapter Five

Record contract or not, life continued pretty much as normal. At some point Pete moved from Crouch End to a flat in the same building as the studio and I moved with him. The new flat was really flash – it ended up being featured in a load of design magazines. But, never missing an opportunity to add a level of random weirdness to life at PWL, Pete didn't always come back to the flat: he slept in the studio, suddenly shouting out instructions from his sleeping bag to the production team that were working nights. I did a bit of recording with Mike and Matt – we did a cover of The Temptations' 'Ain't Too Proud to Beg', which I think was vaguely floated as my first single before the idea was shelved – but I still did my usual duties as a tape op: making the tea, fetching the sandwiches and assisting at mixing sessions. To my slight embarrassment, at one of these mixing sessions it became apparent that they were mixing my version of 'Ain't

Too Proud to Beg'. At least the guy mixing it, Pete Hammond, seemed impressed by my voice. So did Gary Barnacle, a legendary session musician who they brought in to do a sax solo on the track. He mentioned how good he thought the vocal was to Matt Aitken. Matt laughed: 'Don't say too much more, Gary, because the voice belongs to the bloke who just brought you a cup of tea, and he's sitting right behind us.'

One day, they asked me to unpack and help set up a new synthesizer that had been delivered to the studio. I did it very carefully, because it was a Fairlight, the absolute cutting edge of sampling technology. It was too important to call itself a synthesizer – it was, officially, a CMI or 'computer musical instrument' – and, in 1986, a Fairlight cost £60,000. I don't want to sound like the classic Northerner with a chip on his shoulder, but I do remember thinking, *You could buy half a street of houses in Newton for that* as I unpacked it. It was like a keyboard with an actual computer attached to it and a kind of tablet, like an iPad, that you operated with a light pen. It required its own room – the little studio that was supposed to be used for drums, but was clearly never going to be, was renamed the Fairlight Room – and its own specialist operator, someone who understood how to program it. That's what Ian Curnow had essentially been brought in to do: work out how you used the Fairlight. He'd played keyboards live with Talk Talk, who had a very technologically advanced set-up on stage, so he was up to the task.

Ian was still looking at the instruction manual when Mike Stock turned up in the room. He played a few chords on the Fairlight, then sang Ian a melody to go over the top. I went to get Ian a coffee, and when I came back, Pete was there, telling Ian about what he called 'plot tracks' – current records he thought should inspire the sound of the finished song. One was a single by Sybil called 'Falling in Love', an electronic soul track that was big in clubs at the time. The other was something by Alexander O'Neal. I left Ian to it: he obviously had his work cut out for him.

I went back a bit later to see how he was getting on. It sounded pretty great. I'd heard so much stuff that had come out of the studio over the intervening year that I liked to think I'd got quite good at judging which were good tracks and which weren't. Stock Aitken Waterman would never have admitted it because the official line was that everything they did was great, but you could definitely tell when Mike and Matt were more inspired and had nailed something. 'Respectable' by Mel and Kim: yes. The single they did with Roland Rat: maybe not so much. I'd also been in the studio long enough to know exactly what Pete was going to say when he heard this track. Ian was a real muso, and he'd programmed a very complicated, very muso rhythm track that sampled a real drummer and bassist. I loved it, but I knew it was definitely going to go out of the window straight away, which it did, but Pete thought the chords and the melody sounded great.

And, it transpired, they were going to give me a go at singing it, once the words were written. That was why Pete had suggested Alexander O'Neal as a reference point. He knew I loved Luther Vandross, James Ingram, all the great Black American singers of that period, and he wanted a song to fit me, so he tried to give the sound a bit of that American sensibility.

Pete always claims the inspiration for the lyrics was

something I said to him when I overheard him arguing with Gaynor: 'Come on, Pete, you know you're never going to give her up.' It's a good story, but I don't remember it happening. That doesn't mean it didn't take place, of course, although other people have pointed out that Musical Youth released a single called 'Never Gonna Give You Up' when Pete was working with them. And that Barry White released a single called 'Never, Never Gonna Give You Up' back when Pete was a DJ.

But it didn't matter who was never gonna give who up: the lyrics got written, I sang my vocal, they got it up to production level and I thought the results sounded fantastic. Frankly, I thought it almost didn't matter who was singing it, the song itself was so good.

There was one problem: Matt and Mike didn't like it. They weren't sure if my voice fitted the track. They thought it dragged the song down or something. That began the saga of trying to get 'Never Gonna Give You Up' right, which went on and on like one of Pete's monologues. It seemed as if everyone in the PWL building had a go at remixing it except the secretaries in Pete's office. Ian Curnow added more strings and horns. It apparently still wasn't right, although it sounded more than all right to me. I'd run off a cassette of 'Never Gonna Give You Up' and 'Ain't Too Proud to Beg', and I took it home with me to Newton. Everyone I played it to was really impressed: 'There's something in that. It's catchy as hell, that is.' I took the cassette with me when I went on a last-minute holiday just before Christmas with Mike Duffy. He'd mentioned one day that he was going skiing, and I started talking about how much I'd loved the skiing trip I'd been on with school. He suggested I come with him, he was leaving at the end of the week. That was not how holidays abroad had worked in the Astley family at all – you didn't just *go* – but I had a bit of money in the bank thanks to the RCA deal: what was stopping me? So I did, and when I wasn't on the slopes, I played 'Never Gonna Give You Up' over and over again. It got in my head, I kept singing it, even when I wasn't playing the tape. Such a cool song. It sounded like a hit single.

I got back to find that Mike and Matt still weren't happy with the song. Worse, while I'd been away, Pete had had one of his mad, impulsive ideas that no one could dissuade him from. I'd kept writing with Ian Curnow and Phil Harding, coming up with melody lines and lyrics for tracks they had put together. I didn't think much of the results, but that didn't matter: none of them were for me, I was getting a chance to write, and, besides, it was more fun than making the tea. One of them was a dance track called 'When You Gonna', which Pete had clearly heard. Now, apparently, we weren't going to release 'Never Gonna Give You Up' as my first single, we were going to release 'When You Gonna'. *What?* I'd quite enjoyed writing it, but only because it was an interesting exercise in trying to fit my songwriting to a type of music I had absolutely no interest in making myself: I really liked house music, but this was like a naff pop version of house music; it sounded like people pretending to make house music who didn't really know how to do it. I'd thought we were merely throwing ideas around. If I'd had any idea I was going to end up releasing it, I would have done it completely differently.

What the hell was I going to do? Pete was the boss. I'd only recently been promoted from boiling the kettle and fetching lunch from John's caff. It was clearly a fucking terrible idea, but the only reason I had a record deal was because of Pete. Could I challenge him? I didn't think so.

As all this was whirring through my head, Pete was still talking. It turned out this was only the first in a series of fucking terrible ideas he'd had for the immediate future of my career. Apparently, we weren't just going to release 'When You Gonna' as a single, we were going to release it as a duet. A duet? With who? Oh, one of the other juniors has a mate who sings, she's called Lisa. We'll get her in to do it.

Right, so let me get this straight. I've signed up with SAW, who are the hottest pop producers in Britain, so skilled at making hits they can get me a record deal with RCA on the flimsiest of evidence that I'm any good. And now I'm releasing a debut single that SAW don't have anything to do with, that I don't like, and it's going to be a duet with someone I've never heard, never met, and whose main qualification for being involved is that she's mates with someone I work with, and what's more, as far as I can see, there's absolutely nothing I can do about it. What the fuck is happening?

With the benefit of hindsight, I think there might have been some method in Pete's madness. Perhaps RCA were on his back, wondering when this wonderful singer he'd talked them into signing was actually going to come up with some music: 'Never Gonna Give You Up' still wasn't ready, and giving them this would buy Mike and Matt more time to work on it. Or perhaps Pete thought that he needed an ice-breaker, something to get my voice into the clubs, so that DJs – and SAW's target market – were at least a bit familiar with it before 'Never Gonna Give You Up' came out: 'When You

Gonna' was what would now be called a 'soft launch', meaning that everything didn't completely hinge on one song. Either of those ideas seems reasonable, but if Pete had them, he didn't bother explaining them to me at the time. He was too busy talking about promoting it by doing a PR tour of Britain's top nightspots – or at least the Ritzys that were their target market – and getting a choreographer in to work up a little dance routine. *A little dance routine?* Oh, this is getting better and better.

I decided my only option was simply to keep my head down, go along with it and try to stay focused. Lisa came in and recorded her vocal. She could sing, but her contributions didn't make me like 'When You Gonna' any more. There was a photoshoot, but they put the single out like an underground release, in a plain sleeve with a sticker on it. A tour of personal appearances in clubs was booked. We went to a choreographer who, as promised, worked up a little dance routine, despite the fact that neither Lisa nor I could really dance. I mean, we could dance a bit – people didn't point at me and laugh when I got on the floor at the Newtown-le-Willows cricket club disco – but bopping about a bit at a disco is different to learning actual dance steps.

Off we went on the tour of clubs. I didn't want to do it at all, and after the first couple of dates, I wanted to do it even less, if that was possible. I kept trying to tell myself to keep my head down and stay focused, but that didn't work: it was being drowned out by the sound of 'When You Gonna'. I was getting angrier and angrier with every performance of the song and every little dance routine. At this rate, I was going to start smashing things up like my dad before the tour was out.

It all came to a head in Manchester. We'd gone up there with a guy called Nick Aitch, who worked in club promotion for PWL. He was one of those middle-class Southern juniors I'd met when I first started there: a lovely guy, younger than me, but cocky as fuck. Aitch didn't have a licence, so I ended up driving us up to Manchester. It was one of those days when the M6 is solid traffic. It took us about eight hours to get there, twice as long as it should have, which didn't improve my mood much. Then another public appearance – or PA, as it was called – another dance routine, which didn't improve my mood either.

On the way back, we dropped Lisa off and drove to PWL. Aitch lived out near Brands Hatch and was getting the train back from there. When we arrived, I came up with a different plan.

'You know what, Aitch? You don't have to get the train home, mate. I'll drive you there. I'm going home.'

He said he thought I already was home – didn't I live in Pete's flat above the studio?

I shook my head. 'No, I'm going home to Newton. I think I'm done, Aitch. I'm not doing this any more. I quit. I ain't doing it.'

He got really panicky. He said I couldn't go home, or rather he couldn't let me go home. He was obviously worried about what he was going to tell Pete – 'Sorry, Pete, I've lost Rick Astley' – and, moreover, how Pete was going to react. I had to stay here and tell him myself.

'No,' I said. 'I'm going home. I'll fight you if I have to, but I'm done.'

I don't know what I was thinking, offering to fight him.

Big family group photo of my christening in the summer of 1966.
Back row, left to right: Grandad Dean; Auntie Marjorie; Auntie Val with Cousin
Helen; Granny Dean; Val's first husband, Colin. *Middle row, left to right:* Mike
on my dad's lap; me on my mum's lap; my sister, Jayne. *Front row, left to
right:* Cousin Ian; my brother John; Cousin Alan.

St Peter's School nativity. That's me, back row, sixth from left, with
a tea towel on my head.

Butlins. John, me and Mike.

John, Mike and me in the backyard of
Park Road North.

The garden centre with my first pet, Bod the
Jack Russell.

Family holiday in Cornwall. John, Jayne,
Mike and me at the front. Yes, the
parrot and the monkey were real.

Give Way: Phil, me and Geoff. We sounded better than we looked. Red string vest? Suits you, sir.

FBI: Neddy, me, Will, Pep and Chris. Jumpers and brick walls were obviously a thing back then!

On stage at the Battle of the Bands in Warrington at the Parr Hall. We won!

At an outdoor gig – the beginning of the 'no jeans' period of my life.

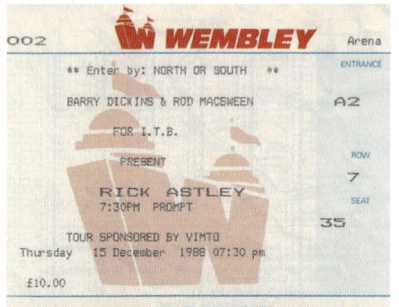

Back row, left to right: Tony Graham; John Preston; David Howells; Peter Jameson; Pete Waterman. *Front row, left to right:* me; Mike Stock; Matt Aitken; Peter Robinson. It felt really good to have RCA/BMG behind us.

Debbie and me with the lovely girls from PWL – Lucy and Sherrie, in front – at an after party in Kensington following the second Wembley show.

Ticket for the world tour on one of the Wembley nights – £10? Bargain! Sponsored by Vimto, a proper Northern drink. What an amazing feeling being able to scream, 'Hello, Wembley!'

Left: Gary Davies presenting me with my BPI/Brit Award for 'Never Gonna Give You Up' on the set of the 'Together Forever' music video. TV producers messed up at the awards show, ran out of time and didn't give me the award on the night. Also, note the infamous shiny sheet in the background of the photo. *Right:* Being presented with a gold record by Bjorn Borg at Stringfellows nightclub.

he suit on the left is by designer Antony Price. It was the look I had been after when I'd bought the one on the right from Next the previous year, for my 'audition' at the reception for RCA.

I'm in between Ray Davies and Steve Winwood at the BMI Awards, 1993.

Lene and me at the BMI Awards. At dinner, she sat next to Ray Davies, chatting away, and didn't recognize him until he got up to receive the big award of the night. I think he quite liked that.

Marti Pellow and me at the Limelight club in London. A lovely man with the best smile in pop!

My dad outside the garden centre in 1987, when 'Never Gonna Give You Up' went to No. 1. I know Mum and Dad loved us; they just had a hard time expressing it. Oh, and that's John in the background.

New York, New York! January 1988. Stock, Aitke who? America didn't care who had made the recorc they just liked it.

London, late 1988. The American top brass came over to present me with my awards for 'Never Gonna Give You Up'and 'Together Forever', both having gone to No. 1 in the US.

Australia. *Left to right:* Tops; tennis ace Peter McNamara; me; our promoter Paul Dainty. Peter was unbelievably kind to come and have a hit. But he didn't go easy! He wiped the floor with us. And, as always, Big Dave was close by.

Me and the lovely Chrissie Harwood, of BMG UK, in Australia – one of our many promo trips together.

Me trying to put up curtains in a hotel in San Francisco. I'd pulled them down by falling into them while doing a somersault over the bed. Somersaulting in hotel rooms was a tradition to offer some light relief after all of the often repetitive interviews.

Tops and me at A&M Studios in LA for the Gary Katz recording sessions. 1990.

The stage for the 1988–9 world tour. The footage in the box was so hard to synch up with because it was all done by ear and eye.

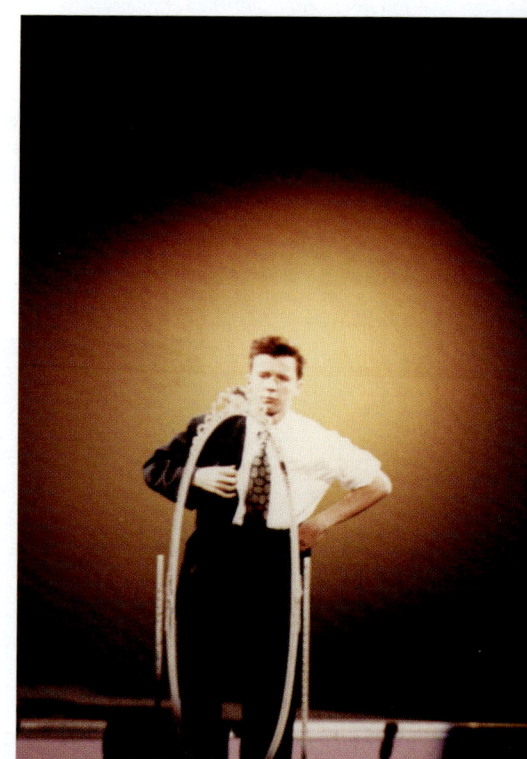

I had the idea to finish one of my costume changes with the frame of an old mirror placed in front of the audience. Simple, but people loved it.

For one thing, Aitch was quite a big bloke, and for another, two men having a punch-up on a Sunday morning in south London over a pop-house single and its accompanying dance routine – it's clearly ridiculous. But forget the prospective fight for a moment: I was standing up for myself, and at twenty-one, I really wasn't big on doing that. I was just used to not having a voice. I was too junior to have one at PWL, and I certainly never had one back at home. If my dad moved us all into a Portakabin or bought 25,000 strawberry plants, there wasn't any point in telling him you thought it was a ropey decision: he wouldn't have taken any notice, he would have simply gone ahead and done it anyway. So I would always just get on with it.

And now, here I was, refusing to just get on with it. Perhaps I'd realized that in fact I had the upper hand, that Pete was going to have to do what I wanted, because the alternative was going back to RCA and telling them that the incredible new singer that he'd guaranteed was going to be huge had walked off, without even releasing a proper debut single. But I don't think it was some grand powerplay like that. I simply knew that the Rick and Lisa thing wasn't really taking off. It's not as if we'd started touring the clubs and the reaction had been so amazing that RCA were demanding we make a video as quickly as possible or talking about a follow-up. The reaction was more 'Yeah, it's all right,' and I wasn't going to die on the hill of 'Yeah, it's all right.' Also, I cannot overstate how pissed off I was with that dance routine.

Anyway, my offer of a fight seemed to do the trick. I got back in the car, drove Aitch back to Brands Hatch and headed back up the M6 again.

A couple of days later, the phone rang at my gran's. It was Tony, one of my managers. Pete had been on to him. He wanted to sort things out. The Rick and Lisa single was being binned. It had already been released – apparently it reached No. 17 in Holland! – but there was to be no more promotion of it. I felt a bit bad for dropping Lisa like that. I felt even worse for her a year later: she subsequently recorded a solo track with SAW, but it was never released – they ended up giving it to Sonia – and that, as far as I know, was that for her singing career. Rick and Lisa was as close as she got to a big break, and I'd pulled the plug on it. But I don't think it was entirely down to me. I think RCA might have had a word, too. Like I said, the Rick and Lisa thing wasn't really working, Pete had doubtless told them about the incredible new song SAW had been working on for months, and they were wondering where the hell said incredible new song was.

When I got back to PWL, yet another version of 'Never Gonna Give You Up' had been mixed, this time by Pete Hammond. Along the way, someone had had the idea of fitting it with drums and a bassline based on Colonel Abrams' 'Trapped', a club track I loved that had crossed over into the Top 5 the previous year. It really changed the song. Pete's mix sounded amazing, but it was nearly eight minutes long. It was fine for a 12", but we obviously needed something shorter and punchier as the main single. Mike and Matt chopped it up, rearranged it and edited it, and they were finally happy.

I had to admit, the finished record was fantastic – better than all the previous versions I'd heard. You could tell it was a SAW production, but it didn't sound like a generic SAW track: it was definitely more 'Respectable' than Roland Rat.

That was good, because there was already a backlash against them brewing, compounded by the fact that there were so many singles by them in the Top 20: Bananarama, Sinitta, Mel and Kim, a track they'd done with the former page-three model Samantha Fox. Their name was becoming a by-word for cheap, production-line pop, which I didn't think was fair, but which they almost encouraged. Pete had started calling their studio the Hit Factory. In fact, they'd started doing things deliberately to wind up people who didn't like them. They put a track out they'd made called 'Roadblock' that sounded like a seventies funk thing. Seventies funk had become huge in really hip London clubs at the time; there was a whole scene around DJs who played the most obscure old tracks they could find: they called it rare groove. Pete thought it was stupid – he'd been playing music like that as a DJ ten years ago – and he knew that the kind of people who loved it would have hated SAW. So he got 'Roadblock' pressed up as a white label 12", with no name on it and a New York phone number, and sent it out to dance shops as a hoax. People fell for it, it got great reviews, then SAW revealed it was them.

It was funny, but I wasn't sure about deliberately provoking people like that, particularly as I was about to release my debut single. After all, they were in the studio all day; it was their artists who went out in public, and it was their artists who really got it in the neck as a result. But I was sure that 'Never Gonna Give You Up' was good.

Chapter Six

I expect that some people walked onto *Top of the Pops* for the first time like they owned the place, as if it was their life's destiny to be there. I was not one of those people. I was terrified, and the audience weren't helping. I don't think anyone actually said, 'Who's he?' out loud, but you could see them thinking it: *I came here to see some pop stars I like, not some bloke I've never heard of.* In fairness, it wasn't exactly a vintage, star-packed episode of the show – there was Def Leppard, there was Wet Wet Wet and Pseudo Echo, an Australian band doing a jokey cover of the old disco track 'Funkytown' – but even so, I got the feeling the crowd in front of my stage thought they'd drawn the short straw. Simon Bates introduced me by saying something like 'What do you get when you cross Newton-le-Willows with Stock Aitken Waterman?' The audience looked as if they couldn't care less what you got, although they cheered on cue. What was I doing here?

No, scrub that: obviously, I knew what I was doing there. I just didn't have a clue how I was supposed to do it.

'Never Gonna Give You Up' hadn't been released in a blaze of publicity and hype. RCA didn't make a video for it, and they didn't do a cover shoot for the single sleeve or the adverts. They simply used a photo of me left over from the Rick and Lisa session. All the record label really did was send it out to radio, which turned out to be exactly the right thing to do. The first time it got played on Capital, it got such a reaction that they kept playing it, over and over again: someone said they played it seventy-two times in the space of a week. I went out on another PA tour, just me, performing to the instrumental version of the song that was on the B-side of the single – they literally used to play the 7" and I'd sing along to it. I played everywhere: nightclubs, under-18s discos on Sunday afternoons, even pubs, those massive 800-capacity pubs where they'd have an unknown singer performing on a Saturday night. One of them was not far down the road from where I live now, and every time I drive past it, I think: *God, I sang in there once.* It was hard work, and I wouldn't say I was completely comfortable singing to a backing tape, but I didn't mind. It wasn't like the Rick and Lisa thing – at least I was promoting a record I really believed in.

And, also unlike the Rick and Lisa thing, it seemed to be paying off. Between the PAs and, more importantly, the radio play, it nudged into the bottom end of the Top 40: No. 32, between Wet Wet Wet and Whitney Houston. I was doing a PA in Glasgow when I got the phone call: the single's really taking off, they want you on *Top of the Pops* next week. I was with Kelly Cooper, a great, vibey Scottish girl at PWL who helped out with artists and styling. I'm still friends with her today. She took me out to buy a new jacket to go on the telly in, a long, black blazer with brass buttons.

I'd assumed that when you arrived at *Top of the Pops* for the first time, someone would sit you down and explain what happened there. But they didn't – they just expected you to know, and I didn't. As the day wore on – rehearsals and dress rehearsals – everything made me more nervous. The fact that the audience all looked to be my age was bothering me – I'd expected them to be younger – and the fact that I could see a couple of girls my age in the audience who I thought were pretty fit bothered me even more. For some reason, the fact that everyone from the BBC seemed to be a Southerner started troubling me: it seemed to be underlining that I was somehow out of place here. I became desperate to hear someone else with a Northern accent, but the only people who sounded remotely like me were Def Leppard. They were from Sheffield, but I didn't think a heavy metal band – a heavy metal band whose current album was in the process of selling twenty million copies – would particularly want to talk to Stock Aitken Waterman's latest protégé. At one point, I went up to the famous BBC bar, but that definitely didn't do anything to make me feel less of an alien. Everywhere you looked, there was a pop star, or an actor you recognized, or two people arguing about camerawork on *EastEnders*. I stood there with my drink, thinking: *What world is this I've landed in?* I'd never been anywhere like it in my life.

Back in the studio, I watched Wet Wet Wet rehearsing and thought: *There's four mates up there. They look like they're having a really good time.* I suddenly wished I was still in a band. If it was FBI's first *Top of the Pops* appearance we'd definitely have been swaggering about a bit, because that's what five lads do together, they sort of egg each other into it. In fact, as I thought about it, I wished I at least *had* a band, a few backing musicians on the stage with me. I felt like a bit of a twat standing there on my own with a microphone. What was I going to *do* while I was singing? And, more importantly, what was I going to do when I *wasn't* singing? It wasn't as if SAW went in for long guitar solos, but there were definitely parts of the song that were instrumental. I couldn't just stand there. Hang on, Marti Pellow was shuffling around. All right, maybe I should shuffle around. People have asked me about the way I danced on that first *Top of the Pops* appearance, and I always say: 'That's not dancing, it's fear.'

Terrified or not, something about that *Top of the Pops* appearance really seemed to strike people. For one thing, they put me on straight after a Mötley Crüe video filled with them riding motorbikes and visiting a strip club and playing guitar solos surrounded by pyrotechnics, so I was definitely a sharp contrast to that. I've never bought into the idea that people assumed I was Black until they saw me, although I've heard that plenty of times. I thought I sounded like a white singer who loved Black music, but I can see that no one who had heard the record expected me to look the way I did. I looked a lot younger than twenty-one and I was very clean-cut. I definitely wasn't Iggy Pop, or one of Mötley Crüe for that matter, and I wasn't some sexy soul singer who was going to try to shag your sister and your mum. I was the boy next door – if you happened to live next door to a Portakabin – dressed up for a night out.

It wasn't a contrived image at all. The nearest I'd had to a stylist was Kelly telling me what shops to go to in Glasgow to get a new jacket. In a sense, it wasn't even an image. I was wearing my own clothes; that was how I dressed. Even before I signed with Pete, I liked how Bryan Ferry and David Sylvian from Japan looked: suits, a shirt and tie. Of course, I didn't look anything like Bryan Ferry or David Sylvian when I put those clothes on. Bryan Ferry is sort of louche and sophisticated-looking, David Sylvian was a bit arty and weird, and I was none of those things. Plus, they were getting their clothes from designers like Antony Price, and I could only stretch to Next and Top Man, so I looked like your older brother's nice mate who was trying to impress his date. I remember one of the engineers at PWL once told me I should wear jeans to work the next day because we would be sorting out the cables under one of the mixing desks so we'd be on our hands and knees all day. I said I couldn't, because at that point, I didn't own a pair of jeans – I was going through a phase where I thought jeans were scruffy. Maybe it was a reaction to growing up with my dad, who looked, more or less, like a tramp. Mind you, there's not a lot of point in dressing like Bryan Ferry if you're running a garden centre.

Whatever it was, the *Top of the Pops* appearance worked: the next week, 'Never Gonna Give You Up' was No. 3. Things went into overdrive: more PAs, more radio appearances, more interviews. Somewhere along the way, I must have done one with *Smash Hits* where I told them that the first song I'd ever written was called 'A Ruddy Big Pig', which was true, in a manner of speaking. I'd certainly made up a song called 'A Ruddy Big Pig' when I was about six, sitting on a bus with my mum and my brother Mike. 'A ruddy big pig came down our street, my mam said "Get it for something to eat," we had it for tea with apple pie, all mixed up with a dog' – for some reason, I thought it was hilarious that it didn't rhyme at the end, but that's six-year-olds for you. Anyway, I mentioned it to *Smash Hits*, and after that I didn't hear the end of it. For years afterwards, they never printed my name without somehow attaching 'A Ruddy Big Pig' to it. If I won an award, they'd claim it was for writing 'A Ruddy Big Pig'. If I was on the cover, there'd be a speech bubble coming out of my mouth, saying something about 'A Ruddy Big Pig'. Maybe that's why it's still permanently seared into my brain: even today, I can recite it straight off, but I'd have trouble telling you half the lyrics from my last album.

There was more TV too. *Good Morning Britain* asked to speak to me and Pete, which was understandable – SAW had four singles in the chart that week, including mine – but it also gave Pete an opportunity to treat the outside world to a taste of the weirdness that went on behind the doors of PWL's studios. He decided that what he really wanted to talk about wasn't music, but model railways. He even brought along the two trains that I'd picked up from Cardiff the previous year. I remember sitting there, on breakfast telly, with these two giant models in glass cases and Pete enthusing about his lifelong love of railways, thinking, *What the fuck is going on here?*

With the single in the Top 3, the record company decided we needed a video, and quickly. Of course they did: it was the 1980s, the highpoint of the music video. Videos were so important and had such a huge impact in promoting a single that they'd turned into a kind of race to see who could make the most striking, lavish production, like a mini-Hollywood film, often by directors who went on to make actual Hollywood films: Duran Duran on a yacht in Antigua; Robert Palmer with a band made up of female models; Morten Harket from A-ha suddenly turning from a cartoon of a teenage heartthrob into the real thing. Our video wasn't like that. I didn't meet the director in advance, or see a treatment, not that I'd have known what that was: in 1987, I thought a treatment was something you got from the doctor if you had piles. To be brutally honest, I'm not certain that I knew what a director was either. If I went to see a film, I didn't hang around the cinema until the end. My preparation for the video involved being told the date and time, and being instructed to bring a bag of my own clothes.

A car was sent to pick me up. It dropped me off in Shepherd's Bush, near where the Westfield shopping centre is today. There was a big old building there that was used by a youth club. Inside, they had set up a stage, an old-fashioned microphone and a bar. I was introduced to a couple of dancers who were going to be in the video, both of whom, I noted, were (a) really hot and, therefore, (b) too hot to realistically be dancing with me. There was another guy there, whose role in the video was to play the bartender who's so impressed by the sound of me singing 'Never Gonna Give You Up' that he stops polishing glasses in order to dance, does the splits in mid-air, leaps over the bar and eventually runs up a wall and does a somersault off it. That didn't seem very realistic either, good as I thought 'Never Gonna Give You Up' was. In fact, there was a fourth dancer, who was the boyfriend of one of the hot female dancers, but you don't see him as much in the finished video. The guy was absolutely enormous – in my memory, he's about 6 foot 9, but that might be an exaggeration – and built like an athlete, and I don't think they could put him in the same shot as me because, next to him, I looked like a twelve-year-old with a quiff.

There were no other instructions: I just had to mime the song and jig about a bit. I mimed the song and jigged about a bit by a chain-link fence in the sunshine. I mimed the song and jigged about a bit on the makeshift stage with the two hot dancers. I mimed the song and jigged about a bit by the arches outside the youth club at night. In fact, I probably couldn't have taken any other instructions in. I was too busy looking at the cameras and the crew – there must have been twenty or thirty people there – and the lights. It really did look how I imagined a proper film set would be. Any sense of movie-star glamour was almost immediately undermined when we started filming by the chain-link fence. As the song kicked into life for me to mime to, someone in a flat nearby leaned out of the window and bellowed: 'Shut the fuck up! I'm on nights, I'm trying to get some sleep, you bastards!' Maybe the same thing happened to Duran Duran when they were singing 'Rio' on their yacht in Antigua, but I somehow doubted it.

When I saw the finished video, I was quite impressed. It looked a lot more professional than you might imagine something shot in a youth club near the A40 while someone shouted at us to shut the fuck up would look. The director, Simon West, went on to make a succession of huge action movie blockbusters – *Con Air*, *Lara Croft: Tomb Raider* and *The Expendables 2*. His films have grossed hundreds of millions of dollars at the box office, he's directed some of the biggest film stars in the world and owns his own production company, but thanks to an accident of pop culture history, if you search for his name online, it's still attached to the video for 'Never Gonna Give You Up', and I can only apologize and say I definitely didn't think that was going to happen.

And, despite how professional the video looked, I wasn't sure about *me* in it. It's hard to judge how you come across at the start of your career. Did I look like a pop star? Or did I just look ridiculous, someone who had no idea what he was doing, waving his arms about in double denim and a pair of borrowed Ray-Bans? Still, I thought: it's only a video. People make a lot of fuss about them, but what are they really? They're simply a promotional device. You make a single, you make a video, people see it and with any luck they'll buy the single, and that's that. You make another single and another video: everyone moves on. It's not as if millions of people are still going to be watching it in thirty years' time, right?

Chapter Seven

I can't remember where I was when I got the phone call to tell me 'Never Gonna Give You Up' was No. 1. I know I wasn't at home, because I was in a hotel, but where the hotel was I've no idea. I have a feeling I was in Scotland but, in truth, I could as easily have been in Surbiton: the weeks after the single's release are just a blur of local radio stations and interviews and public appearances. It was bedlam.

But I do remember how I felt. I was excited and thrilled and disbelieving and all the things you'd expect to be when you're told your first single has gone to No. 1, but there was another very distinct feeling as well – I'm saved. I don't have to go and live in a Portakabin ever again. I don't have to put up with my dad's shit ever again. I'm saved. There was a version of 'Never Gonna Give You Up' on the 12" called the 'Escape from Newton Mix'. It was a daft title Pete had come up with: he was always giving remixes stupid names, the 'Cake Mix' or the 'Mortgage Mix', or the 'Duck-billed Platypus Mix'. But that time, he accidentally hit on something quite insightful and profound.

In a way, it was stupid to feel like that, to assume I'd suddenly achieved the safety and security I wanted just because I'd got to No. 1. Plenty of people have had a No. 1 single and never been heard of again. But I had a weird feeling it wasn't going to work out like that. It could have been the same blind belief I'd had back when I was in FBI. Or perhaps I was thinking about it a bit more rationally than that. After all, I had Stock Aitken Waterman behind me, and they seemed to have the Midas touch: Mel and Kim's career had gone off like a rocket; they'd turned Bananarama's career around; they'd even managed to transform Sinitta from a minor West End actress into a hit-making machine. And the longer 'Never Gonna Give You Up' stayed at the top of the charts, the more I thought that it might have crossed over from the people SAW had aimed it at, to a wider audience. It was No. 1 for five weeks and it stopped much bigger, more established artists than me from getting to No. 1: the Pet Shop Boys, U2. People started saying it was going to be the biggest-selling single of the year. I didn't think there were enough Daves and Traceys in Britain to do that. Perhaps their mums and dads were buying it – the strings on it made it sound a bit like an old disco record, so maybe it reminded them of their youth. Perhaps their grandmas were buying it because they liked my clean-cut image: *Oh, that Rick Astley's a lovely young lad.* Perhaps people fell in love with it because they couldn't ignore it – the song was never off the radio or TV. It was inescapable. Mind you, that seemed to be annoying people more than making them love it, if the man in the street was anything to go by, because after a couple of weeks at No. 1, I noticed that the man in the street – or more usually the man on the scaffolding – quite often felt the urge to shout 'Wanker!' if I walked past him.

Still, there's nothing like complete strangers feeling free to call you a wanker to make you understand that you've hit a completely different level of fame. In the late eighties, a new artist going straight to No. 1 for five weeks with their first single (the whole Rick and Lisa thing seemed to have been entirely wiped from history, much to my relief) felt like a national event, at least if you were the new artist in question. You were suddenly everywhere. It literally changed your life, as I discovered when I went back to Newton for a night. Everything was fine with my sister and brothers. They were proud, and they were excited, but they didn't treat me any differently than they had before I had a hit single: I got the feeling that if John had needed some help putting sheds up, he wouldn't have thought twice about asking me, which was perfect. But things really were different with my mum. The minute I came through the door, she produced a pile of things for me to sign. She'd invited the neighbours over – 'Bob and Mary are coming. I've told them to bring their kids and their nieces round to meet you.' She didn't seem to get that I just wanted a cup of tea and a chat, a bit of normality, a break. I realized that popping to the Legh Arms was probably out of the question, but I thought I could go out to a local nightclub with a couple of mates. I couldn't. Well, I could, and I did, but it was chaos. There was a certain novelty in walking into a nightclub where loads of girls wanted to meet you – that had certainly never happened before – and half the blokes wanted to thump you because their girlfriend wanted to meet you, but the fun wore off pretty quick. They ended up having to assign us two bouncers. They planted themselves in front of us while we stood in a corner having a drink, looking at the bouncers' backs. We might as well have stayed at home and had a couple of beers in front of the telly. Lesson learned.

You were tabloid fodder. Journalists had only worked out that pop stars sold newspapers a few years before, and now they were desperate for stories about you. My dad was happy to oblige. When 'Never Gonna Give You Up' got to No. 1, he had a sweatshirt made with I'M RICK ASTLEY'S DAD on it and wore it round the garden centre. Then he built a huge sign – WELL DONE RICK ASTLEY – YOU'VE ALWAYS BEEN OUR NUMBER ONE – and put it at the entrance. The tabloids went and took photos of him by it, wearing his sweatshirt, giving a thumbs up. Then they found out about his living arrangements and that became a different story: 'Chart-Topping Rick's Dad Lives in Portakabin'. Oh, for fuck's sake: it was like that girl in Miss Jackson's English class – 'Miss! Miss! Rick Astley lives in a tin hut!' – but on a national scale. Worse, it carried the implication that this was somehow Chart-Topping Rick's fault, that I should have done something about it, as if I could. I confess, Chart-Topping Rick might have laughed a little bitterly at the irony of that when I read it, but what was I supposed to do? I could hardly go to *The Sun* and tell them the truth. 'Chart-Topping Rick: My Dad Is So Completely Bloody Bonkers He Actually Wants to Live in a Portakabin, Unlike Me'. I didn't think that was going to do anyone any good.

So I wasn't sure about being in *The Sun* and the *Daily Star* at all. On one level, their interest definitely signified something – *Oh my God, there are two pages in the middle of the biggest-selling newspaper in Britain and you're on both of them: this is massive* – but on another, there was a part of me that really wanted to be in the *NME* and *Melody Maker* instead. Ideally, I wanted to be seen as a musician, but I knew that was out of the window the minute SAW became huge. If you're working with them, you're a pop star, you're a bloke with a funny dance, and the *NME* isn't going to be interested. That's the deal you've done, and there's no point complaining about it.

Besides, most of the time, I never really saw what the tabloids wrote about me, good or bad. If it was nasty, I think people at PWL did their best to keep it away from me, or at least not draw attention to it, because why would you? It's not a great conversation starter: 'Morning, Rick, *The Sun* says you're an arsehole – have you read it?' But they didn't have to make that much effort to keep it away from me, because I honestly wouldn't have had time to read it. There was so much going on. I'd thought things were hectic before I got to No. 1, but it turned out that had only been a dry run for what happened afterwards. Every day was completely ballistic from the moment I got out of bed until the moment I eventually got back into it: radio, TV, interviews. I got used to waking up and my first thought being that I was running late.

It wasn't just promotion for 'Never Gonna Give You Up'. There was the small matter of what we did when it wasn't No. 1 any more. I hadn't got a follow-up. I don't mean we hadn't finished the follow-up, or that we hadn't recorded the follow-up yet. I mean we hadn't discussed it or even thought about it. We'd literally only recorded one song – if you turned 'Never Gonna Give You Up' over, there wasn't another song on the B-side, only an instrumental version of 'Never Gonna Give You Up'. The whole thing had simply been done on spec, released to test the waters and see what happened, and what had happened was . . . this: No. 1 for five weeks, the biggest-selling single of the year and absolutely no idea what we were going to do next.

You had to hand it to them, SAW didn't seem panicked by this at all. Pete said it was no problem, they already had the perfect song. There was an old single that O'Chi Brown had put out in 1985 called 'Whenever You Need Somebody'. It had sunk without trace, which sounded remarkably like a problem to me – your big idea is that I'm going to re-record a flop single from eighteen months ago? – but Pete was convinced its failure had nothing to do with the quality of the song itself. It was a guaranteed hit, despite the fact that it clearly hadn't been a hit: O'Chi Brown's record label had simply screwed up the release of it; they hadn't pressed up enough singles to meet demand. It had only stalled at No. 98 because no one could buy it. All they had to do was change the key of the song so I could sing it, re-record the backing track so it sounded a bit more up-to-date, a bit more like 'Never Gonna Give You Up', and there was my follow-up.

The whole thing was done in four or five days. Whatever you thought of them, you had to be impressed at how quickly Matt and Mike could turn things around, although at the time I just took it as read that it was how records were made. It wasn't until years later, when I worked with other producers and songwriters, that I realized how mad SAW's approach to music was: *What do you mean the song will be ready in a couple of months?* Mike and Matt could make an album in the time it takes some producers to decide what the snare drum on the opening track should sound like. It wasn't that they didn't care – they could be very painstaking when they wanted to be, as the saga of 'Never Gonna Give You Up' showed. But most of the time, they were very confident that they'd distilled their sound down into a kind of formula: we don't need to mess about, this is how we do it. There were good and bad aspects to that approach, but that's how they ended up with so many hits in the charts at once: they could work really fast.

When they delivered 'Whenever You Need Somebody', RCA loved it. This time, they commissioned a video in advance of release. It was a bit different to 'Never Gonna Give You Up' in that it had a plot, although not one that required me to do anything more than jig about a bit while miming again – in a recording studio, in front of a screen that silhouetted my backing singers, and, I thought, with a bit more confidence than before – and not one that made a lot of sense. Attractive girl goes on holiday, keeps seeing me singing 'Whenever You Need Somebody' on a variety of televisions – one of them balanced on the edge of a swimming pool, which doesn't say a lot for her hotel's attitude to health and safety – and is so impressed that she cuts her holiday short in order to fly back to Britain *on Concorde*, track down the studio where I'm busy miming and jigging about a bit, and throw herself at me. Once again, this seemed to be slightly overselling both the song and my personal magnetism, but it didn't seem to matter. Pete was absolutely right: 'Whenever You Need Somebody' was in the Top 10 before 'Never Gonna Give You Up' had even left the Top 40.

*

Something else happened the minute 'Never Gonna Give You Up' started slipping down the British chart. It took off in the rest of Europe. The next thing I knew, it was No. 1 everywhere: Belgium, Germany, Holland, Italy, Norway, Spain, Denmark, Finland, Greece, which meant a lot of travelling to promote it. I never played live – I would have liked to, but the record company and PWL weren't keen. In those days, a pop artist, and therefore their label, made money from record sales, not gigs. They thought it was much more efficient for me to appear on TV shows and reach millions of people at once. So that's what I did. All across Europe, I became intimately acquainted with whatever was the local version of *Top of the Pops*.

It was really exhausting. Up before dawn to catch a 5 a.m. flight, get taken to a radio station for the breakfast show, then somewhere else to do press interviews, then to the TV station to mime the song, which, with all the run-throughs and rehearsals involved, took hours. For someone who really hadn't been abroad a lot, it was weird how quickly you got used to it, and how quickly every country you visited started to seem the same. Obviously, they're all completely different to each other, but I never really had time to see anything other than the inside of cars, radio stations and TV studios and, with the greatest of respect, a TV studio with an audience full of kids in Germany really doesn't look that different to a TV studio full of kids in Spain. In fact, my main memory of that time in Europe is of corridors. I seemed to spend an inordinate amount of time standing around in corridors of studios, waiting to be called to pretend to sing for three and half minutes. It was as close as I got to a social life, because you'd bump into other British artists doing exactly the same thing: Climie Fisher, Boy George, Kim Wilde.

I'd love to tell you that afterwards, I rounded up Climie Fisher, Kim Wilde and Boy George, and we went out and got absolutely trolleyed, laying waste to the capital cities of Europe in an orgy of rock-and-roll debauchery, but I didn't. I never did anything like that. Partly because, by the time I'd finished working, I was exhausted and usually knew that I had to be up at 4 a.m. the next morning to go to Norway or wherever. And partly because, most of the time, the only person with me was Tops, who PWL had lured out of his shed on the roof in order to look after me on the road – or whatever my version of being on the road was – and Tops definitely wasn't into going clubbing. He didn't even drink. He'd occasionally come to the hotel bar and have a glass of Coke, but that was about it. He preferred to be up in the morning and, on the rare occasions when there was any spare time, to play tennis. I started playing with him, even though I could never beat him.

I began to develop a real bond with Tops on those trips to Europe. He was an intriguing character. I could never work out what his background was. I got the impression he might have been in the army at some point – something about his bearing, plus he seemed to know a phenomenal amount about guns. I never actually asked him, and he never volunteered the information.

And he was great at his job, really organized and firm. Whenever we turned up somewhere in Europe, he'd immediately ask to see the schedule they'd put together for me. If there was anything on it that he hadn't agreed to in advance, it was a 'no': 'If the Pope asks to meet you, Rick, and it's not in the schedule, I might say yes to that, but he hasn't asked yet.'

That was good – there was more than enough in the schedules to keep me very busy – and so was Tops' wariness about photographers. It wasn't as if the paparazzi were a problem in so far as they might catch me out doing something I wasn't supposed to be doing – I didn't have time to be doing anything I wasn't supposed to be doing – but weird things could happen when they were around. They'd ask for a photograph and then ask if you could hold something while they took the photograph, and the next thing you knew, you were in the papers personally endorsing whatever it was you were holding. Or they'd get a load of pictures and make an official Rick Astley calendar out of them. Stupid stuff like that.

So I didn't have the time, or the inclination, or the partners in crime for any riotous pop-star lifestyle. In fact, during that first bit of fame, I remember going out to a nightclub precisely three times. Once was the club back at home, and we all know how well that turned out. One of the other times was to the Limelight in London, where there was some SAW event happening: Sinitta was doing a PA or something. I remember it because I got talking to Wet Wet Wet. It wasn't a particularly memorable conversation – the way my life was at that particular point in history, I didn't have much to talk about except what the corridors at various different European television stations were like – but I do recall feeling a certain kind of kinship with them, just because they were Scottish. *You're a bunch of working-class blokes from Clydebank, I'm a working-class bloke from Newton. We're really not supposed to be in some glitzy nightclub in the West End. All this is a bit weird, isn't it?* But what I remember most of all is that there was a guy pestering us. He had a camera and he wanted a photo. Then he wanted another photo, and another one. I'd have probably put up with it all night, but Marti Pellow wasn't in the mood. He turned to the guy and his voice changed. It got lower and deeper and much more Glaswegian. I have no idea what he said to him, but it didn't sound very friendly – it sounded a little like the noise a dog might make immediately before it bit you, only Scottish. After he said it, the guy suddenly decided he'd got more than enough photos and scuttled off. Marti Pellow turned to me, flashed the famous charming Marti Pellow smile, and asked if I fancied another drink. I have to say, I was incredibly impressed.

The third time I went to a nightclub around that time was in Denmark. I flew in with Tony, my co-manager, and Andy, a guy who worked at Bertelsmann Music Group (BMG). There was a little deputation of people from the Danish record company waiting for me at the airport. One of them was a blonde girl, who introduced herself as Lene. She seemed incredibly well organized – she'd turned up with a clipboard and a folder – which was very impressive: sometimes you'd get to a foreign country and the record label would barely know what was supposed to be going on. She seemed to have really thought about my whole trip. She'd even arranged for a local fashion label where her friend worked as a designer to give me a huge pile of clothes. And I couldn't help but notice that she was also breathtakingly beautiful. She sort of burned herself onto my brain, to the point where even today I can still remember exactly what she was wearing when I saw her at the airport: black cowboy boots, black tights, a long black coat.

I spent the afternoon in a hotel, doing one interview after another. At one point, there was a knock on the door of the room. It was Cliff Richard, who turned out to be staying in the same hotel, playing a gig in Copenhagen that night, and he wanted to know if I could come. Lene, Tony, Andy and I had an early dinner in an Italian restaurant, then went to Cliff's show. He'd only played about four songs when Lene turned to me and asked if I wanted to leave. She had friends who were DJ'ing at a club around the corner – we could go to that instead. With all due respect to Cliff, it wasn't much of a competition: did I want to go out clubbing in Copenhagen with a breathtakingly beautiful girl, or did I want to sing along to 'Living Doll' and 'Bachelor Boy'? I don't think I hesitated before choosing option (a). When I agreed, she just walked up to my manager and the people from her record label and told them we were leaving, and furthermore, we were leaving without them. Hang on, could you *do* that? I seemed to spend my entire time agreeing to things, doing stuff out of obligation, being told what to do. Apparently you could. We left.

We went from one club to another club, to a bar, to another club. Lene seemed to know everyone in Copenhagen. The whole time, we kept talking. It turned out that she'd lived in London, working for Island Records. She'd gone back to

Denmark and worked for EMI and a label I'd never heard of called Les Disques du Crépuscule, who turned out to be incredibly hip; they were like a Belgian equivalent of Factory Records. There was something about her personality that was unbelievably attractive. She was confident and sophisticated, she appeared comfortable in her own skin, and we seemed to have a lot to say to each other. We were still talking in my hotel bar at 5 a.m., when the staff started pointedly hoovering and putting chairs on tables all around us.

I ended up kissing her in the lift of the hotel – I kept pushing the buttons in the lift, to send it to different floors, trying to prolong the moment – but that was it. We kissed, she went home, I got up two hours later for a television interview, still a bit tipsy. My whole second day in Copenhagen was blocked out with press and radio. I ended up giving interviews lying flat on my back on a sofa, because every time I sat up I thought I was going to be sick. Lene was back, looking on, in her record label capacity. She seemed to think the whole thing was hilarious. Who *was* this woman?

She turned up later to take us back to the airport, and the atmosphere was very weird, but I couldn't find a way to speak to her in private. Tony and Andy were there, they knew we'd been out together the night before, and I didn't want it to look suspicious. So we hugged at the airport and that was that.

Or, rather, that was nearly that. A few weeks later, at the end of the year, I saw her again, in London. The label I was signed to had also signed a band from Australia called The Church, a kind of psychedelic alt-rock thing. There was a showcase gig at the Marquee, to unveil them to the marketing staff around Europe. I made a few enquiries, discovered that the audience included a deputation from Denmark and suddenly became incredibly interested in Antipodean psychedelic alt-rock and what it sounded like live. I saw her as soon as I arrived. I walked straight up to her, which I think caused a few raised eyebrows among the assembled heads of record labels. I ushered her outside, desperate to talk to her. Virtually the first thing she told me was that she had a boyfriend, who she was meeting for dinner after the gig. Oh well. I gave her the number of my hotel anyway – I'd moved out of Pete's flat and BMG were putting me up in a place around the corner from their offices – but she never rang. Perhaps that was for the best. After all, I had a girlfriend, albeit one I hardly saw.

*

Back at PWL – or the Hit Factory as everyone was now calling it – there was a bit of a scramble going on to put together my debut album in time for Christmas. Matt and Mike had a couple of songs for me. They'd written 'It Would Take a Strong Strong Man', which was a kind of retro soul track, but most of them were in the vein of the two previous singles. 'Together Forever' was like 'Never Gonna Give You Up Part 2', or 'Never Gonna Give You Up' with two extra spoonfuls of sugar in it: great melody, just not quite as good. In fairness, even if they had wanted to think of doing something radically different, they didn't have time; they needed to get it done.

There was other stuff happening at PWL as well. They had a new artist, an Australian actress called Kylie Minogue. The soap opera she was in, *Neighbours*, was huge in Britain at the time, and she'd already released a single in Australia, a cover of 'The Loco-Motion': my friend Mike Duffy had produced it, very much in the style of SAW. He told me she was great, but I've got to be honest, when I first heard about her, I thought it was Mandy Smith all over again, SAW making a record with someone because they were famous, without any thought as to whether they were a singer: *God, as if people don't think they're naff enough already, now they're making a record with a soap star.*

My snootiness lasted about ten seconds after I met her face to face. She was fantastic. She was so warm and lovely, so completely without airs and graces, so normal, despite the fact that, at that moment, *Neighbours* was on TV twice a day, eighteen million people watched it, and she was definitely the star of the show. In a way, I felt sort of protective towards her, because I knew what she had coming now. 'I Should Be So Lucky' was obviously going to be a huge hit, which meant that she was going to be in the same place that I was: the tabloids, the workload, the blokes on the scaffolding telling you what they thought, although I supposed they'd be wolf-whistling rather than shouting 'Wanker!' She was already recognized everywhere, but this was going to make her even more famous, altering her life in the same way that mine had, and it was hard work.

I was absolutely knackered. As we'd done in Britain, as soon as 'Never Gonna Give You Up' started slipping down the charts in Europe, we released 'Whenever You Need Somebody', and it was another huge hit: No. 1 in seven countries. It was really exciting. I obviously wasn't a one-hit wonder now, but it meant the whole process started again, or rather it continued, because there was never a point where it had stopped: up at 4 a.m., airport, breakfast show, TV studio. I was so tired I was struggling to get the vocals done for the album. Kylie seemed such a sweetheart, I hoped she was ready for it. Still, I thought, it won't last long for her – it might even be a one-off. She's bound to go back to acting, it's not as if she's going to make a career out of being a singer.

Kylie added to Matt and Mike's workload: they were juggling me, her, Bananarama, Sinitta, Mel and Kim and God knows who else. It meant they had nowhere near enough material to fill an album, and there wasn't time for them to write any more. Pete asked me if I had any demos, which I suppose had the added bonus of underlining the story he'd fed Peter Robinson at RCA about what a great writer I was. I played him some songs, and he thought they were good enough. Mike and Matt only wanted to produce songs they'd written themselves, so I recorded the songs with the B team of producers, Phil Harding and Ian Curnow and a guy called Daize Washbourn, although the end results sounded more or less identical to Mike and Matt's productions because everything was done to quite strict rules they set up: we use this synthesizer with this sound, so you use this synthesizer with this sound; we use this drum machine, so you use the same drum machine. My songs turned out OK, but there still wasn't enough material there for an album.

That was when Pete came up with one of his ideas. As usual, the logic behind it didn't really stand up to close examination. He'd read something in a newspaper comparing me to Elvis Presley, which would have been the most ridiculous thing anyone had ever said about me – I had nothing in common with Elvis apart from the fact I had two arms and a quiff – were it not for Pete's response: 'No, he's more like Frank Sinatra.' I suppose what he meant was that Elvis was initially seen as feral and sexy and threatening – not words that anyone was going to use to describe me. I wasn't the kind of artist who was going to swivel my hips and scare people's parents: I was more the kind of artist who might put on a shirt and tie and sing a ballad. He got it into his head that I should do the kind of song Frank Sinatra might have sung, and that it should be 'When I Fall in Love'. Everyone from Doris Day to Donny Osmond had done a version of it, but the most famous one was by Nat King Cole.

On the one hand, that was pretty daunting. Nat King Cole was one of the greatest singers that ever lived and I was a kid. Nevertheless, however Pete had arrived at the idea, it was kind of brilliant. It was the last thing people expected me to do – up until then, I'd done dance-pop – and he was right: it did sort of fit with my image, the boy next door wearing the nice blazer. So it turned everything on its head, but it also worked. And, with the benefit of hindsight, it was really ahead of its time. This was decades before Robbie Williams made a swing album and pop stars started dipping into the Great American Songbook as a matter of course. We're used to it now, but in 1987 no one like me sang songs like that. It was music my dad liked, and my dad hated pop music.

Looking back, I wish they'd really gone for it: hired Abbey Road and an orchestra, used the original arrangement, done it live, filmed the whole thing, turned it into a real moment. But maybe I wouldn't have had the vocal chops to do that back then. Besides, that simply wasn't the way SAW did things. So Ian Curnow was called in, the strings were samples from the Fairlight, and they got me to sing it line by line, which is the way most people record vocals today. I've got to say, Ian did an amazing job given the technology he had to work with, and my vocal isn't awful, although there's no way anyone's going to convince me I did the song justice. When you play my version next to Nat King Cole's, there's no comparison. But as soon as we'd done it, RCA went nuts: they thought it was a Christmas No. 1. They made a video with crackling fires, snow and log cabins, me in a scarf and a long woollen overcoat. I wasn't required to jig about, just lean on a mantelpiece, looking earnest. We flew all the way to the Arctic Circle in Sweden to shoot it, in a tiny aeroplane that landed on a runway covered in ice, although I didn't think you could tell: it could have been shot in Brentford with a load of fake snow.

It went straight into the charts at No. 2, and it stayed there. Pete has always maintained that it was kept off No. 1 by a dastardly conspiracy involving the Pet Shop Boys and their label EMI, which rush-released Nat King Cole's original version as a single. It got into the Top 20, and fair enough – Nat King Cole's version was better than mine – but Pete thought they did it deliberately to detract sales from us, thus ensuring the Pet Shop Boys' cover of 'Always on My Mind' was the Christmas No. 1 instead. I'm not so sure. For one thing, the Pet Shop Boys were massive at that point – they'd already had a No. 1 that year, with 'It's a Sin'. For another, their version of 'Always on My Mind' was fantastic. And even if their record company had done it deliberately, well, that's the music business for you. Pete would have done exactly the same thing in their position. Anyway, the previous

Christmas, I'd been a tape op at PWL, wondering if they were ever going to get around to coming up with a finished version of 'Never Gonna Give You Up'. Twelve months on, I'd had a No. 1 single, a No. 1 album and two Top 3 hits in Britain. 'Never Gonna Give You Up' had been No. 1 in fifteen countries. The album had gone platinum across Europe. I really wasn't in the mood to complain about being cruelly denied success.

There was one postscript to the saga of 'When I Fall in Love'. After it was recorded, SAW realized that, in most of Europe, it would come out after Christmas: my singles were released a month or so later there, because 'Never Gonna Give You Up' hadn't come out until after it was a hit in Britain. So the whole Christmas angle of the video wouldn't work, and in any case, other countries might not like such a dramatic shift in style. They hurriedly decided that the answer was to make it a double A-side single, with a new song more in keeping with 'Never Gonna Give You Up' and 'Whenever You Need Somebody' on the other side. They came up with a song called 'My Arms Keep Missing You'. It was written and recorded in such a rush that it made the rest of the album look like it had been painstakingly assembled.

Just how much of a scramble it had been to record 'My Arms Keep Missing You' only became apparent after Christmas, when I was on a TV show in Holland. I sang – well, mimed – 'When I Fall in Love'. After I finished, the producer approached me and said they'd love me to sing the other song as well – they could tape my performance and use it the following week.

I frowned. 'Other song?'

'Yes.' He smiled. '"My Arms Keep Missing You".'

I stared at him, hoping I didn't look like I was panicking as much as I was. 'Right,' I agreed. 'Could you give me a minute?'

Tops looked up as I burst through the dressing-room door. 'They want me to sing "My Arms Keep Missing You"! What am I going to do?'

Tops suggested that, under the circumstances, what I should do was sing 'My Arms Keep Missing You'. It didn't seem that unreasonable a request: it was, after all, being promoted as the A-side of the single in quite a lot of countries and was, in fact, already in the Top 10 in Germany and Spain.

'I can't. I've got no idea what it sounds like. I sang it once, and heard it once. It was months ago. I've not listened to it since. I can't remember how it goes.'

Tops agreed that an artist not having a clue what their own single sounded like was definitely a problem. I couldn't bluff my way through it – I didn't even have a vague memory of it. The tune, the lyrics: nothing. I went back to the studio, wearing what I imagine was quite a sheepish expression.

'I'd love to sing it for you,' I told the producer, 'but I don't actually know it.'

He let me off – he didn't really have any choice – but he was still looking a bit stunned when we left. I was a bit stunned too. *Fucking hell*, I thought, *and you wonder why people say the stuff they do about SAW and their artists*. On one level, it was funny, because it was so ridiculous. A pop star who can't actually remember what his new single sounds like: if someone put that in a drama about the bad side of the music industry, people wouldn't believe it could possibly happen. But there was another side to it that wasn't funny at all. I felt ashamed. Not for the last time, I was unbelievably embarrassed about the way my career was panning out. You couldn't argue with the success, but doing things this way wasn't what I'd signed up for at all: I'd heard 'You Spin Me Round' and 'Say I'm Your Number One' and thought I was getting involved with master pop craftsmen, not people who seemed to be just knocking things out. They had the Midas touch, so it must be great.

Worse, there was something familiar about that feeling. It was how I'd felt when I was a teenager: ashamed of living in a Portakabin, embarrassed about the way my dad behaved, doing what I was told to do without question, just getting on with it and not answering back.

Everything had changed, but in a sense, nothing had changed at all.

Chapter Eight

Ifinally got my own place in London, a flat in Maida Vale. The rent seemed ludicrous. I could hardly believe the figure I was writing on the deposit cheque. I had the money – I'd started earning a bit from record sales and royalties – but I was a pop star. How did anyone who wasn't a star afford to live in this city? I wasn't even sure I wanted to live there. I'd been in London for two years, and it still didn't feel like home. I'd never liked going on the tube much and I couldn't seem to get a sense of the city at all, where anything was in relation to everything else. But it made sense for me to be here – PWL was in London, so was my record label, so was virtually the entire British music industry – and it seemed practical for me to get my own place. For one thing, I couldn't live in hotels for ever. For another, I hardly ever had time to go back to Newton, which meant I hardly ever saw Debbie. She had a job in a shop in St Helens, but I thought that, if I got my own place, she could come down and live with me. I was still travelling all the time, but we'd see each other more than we currently did.

It didn't really work the way I'd hoped it would. I was away a lot, and when I was home, I was too knackered to do anything. Besides, I was too famous to do anything normal: you couldn't just go to the pub on a Friday night like any ordinary couple would because the minute I walked in, I'd start getting mithered by people: it would have been 'Can I have your autograph?' or – on a bad day – 'Wanker!' So when I was home, we just stayed in: got a video and a takeaway and a bottle of wine. In a way, that was great – it was a quiet weekend, which was exactly what I wanted – but it didn't amount to much of a life. Maybe it would have been different if I'd been with someone who'd been there and done that and was really confident, someone who just went, 'Fuck it – let's go out and rock this town!', but Debbie wasn't like that, and she didn't like London at all. She missed her friends and her mum and she struggled a bit with the music business. It just didn't suit her. Even when I'd been in FBI, she'd never been particularly bothered about the band. She definitely wasn't the kind of girlfriend who went to every gig, which wasn't a problem at all, but I don't think she realized how committed I was to it. I think she saw it as something I did in my spare time, almost like a hobby. Now something that might have looked like a hobby had suddenly turned into a full-time job in a studio in London, and then it had suddenly turned from that into being on *Top of the Pops* and never coming back home at all. It was a massive adjustment for me to make, and it must have been even weirder for her. She got on OK with the girls who worked at PWL, but I could tell she wasn't really comfortable. We went out together to a couple of events. There were paparazzi outside shouting, 'Is that your girlfriend, Rick?' She hated it, and after that she didn't really want to go to anything like that. In a way, I think she kind of resented the music business a bit, because it was the thing that kept taking me away; it was the thing that was stopping us being together. I understood, but equally, this was my life now. I didn't want to stop. So where did that leave us?

It was definitely a problem. It made things awkward between us, because I didn't feel I could talk much to her about what was going on outside of our lives at home. On the rare occasions when something interesting happened when I was away – like when the record label took me out for a fancy meal in a posh restaurant – I didn't want to mention it, because it sounded like I was bragging about some glamorous life I had that she wasn't part of, and moreover didn't really like. But it wasn't a problem I had much time to address properly. The record label I was signed to, RCA, had been bought by a German company called Bertelsmann. They already owned Arista Records and merged it all into a new company called the Bertelsmann Music Group. BMG really wanted to be seen as a big new world force in pop, a home of huge stars – they had Whitney Houston, the Eurythmics, Dolly Parton, Aretha Franklin – that could also make new artists into huge international stars. And, apparently, that meant me. Someone in America must have seen how 'Never Gonna Give You Up' had sold in Britain and decided it could be a hit in America as well. I'd never really thought about the States before; it wasn't exactly as if I'd had much of a career plan in the first place. Besides, Stock Aitken Waterman sold a lot of records in Europe, but they never did anything in America: no one over there really knew who they were. Bananarama had a couple of big hits, but that was the exception. The Americans seemed convinced about me, though. They wanted to release 'Never Gonna Give You Up', and they wanted me to come over to promote it. And, of course, I wanted to go. Heading off to the States obviously wasn't going to help the situation with Debbie much, but I was a bit in love with the idea of America. It was where all my favourite artists came from; it was kind of the holy grail of success for British artists – 'if you could make it there, you could make it anywhere', all that sort of thing. I had absolutely no idea if I could, but it was probably worth a try, wasn't it?

*

Everything about my first trip to America was weird. We flew into New York, and the city completely freaked me out. Maybe it was the combination of it seeming incredibly famil-iar – you'd seen it so many times in movies and on TV, and it looked exactly like it did on screen, with the yellow taxis and the steam coming out of manhole covers – and feeling a very long way away from home. In 1988, New York wasn't the way it was in the 1970s, when the police literally used to hand visitors a leaflet called 'Welcome to Fear City', with a skull on the front, but it definitely wasn't the way it is now. It was still rough enough around the edges to make London look cosy by comparison. I remember driving in from the airport and there were piles of rubbish by the side of the motorway – just stuff people had dumped, which I'd never seen in Britain.

Some of the piles of rubbish had people sitting on them. I thought it looked a bit post-apocalyptic, although that was probably me projecting my own ideas about New York onto it. I'd heard so many stories about how dangerous the city was supposed to be that I spent my entire time there absolutely terrified, my fears amped up by how full-on the place was: the number of people, the traffic, the noise, how the height of the skyscrapers made it feel strangely oppressive to me. Plus, I had no idea about good areas and bad areas. I assumed everywhere was dangerous. So I'd be walking down Fifth Avenue, past Saks, worrying I was going to get murdered or mugged at knifepoint at any minute.

Tops and I had been told to hook up with a guy called Sal Michaels while we were out there: Tony and Dave were looking for American management for me and had decided he was a suitable candidate. When we met him, he wanted to take us to meet his boss, a guy called Norby Walters. We went to his office, a really plush place. The walls were covered with photographs of celebrities – pop stars, sportsmen, all sorts. Norby Walters was like the archetype of a big-shot American manager – 'Hey, Rick, I really like ya, ya gonna be the next big thing, I like ya' – but both Tops and I agreed there was something a bit off about the whole situation: nothing we could put our finger on exactly, but just a feeling that it wasn't quite right.

A few days later, we turned the TV on, and there was Norby Walters, being arrested: he was charged with bribing athletes to sign secret contracts with his company, and, the prosecution claimed, backing the contracts up with threats of violence involving the Mafia. His conviction was eventually overturned, but even the judge who overturned it called Walters 'a nasty and untrustworthy fellow'. Clearly, the idea of being managed by him went out of the window, but the whole business just added to the bizarreness of my first American trip.

We went to the new BMG offices on Times Square, and that was weird too. It was enormous, this huge glass thing. You felt as if you were in a movie, that you'd look up and see Tom Hanks sitting behind one of the desks. The higher up the building you went, the less American it became. On the top floors, where all the really important executives were, everyone was German, even the secretaries; you could have been in Dusseldorf, rather than the centre of Manhattan. Everyone you were introduced to was called Rudi or Heinz. And the more you talked to people, the more you realized how different the music market in America was from the UK. You'd mention some artist who was absolutely huge in Britain, and find out that no one in the US had a clue who they were: 'Things from Britain don't always work over here.' The fact that I was massive in Europe was the reason they thought I *might* be successful in the US, but it really counted for nothing. We were obviously starting from scratch again, which wasn't a problem at all; fine with me.

It also had a plus side, although that was a bit weird too. All the British perceptions of me, the kind of artist that I was, didn't matter. I noticed it when we started doing public appearances. Most of them were pop shows. I remember meeting Debbie Gibson at one, this little sixteen-year-old girl who it turned out wrote and produced all her own hits, which I thought was hugely impressive. But one of the first

PAs was in New York, and when we arrived at the club, it became clear that Tops and I were the only white people there. *Oh God,* I thought, *this is taking the piss*. It's a club for a Black audience, who want to hear Black music. Why are you putting a twenty-one-year-old Northern white bloke on a podium in the middle of it, singing a British pop version of the music they love? But they didn't care. They seemed to love the song. I guess they heard a song that had a Colonel Abrams-style bassline and strings that made you think of an old Philadelphia International track from the seventies and didn't really care that it was sung by a ginger-haired kid from Lancashire and produced by three middle-aged white guys.

It made me think that 'Never Gonna Give You Up' might sound different outside the context of SAW: a bit cooler than it was perceived to be in Britain. And America definitely did see it outside the context of SAW, because America didn't have a clue who SAW were. I noticed this when we started doing interviews at US radio stations. They seemed different from the usual interviews, but at first I couldn't work out why. Then I understood: no one ever asked me about Pete, Mike and Matt. I'd got so used to them coming up every time I did an interview. In Britain, entirely understandably, people were fascinated by this bunch of producers who seemed to have taken over the singles chart, who you couldn't get away from no matter how hard you tried. What are they like? What are their other artists like? How do they make records? Is it true you were the teaboy at their studio? In America, they weren't mentioned. Or if they were, the DJs got me off the topic really quickly, as if they thought the audience wouldn't care who produced the single and might switch off if we talked about them too much. I thought that was quite nice and a bit of a relief.

*

Back in Britain, 'Together Forever' had been released as a single. I'm not saying that video directors were running out of ideas for places for me to mime and jig about a bit in the company of hot dancers I'd never met before, but this time, they settled for getting me, and them, to do it in front of a large shiny sheet: a large shiny sheet that was being shaken vigorously, which made it look remarkably like a large shiny sheet that was being shaken vigorously. I cringe a bit looking at it now, but I think that's got less to do with its lack of high production values than with seeing myself at twenty-one or whatever I was. It's like being shown a photo of your first day at uni or your first day at work.

The single went to No. 2 – as predicted, Kylie was at No. 1 with 'I Should Be So Lucky' and me and my vigorously shaken shiny sheet could do nothing to dislodge her. But it felt that I'd hardly been back home five minutes before the American record label said they wanted me to return to the US. 'Never Gonna Give You Up' had started picking up a lot of radio play. Radio was even more important in America than in Britain, because in America the amount your song gets played on the radio counts towards your chart position, and the song had started climbing the Billboard Hot 100, albeit in the lower reaches and albeit very slowly: No. 61, No. 52. So back we went, this time to the West Coast, for another round of radio station interviews and daytime TV appearances and occasional PAs. It seemed to work: 'Never Gonna Give You Up' kept slowly inching its way up the charts, until it was just outside the Top 20.

In Los Angeles, Tops and I stayed at the Sunset Marquis, the more upscale of LA's two famous rock-and-roll hotels; the other was the Hyatt House, where Led Zeppelin had entertained groupies and Keith Moon blew things up and threw things out of windows. The Sunset Marquis was a bit more sedate, although these things were relative. Sometime in the 2000s I once walked into the bar at the Sunset Marquis; it was very late and I'd had a few already. Out of the corner of my eye I noticed a child wandering about in the bar. *That's a bit off*, I thought, only to realize it was an adult, but a very small one. All of a sudden this guy is throwing punches at a man a lot bigger than him and I decided that it was probably time to go to bed, but as I left, I bumped straight into Kylie Minogue, who was accompanied by a guy I didn't know. They were both soaking wet, because they'd jumped in the swimming pool fully clothed.

I loved the Sunset Marquis, in fact I loved LA – something about the weather made it feel like you were on holiday, even if you had work to do. And the Marquis was incredible. The place was heaving with models and film stars. I saw Roy Schneider, baking in the sun by the swimming pool, reading a film script. It had been a few years since he'd been in a huge movie, but that didn't matter – it was Chief Brody from *Jaws*, the film that had stopped me wanting to go anywhere near a swimming pool when I was a kid. There were even more pop stars than there were models or actors. You'd come down for breakfast and see Bono and The Edge discussing the menu.

Robert Plant would be on the next table. Bruce Springsteen stayed there, parking a massive Winnebago outside. Me and Tops taught Phil Collins's daughter Lily how to dive at the Sunset Marquis swimming pool while her dad was plough-ing his way through a film script. She was about four years old, and called Tops 'big boy' – he was quite barrel-chested – and me 'little boy'.

The Sunset Marquis should have been an intimidat-ing environment for someone like me. It was all rock stars, hair-metal bands and hip indie bands, the kind of people I assumed would ignore me because they thought I was a complete twat – a SAW-manufactured pop star, someone who might be successful but definitely wasn't allowed to be part of their world. But it didn't seem to be like that at all. People came up and introduced themselves, they had a chat, they behaved as if I was exactly the same as them.

One night, in the bar, I saw Andy Rourke and Mike Joyce from The Smiths. *Oh my God.* At the height of my Smiths obsession, I'd seen Andy Rourke out shopping in Manchester and had decided to follow him around for a bit. I didn't stop him, or speak to him, or ask for an autograph, I just trailed around after him; for about ten minutes, I was his stalker. I've no idea what I thought I was doing. I simply couldn't believe I'd seen one of The Smiths in real life.

And now there were two of them, sitting in the Sunset Marquis bar. No way was I going to go over and talk to them: however much I loved The Smiths, I was sure I was the type of artist that members of The Smiths would prefer to ignore. Apparently not – they beckoned me over. I thought they were going to take the piss out of me, but no. They wanted to know how it was going, what I was up to – they were just lovely, incredibly nice. They couldn't give a flying fuck whether the music I made was considered cool or not.

Maybe it had something to do with the fact that we were all British musicians together in a foreign country. Or maybe not, because something similar happened in Britain later in the year. I got asked to perform at the Prince's Trust Rock Gala at the Royal Albert Hall. The bill was ridiculous – Elton John, the Bee Gees, Mark Knopfler, Eric Clapton, Joe Cocker, Peter Gabriel – and so was the backing band. I hadn't played a gig, with actual musicians, since I was the lead singer of FBI, and now I had to play one with Phil Collins on drums, Midge Ure on guitar, Howard Jones on keyboards, Mick Karn from my teenage favourites Japan on bass, and Brian May on lead guitar. I have to walk in and introduce myself – 'Hi, I'm Rick, I'm here to rehearse!' – while being both terrified and completely convinced that the last thing this kind of legendary musical talent wants to play is 'Never Gonna Give You Up'. And they're about as lovely as it's possible for human beings to be. Phil Collins comes up to me and goes, 'Is it OK if Mark Brzezicki and I both play drums on this?' *Yes, Phil, I'm pretty sure it'll be all right if both the drummer from Genesis, a band I spent hours and hours listening to my sister play as a kid, and the drummer from Big Country, a band whose songs I used to cover in the Legh Arms in Newton, play on my song.* Then Brian May wanders over: 'So, Rick, I'm thinking of doing a guitar solo here. What do you think?' *Well, I think you can play a guitar solo that starts at the beginning of the song and finishes when it ends, completely drowning out my vocal in the process if you want, because you're*

Brian fricking May from Queen. No one was sniffy, no one talked down to me, everyone was incredibly friendly.

It was the same at the Sunset Marquis. Perhaps people didn't think I was as much of a twat as I'd imagined they did. Perhaps they simply saw me as someone else who made music, just not the same kind of music that they made. They knew how lucky we all were to do that for a living; they understood the ups and downs of doing it, the good side and the bad side, all of that. Whatever it was, it kind of blew me away. It wasn't validation or anything like that, but it did feel like someone giving you a hug.

Even so, staying at the Sunset Marquis could occasionally remind me that I wasn't *quite* made of the same stuff as some of its other guests. That happened when I met Martin Gore and Andy Fletcher from Depeche Mode. They were becoming huge in the States, and they were thought of quite differently there from the way they were seen in the UK. In Britain, they'd been a synth-pop band who got a bit more edgy and sophisticated, but none of their early singles were hits in America, so they only saw Depeche Mode Mark 2, a gothy alternative band that had more in common with The Cure than a pop band. There was something a bit dark and dangerous about them, but Martin and Fletch were really friendly. They said it was the last gig of the tour that night and asked if Tops and I wanted to come along. We couldn't: I was working. No problem, they said, there was an end-of-tour party happening after the gig, in a club near Melrose Avenue – why didn't we come along to that?

When we arrived, the end-of-tour party was in full swing. The club was like a series of interconnected rooms,

The Prince's Trust concert comprised some of the world's greatest artists . . . and me.

Meeting Princess Diana before the Prince's Trust gig at the Royal Albert Hall, 1988.

Meeting Prince William, at the Royal Albert Hall again, this time for the Royal Variety Show, 2023.

Family time with Emilie,
in the pool of the
Sunset Marquis, 1993.

Emilie and me in Italy in the mid-nineties.

Emilie and Lene skiing in Val-d'Isère,
also mid-nineties.

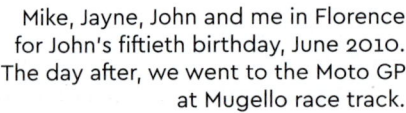

Mike, Jayne, John and me in Florence
for John's fiftieth birthday, June 2010.
The day after, we went to the Moto GP
at Mugello race track.

My band and crew in 2024. I can't do it without them and I wouldn't want to. My name is on the ticket, but it takes every single one of us to make this happen.

Band and crew rehearsals, Putney, 2022.

All my band on stage with KT Tunstall for the post-Covid free concert we put on for NHS staff and careworkers, Wembley, 2021.

New Kids on the Block tour in the US, 2022, with Salt-N-Pepa and En Vogue. You guys!

So amazing to be on tour with Gary, Mark and Howard! Take That quite literally rule the world. I love them!

On tour in Australia and New Zealand with A-ha, posing in Perth, 2022.

The Royal Albert Hall, Swinging Christmas, December 2022. I cried at rehearsals and on both nights performing. I wish my mum and dad could have seen me do these shows.

Possibly the greatest drummer in rock and roll. . . oh, and Dave Grohl on guitar. He's nuts!

With Kylie at Radio 2 in the Park, Leicester, September 2023. Is she 'lucky'? No, it's talent and hard work. Love her!

The Luddites: me in the middle; Simon Mattacks on bass; Graham Stack on guitar. All of us in bowler hats and kilts. Well, why not?

Glastonbury, 24 June 2023, midday. Lene and I walked on the stage to see an empty field twenty minutes before start time . . . then this happened. It doesn't get any better!

Glastonbury, 24 June 2023, 6 p.m. Blossoms and me about to take the stage at Woodsies. Love these lads.

On the Woodsies Stage, giving the mic a twirl in the heat of a moment that I will never forget.

Royal Albert Hall, April 2013. Lene and me at soundcheck. Our company is called 50/50. It's a partnership in every way.

The new BMG: Alistair Norbury and Peter Stack presenting me with an award for 5 million single sales in the US of 'Never Gonna Give You Up', backstage at the Royal Albert Hall, November 2022.

With Simon Moran and Peter Kay at the Manchester AO Arena, September 2017. The gigs with Peter really helped to kick-start my career again.

Jimmy Jam and Richard Weitz, LA, June 2022. I wish I had met these amazing guys much earlier in life.

really dark and crowded, a DJ blaring out, people drinking cool-looking cocktails. We briefly saw Fletch from Depeche Mode – 'You made it in the end! Great to see you, have a great night!' – then we went to the bar. I had a beer, Tops had his usual Coke. We didn't really know anyone else there, so we were standing chatting to each other when a girl in a short skirt came up to us and started making small talk. She was about my age, and absolutely stunning. She kept dancing while she was talking to us. Then I noticed she was slowly pulling her skirt up as she talked. What was she doing that for? I caught Tops' eye: *This is a bit weird, right?* He gave me a look that indicated that, yes, he'd noticed she was pulling her skirt up and yes, he thought it was a bit strange too. We kept talking, she kept pulling her skirt up and it slowly dawned on us that she was hired for the party as an exotic dancer. I then noticed there were a few of them, dotted about the room – men as well as women – taking their clothes off. Which was fine; I suppose it all added to the air of decadence and debauchery if you liked that sort of thing, but what if you didn't? What if you were, say, a twenty-one-year-old bloke with a steady girlfriend – and his happily married road manager – and you didn't want someone sort of stripping . . . well, *at* you, no matter how stunning they were? Tops and I decided the best option was just to bore her into stopping. We kept asking her really dull questions. Where was she from? Oh, Nevada? I'll bet it's hot there? Did she have any brothers and sisters? How did she get here tonight? Did it take her long? Eventually, she pulled her skirt down and danced off to entertain someone else. We decided to call it a night. Sometimes you've got to be honest and admit to yourself that the rock-and-roll lifestyle isn't really for you.

So maybe I was a bit clean-cut and innocent. I certainly wasn't averse to getting pissed, but I was never going to be the kind of person who's the last one standing in the bar at 4 a.m., raising his glass of Jack Daniels: 'Hey, man, here's to rock and roll.' Honestly, in the whole time I was successful, I never even saw a drug. Not a joint, not a line of coke, nothing – I think Tops and I just gave off a vibe that said, 'Nah, that ain't us, it's not our bag,' so no one ever offered it. I mean, I must have been *around* people who were on drugs at some points – I was a pop star in the eighties; the likelihood of me never meeting anyone who was on cocaine was basically nil – but the truth is, I wouldn't have known if they were. And that one night in Copenhagen aside, I certainly wasn't interested in chasing girls. I had a girlfriend, although admittedly I knew in my heart of hearts that things weren't really working out with her.

I felt awful that Debbie had moved to London and basically ended up sitting in a flat on her own while I was flying around the world. She used to get her friends or her mum to come down and keep her company, but I didn't know what else I could do about it. It had got to the stage where I'd started thinking we might be better off apart, but I couldn't work out how to bring it up without looking like a total git: 'Right, so you know how we've been together since we were at school? Well, now I'm a massive pop star and I'm making loads of money I've decided I'm dumping you.'

It's almost laughable how strait-laced I was all the way through that part of my career. There were times when I had so much on that I even joined Tops in his teetotalism for a few months. You could see it all as a terrible missed opportunity if you wanted, but I'm glad I did it that way. Besides, in the spring of 1988, I didn't really need rock-and-roll excess to make my life seem crazy. In March 1988, 'Never Gonna Give You Up' knocked George Michael off the top of the Billboard Hot 100. I was No. 1 in America.

I was in a hotel in Spain when I found out. I remember sitting on the edge of the bed, trying to take it in, but all I could think was: *Wow.* I was really proud of my success in Britain and Europe, but there's no getting around the fact that, for a British artist, success in America changes things, especially for an artist like me. It didn't make me any more cool, but I think it did change perceptions a bit. It meant I wasn't just more standard SAW fodder; I'd done something that hardly any other SAW artist had done.

*

Maybe that shift in perception explains what happened when I submitted my next set of demos to Pete Waterman. I was still writing songs and still looking for Pete's approval when I did: after all, I'd sung the hits, but SAW were the hit-makers. I knew he loved 'I Wanna Dance with Somebody' by Whitney Houston, so among my new songs there was one where I tried to come up with something a bit like it: a white, immature pop version of 'I Wanna Dance with Somebody', if you like, called 'She Wants to Dance with Me'. I told him I'd come up with some new stuff and left the tape on his desk. About ten minutes later, Pete comes screaming out of his office, yelling that I've written my first single. Really? I wasn't sure about that at all, but Pete was already off around the studios, rushing into other people's rooms, shouting up the stairs: 'This song is amazing! Rick's just written his first single!' He told everyone, from the secretaries to the girls who worked in the publishing department. He couldn't have broadcast it any more loudly without hiring a plane with a banner hanging off the back and flying it over London. I mean, obviously I was pleased and flattered, but equally, I'd known Pete long enough to realize that he had a habit of saying some pretty mad things that weren't necessarily true, and of acting a bit rashly. And I couldn't help notice that the one place in the PWL building he didn't barge into and announce that I'd written a hit single was the studio where Matt and Mike – the people who were in charge of coming up with hit singles themselves – were working. Hmmm.

It was a strange incident, but I didn't think any more about it. There were more pressing things I had to attend to. While 'Never Gonna Give You Up' was still in the charts, the US label released 'Together Forever' as a follow-up. It did exactly the same thing: slowly climbed the charts, then knocked George Michael off No. 1. Clearly, the American public weren't bothered by the video, with its vigorously shaken shiny sheet, but for the next single, the label in the States decided to take matters into their own hands. They didn't release 'Whenever You Need Somebody' – they'd clearly had enough of singles by me that went bom-chibom-chibom – so they put out 'It Would Take a Strong Strong Man' instead. That was fine by me. It was good song, it was different, and it really showed off another side to my voice. And they decided to commission a video themselves. If you wanted evidence that everything about success in America was on a grander scale, then here it was. They hired a big-name video director. There was a full backing band, performing behind me on a nightclub stage. There was a script, which I read with increasing horror. Acting, of a sort, was required from me. So was a female co-star. I had to walk through the streets of LA with her and have a mock argument. *Oh God, I had to kiss her.*

They told me they were holding auditions for the role of my love interest, and I asked if I could meet the successful candidate in advance – maybe we could have a coffee or something. I simply wanted to be spared the embarrassment of turning up on set and immediately having to snog someone I'd never met before.

When the successful candidate arrived at the Sunset Marquee, even Tops – who'd previously given the impression of being completely unflappable, having seen it all before – looked a bit startled. She was called Blueberry – *Blueberry!* – and she was, apparently, a *Playboy* model. She was a brunette, curvaceous, very beautiful and about 6 foot 1. She seemed perfectly nice, but in her high heels she would literally have to bend down to kiss me. It was as if they'd picked her deliberately to make the experience of kissing someone you barely knew in front of a load of cameras even more excruciating than it already was.

We had a coffee, she left, and I hurriedly rang the record label with the polite suggestion that they could perhaps try to find someone else, preferably someone I could kiss without the aid of a ladder. A couple of days later, they got back to me with the name of a replacement actress. She was called Mädchen Amick – she went on to have a big role in

Twin Peaks – and I asked the same thing as before: would it be possible to meet her in advance? They said they would see what they could do.

They rang back, saying that she wasn't sure she could do that, but if she did, could her boyfriend come with her? I was a bit confused, then I suddenly realized how it must have sounded: *Right, this pop star from England whose video you're going to be in wants you to go and meet him at his hotel.* Oh, Christ, no: I didn't mean it like *that.* Great, now I've got to kiss someone who I don't want to kiss anyway and now she thinks I'm some kind of . . . *sex pest.*

So she didn't come to the hotel, but she did turn up for the video. So did her boyfriend, who spent the shoot more or less glued to her side, looking at me suspiciously. I eventually went and talked to him – turned out he was a musician – which diffused the situation. I think he realized pretty quickly that he wasn't dealing with Newton-le-Willows' leading pop Lothario, and that the only immediate danger his girlfriend faced was that I might die of embarrassment while kissing her. The video got made. It looked great. The single made the US Top 10.

In fact, things in America seemed to keep snowballing. 'Never Gonna Give You Up' turned out to be the fourth biggest-selling single of the year. I got nominated for a Best New Artist Grammy. The producers of a new Tom Cruise movie called *Cocktail* contacted Pete Waterman Limited, asking if they could use one of my songs on the soundtrack: they gave them a song I'd written called 'You Move Me'. I remember Pete excitedly dragging me into his office to show me a VHS of the trailer: 'You're not gonna believe this, kid.' There was 'You Move Me' booming out over footage of Tom Cruise throwing bottles in the air and smooching with Elisabeth Shue on a Caribbean beach. It might have been better if Pete had bothered to mention that they'd decided only to use my song in the trailer and not in the film itself – nor, for that matter, on the multi-platinum-selling soundtrack album – but no, he just carried on as if it was the theme song. I should have been furious, or crushingly disappointed, but I had to laugh at the absolute Pete-ness of that moment.

Then Coca-Cola got in touch, asking if I wanted to be in a TV commercial. Being in an advert might not sound like much, but at that point, appearing in a Coca-Cola or Pepsi ad was a very, very big deal. It was the height of the eighties cola wars and one of the weapons in each company's arsenal was to lure the biggest stars imaginable to be in their commercials: Michael Jackson, Whitney Houston, David Bowie, Elton John. And now they apparently wanted *me*. It was unreal. And, as someone pointed out, being on a Coca-Cola commercial was like getting $10 million of promotion: you and your song were going to be on everyone's telly, all over the world, all the time, for months. And they were paying *you* to do it. Incredible.

More incredible still, I didn't do it. I wanted to, but then some weird thing blew up about how much Coca-Cola were going to pay me. Someone on our side of the deal decided that the fee they were offering wasn't enough and the deal fell through. I couldn't believe it – I thought it was supposed to be $10 million worth of global promotion; who gives a monkey's about the fee? – but there didn't seem to

be much I could do about it. It was all bound up with lawyers and stuff like that, things I didn't get much involved in.
I was still only twenty-two and no one wanted me to get
caught up in the complexities of the business side. Still, the
fact they they'd thought of asking me in the first place, the
fact that, somehow, Coca-Cola saw me in the same context as the kind of artists they usually asked, seemed nuts.
In fact, everything that had happened since 'Never Gonna
Give You Up' was first released seemed nuts if I stopped
to think about it: No. 1 singles, awards, an album that had
sold, by that point, 8 million copies. And it had all happened in less than a year.

I suppose it was the kind of sudden, dramatic fame that
could go to your head, but I wasn't in any danger of turning
into a diva. I'm just not the sort of person who goes round
clicking their fingers and demanding people do things for
me. Maybe it's got something to do with my upbringing: one
thing I got from my dad was that if you could do something
yourself – whether it was fixing a car or putting up a fence or
whatever – you did it yourself, rather than getting someone
else to do it. And I instinctively knew the way to play all of
this, even if you've had a massive hit and sold millions of
records, is to be humble, be nice, be polite. Just don't be an
arse: I mean, that's true regardless of what you do, isn't it?
Doesn't matter if you're a pop star or working in a petrol station, or indeed a garden centre: don't be an arse. It really isn't
that hard to work out and it really isn't that hard to put into
practice either, although a remarkable number of people in
the music business seem to struggle with the whole concept.

Chapter Nine

E ven if I had been inclined to let success go to my head, there was something about Stock Aitken Waterman that could bring you back down to earth with a bump. At some point, when I'd been shuttling backwards and forwards from Britain to America, it had been pointed out that we needed to make a new album, and that we'd have to start soon if we wanted it to be ready for the end of 1988. It was a tricky job, following up an album that had sold 8 million copies and produced two US No. 1s. They wanted me to write more songs, but Mike and Matt were definitely going to come up with the first single. It was really important that we got it right. Plus, at that point, the idea of the Coca-Cola commercial was still in the air. If we were going to put out something that was going to be on TVs during ad breaks around the world for months – albeit with its lyrics changed to sell cola – it had to be good.

I'd just landed back in the UK when I got a call to come to the studio: they had a track that was right. I arrived, and they told me the song wasn't ready yet – I should hang around for a bit; they'd be finished soon. I waited in what was now called the Missile Room, where Pete had hung the decommissioned missile that he'd got from God knows where. The hours went by, and the song still wasn't ready. I waited all day. Still nothing. They told me to come back tomorrow, that it would definitely be ready by then.

I didn't say anything, didn't kick up a fuss, but I was angry: not because the song wasn't finished, not because I thought I was too important to wait around, but because it was a day off wasted. I hardly *ever* had a day off. I could have been spending time with Debbie, I could have been getting my laundry done – anything, it didn't matter. Instead, I'd spent it pointlessly sitting around in the Missile Room, doing nothing. I'd have been better off making the tea and fetching sandwiches, the way I had been eighteen months ago. If they'd called in advance and told me they weren't finished – 'Look, sorry, Rick, stay at home, mate, we haven't quite cracked it yet' – that would have been absolutely fine.

I don't think it was done deliberately at all. It wasn't a case of, 'You think you're a star, but you're nothing special here.' I feel it was simply done without thought. In a way, that was more annoying. I believe they didn't have a clue how hard I'd been working. I hate saying things like that, because I'm a pop star and, like I said before, it's a privilege to do what I do: I wasn't digging ditches for a living, or saving anybody's life. But I was on a plane every other day, I always had something to do, somewhere to be. If you think this book is lacking a bit of colour about my personal life, it's not because I'm being secretive about it, it's because – at this point – I didn't really have any kind of personal life to tell you about. I didn't have time to do anything other than work. Even if there had been time, I had that kind of tabloid fame that means you've got no privacy to do anything normal anyway.

Rant over. I went back to the studio the next day. The song was finished. It was called 'Nothing Can Divide Us'. They played it to me, with Mike singing the vocal. It was . . . OK. Nothing special. It wasn't even 'Never Gonna Give You Up Part 2', like 'Together Forever' had been. It just sounded like generic SAW, the sort of thing they'd been pumping out while I was in the States. And maybe that was the problem: I'd been in the States. I'd been round every radio station and TV show that would have me, and in the process, I'd got a sense of the kind of pop music that was really selling over there: George Michael, Bobby Brown, INXS, Terence Trent D'Arby, a lot of new jack swing like Al B. Sure! and Tony! Toni! Toné! It wasn't that I wanted to make R&B records, but I did want to make something good enough to com-pete with those kinds of artists, and 'Nothing Can Divide Us' wasn't it. I'm not sure that SAW really cared about America – they were focused on what would work in the UK. Their world was Capital Radio, Woolworths, Tracey and Dave in the Ritzy clubs. Their records didn't usually sell in America, and that was fine with them. But it wasn't fine with me: I'd worked really hard, I'd sold millions of records over there, I had a real chance to keep doing well, and I didn't want to squander it on some song I knew wasn't right.

Still, I went ahead and finished the track, and finished

it properly: I didn't want to kick up a fuss, or act unprofessionally. While I was recording my vocal, I overheard Matt talking to Mike. He laughed and said, 'What colour do you want your Testarossa, then?' I don't know whether he didn't realize the talkback microphone was on and that I could hear him in the studio, or whether it was daft banter that I was meant to hear, but I was really hurt. *That's the problem, right there,* I thought. You think you've cracked it again, you think this is another big hit, one that's going to earn you another Ferrari. You're so successful in the UK that you're sure everything you do is automatically fantastic. And it ain't. *This song isn't good enough.* How can you not see that? Why hasn't one of you said: 'Stop everything, we've sold 8 million albums with this lad, Coca-Cola want to do an advert and stick him on American telly every day for the next six months – this is on a completely different scale, we have to get this right, even if it takes us a month, we can't simply palm him off with something that we've knocked together in a rush, overnight'? *This song isn't fucking good enough.*

But I still didn't say anything. We finished the song. Mike and Matt seemed very happy. I went home. I rang Tops, and then I rang Tony, my co-manager, and I told them both the same thing. 'I'm not doing it. Even if they sack me, or terminate my contract, I'm not doing it. I quit.'

Tops thought we should go and see Pete straight away. He was up in Warrington – he'd bought a house there, to be closer to Gaynor – but if we set off now, we'd be there late in the evening. I wasn't sure. I hate confrontation, but Tops pointed out that nothing was going to get sorted out without a conversation. Even if all I ended up doing was effectively handing in my resignation, I should do it face to face. He had a point. He called Pete and then came and picked me up.

Tony met us at Pete's house. It was him who told Pete I wasn't going to do 'Nothing Can Divide Us', that I'd rather quit than release it as a single. I didn't know what response to expect, but Pete was very keen to smooth things over: he was very pragmatic about the whole thing. He'd sort it out. We'd get another song. I should submit some, and Mike and Matt would write some more, and we'd pick the best between us.

In retrospect, I think he was just tap-dancing, trying to stop the situation turning into a black hole, because that plan didn't happen. It was simply decided that 'She Wants to Dance with Me' was going to be the first single off the album. That wasn't really what I wanted, and I'd certainly never pushed for it at all. It was Pete who had gone round the building yelling at everyone that it was going to be a hit single, not me. I never thought that. 'She Wants to Dance with Me' is all right – it's certainly a better song than 'Nothing Can Divide Us' – and people still love it when I play it live, but it's not a total belter, a song that's going to stop you dead in your tracks. I wonder if it was made the single because that was the story he told Mike and Matt. Rather than say to them, 'Rick's refusing to release your song because he doesn't think it's good enough,' maybe it was easier to say, 'Rick's gone totally mad, he's insisting that a song he wrote should be the first single.'

However he pitched it to them, it still caused bad feeling. They really didn't like artists throwing their weight around in any way. They wouldn't produce 'She Wants to Dance with Me' – that was the deal; they only produced songs they'd written – and the next time I went into the studio, there was a really weird atmosphere. I saw Mike and he blanked me. I was sorry if I'd hurt his feelings and I could sort of understand how he was thinking – *He's only famous because of the songs we wrote, and now he's refusing to release them, the ungrateful little bastard* – but I thought it was a bit childish, and a bit sad. PWL had always felt like a team: the producers, the artists, everyone who worked there. I suppose because of all the negative press PWL and SAW received, there was a bit of an 'us against the world' mentality. Suddenly, it didn't feel like a team any more; it felt as if it was me against them. All it had taken was for me to question their judgement *once*. I wasn't asking to take some mad new musical direction; I wasn't demanding to make a heavy metal record or a jazz album; I wasn't even asking to get other musicians in. I just wanted them to think a little more about what they were doing, to make it as great as it had been the first time around.

And anyway, I was right. SAW never really had another successful artist in America. They had a hit single with Kylie's version of 'The Loco-Motion', but none of her follow-ups were successful there; she didn't have another American Top 10 hit until 'Can't Get You Out of My Head', thirteen years later, long after she had split from them. They were perfectly capable of making US hit singles if they tried – 'Never Gonna Give You Up', 'Together Forever' and 'It Would Take a Strong Strong Man' proved that, as did the stuff they'd done with Bananarama – but they were too cocky about what they did, and their attitude towards the whole country was weird, as if they had a chip on their shoulder about it: *Everything we do is incredible, Americans just don't get it, so fuck them.* Meanwhile, they gave 'Nothing Can Divide Us' to Jason Donovan as his first single. At that point, Jason Donovan was so popular – he'd been in *Neighbours* with Kylie – I thought you could have released a single of him playing the banjo and farting and it would have gone straight to No. 1. 'Nothing Can Divide Us' stalled at No. 5. As I said: the song wasn't good enough, whatever Matt and Mike thought.

*

In some ways, the fallout from the whole 'Nothing Can Divide Us' thing was good. It hadn't turned out as I'd hoped, but it gave me a bit more confidence to say no to things I wasn't happy about. SAW still seemed intent on winding their critics up: if people said their records were knocked out with no effort, they were happy to play up to that image. There was some stupid suggestion of making a record with a journalist – it might even have been a critic who'd been slagging them off – to prove that they could have a hit with anyone. There was an even worse idea to get in *The Guinness Book of Records* by making the fastest single in history. I was supposed to sing it and it would be mixed, mastered, pressed and in the shops within twenty-four hours. They wanted me to do it live on TV: I was to go to the Trocadero, a sort of touristy shopping centre in Piccadilly Circus where Guinness World Records had an exhibition, and record it there. I thought it was a terrible idea, really gimmicky – you might get a hit out of it, but it just looked awful, as if you didn't care about the quality of what you were doing, you only wanted publicity – and even worse, it involved me singing in the middle of a shopping centre in central London, like a complete twat.

A year before, I suppose I might have gone along with it. Now I told them I absolutely wouldn't do it, and the idea was dropped. And I started pushing harder to be allowed to tour when my second album came out. As I said before, no one at the record label or PWL was particularly interested in me playing live at the time; they thought there was no need and no money in it. But I'd always loved being on stage, even if it was only at the Legh Arms with FBI. I thought singing live was something I was good at. I wanted to do it. So I kept nagging away about it until they gave in: a world tour was booked to follow the new album's release.

I really enjoyed working on my own songs for the second album. Things with Matt and Mike rectified themselves enough that we worked together on three songs they wrote, and it was fine, but most of it was done by me, Phil Harding, Ian Curnow and Daize Washbourn. It was decided that we wouldn't record at PWL. Although the relationship with Matt and Mike had improved, the atmosphere in the studio still felt a bit odd when I wasn't working with them. I got the sense that I wasn't really wanted in the building any more, unless I'd been asked to be there. So we went to the Workhouse, a studio on the Old Kent Road that had been built in the sixties by Manfred Mann and that Pete had some kind of financial interest in, which suited me fine. I loved it there. It had a bit of history – Ian Dury had recorded there, and so had Echo and the Bunnymen and Joe Cocker – but it wasn't a tacky old studio, it was really modern: people like Depeche Mode and Paul Young made hits there. It obviously had links to PWL, but it somehow felt outside the whole SAW empire. We really cracked on there. I turned up with full demos of songs and we rearranged them. I was a bit more involved with the whole recording process. I even played a bit of guitar and keyboards on my own record, and got a co-production credit. I suspect Phil and Daize did that to placate me a bit – you know, 'He's lost his temper at Matt and Mike, we'd better let him play keyboards because that'll make him feel better' – but it still felt very different from working at PWL, where you were just expected to sing the songs you were given.

Midway through recording, I took a proper holiday with Debbie. Things had been pretty strained between us, and I'd even tried to end it a couple of times, but whenever I did, it only ended up with floods of tears and me backing down. We went to Mauritius together and we genuinely had a fantastic time. It was the first proper break I'd had since I'd gone skiing with a cassette of 'Never Gonna Give You Up' in my pocket, wondering if it would ever be released. For a fortnight, the music industry felt a long way away. I even stopped thinking about work and the situation with SAW for a bit – at least until the house band at the hotel asked me to sing with them. I said no, but they really knew how to put the pressure on: 'Oh, Eric Clapton was staying here recently and *he* played with us.' So I did too.

I arrived back in London ready to start work at the Work-house again, only to find out that the Workhouse didn't exist any longer, or rather half of it didn't: it had been destroyed in a fire while I was away. And it was the half that we'd been working in. All the tapes of everything we'd done had gone up in flames. There were all sorts of mad rumours flying around about what had happened – it was arson, it was an insur-ance job – but they seemed pretty far-fetched to me. And it honestly didn't have that much impact on the album. Everyone connected with SAW was required to use exactly the same equipment that Mike and Matt did, to give everything a uniform sound. They had their preferred armoury of synthesizers, and they duplicated it in every studio. It wasn't like trying to perfectly recreate *Sgt Pepper* or a Steely Dan album or something like that: music where a particular recording from a particular group of musicians in a particular studio at a particular time has a special feel that is impossible to recapture. You could replicate the sound we'd made again with the same equipment. I've actually got a feeling that Daize had kept the floppy disks from the sequencers with him, rather than leaving them in the studio. All he had to do was stick them in the same type of sequencer in another studio, plug the keyboards in, and we were most of the way there: all the creative work and choices had already been done. I had to redo all the vocals, but that was actually a good chance to have more experience in the studio.

The second album, *Hold Me in Your Arms*, came out in November 1988. It did well: 'She Wants to Dance with Me' was a Top 10 hit in Britain and America; the album went platinum or gold all over the place.

*

I now had some money, enough to buy a house back up North, the sort of thing a Manchester United footballer would live in: six bedrooms, a front drive you could park twelve cars on, overlooking a golf course in Mere, in the really posh bit of Cheshire, near Knutsford. It kind of made sense to buy it. Debbie wasn't happy in London, and I wasn't mad about living there either. Back then, I still had a bit of a Northern chip on my shoulder about everything, from the price of stuff in the capital to the way everyone spoke. I assumed that if you pronounced bath without an 'r' in it, people in the South secretly thought you were thick. That was only a niggling thing. The real problem I had was that I genuinely wasn't keen on the amount of attention I attracted in the street because I was famous. I'd found I had started to steel myself before leaving the flat in Maida Vale. I liked the idea of having a big driveway and a gate, not walking out of my front door straight onto a pavement packed with people, and counting the seconds before someone shouted my name, or my name followed by the always welcome information that the person shouting it thought I was a wanker.

So we went back up North. Maybe I also thought the move would help things along between Debbie and me, because I was still full of doubts about where, if anywhere, our relationship was headed. I couldn't quite get that girl I'd met in Copenhagen out of my mind, but it really wasn't anything to do with her at all: I hadn't seen her for a year, I had no plans to see her and anyway, she'd made it abundantly clear she had a boyfriend. I just knew my relationship wasn't working, but I couldn't seem to break up with Debbie. And if I couldn't seem to break up with her, maybe it deserved another chance, in more familiar surroundings. The new house was twenty minutes from the town where Debbie's family were, and fifteen minutes from Newton, close to Manchester Airport, so I could fly to London easily. It was also in Cheshire's top burglary hotspot, which we discovered after a visit from a local policeman soon after we moved in.

He proceeded to regale us with lurid stories about a gang who robbed houses in the area wearing ski masks and threatening anyone they encountered with a hammer. So we bought a German shepherd dog.

*

Another hit album, a big new pop star's house, I should have been on top of the world. But I wasn't, and not only because of the situation with Debbie. I knew something about my career had changed, that something was over. I remember making a video for 'Take Me to Your Heart', one of the tracks Mike and Matt had written, which was scheduled to come out as the second single in the UK and Europe, and thinking, 'This is the last time I'm going to make a video for a SAW song, because this is the last time I'm going to release a SAW song.'

I'd simply had enough: of Pete saying things without thinking and acting impulsively, of Matt and Mike's egos, of their unshakeable belief that everything they did was automatically amazing, of their response when anyone dared to suggest that it wasn't, of their increasing inability to work out that some of their songs were better than others, of feeling ashamed about the tacky side of what they did – the tacky side of what *I* did. I was very grateful to have been with them when they were really on fire, and I knew even then that I owed pretty much everything to 'Never Gonna Give You Up'. But I didn't want to do it any more, not after the way things had played out with the second album. That obviously left a lot of big questions unanswered, not least what I was going to do next, and whether anyone would be interested if I wasn't working with SAW. But, for the moment, I put them out of my mind. I had a world tour to go on: Europe, Australia, Japan, North America. By the time it was over, my life would have changed more than I could have possibly imagined.

The tour was a big production. There were ten musicians and three backing singers – thirteen in total, including a horn section – which I loved. It was like being in a band again, plus I thought it made a statement: I'm doing this live, it's not just a singer with a backing tape and a shiny sheet. It worked, too – I thought I had a point to prove, and at the gigs I thought I proved it: I felt like the audiences were truly won over. It was really enjoyable and rewarding. There were costume changes and a lot of special effects that seemed incredibly cutting edge for the era, but by the standards of today were basically steam-powered. We built a 35 mm projection screen into the stage, got a projector from a cinema, and had films made that I interacted with, not that anyone ever used the word 'interactive' in 1988. This is how low-tech it was: on stage, I had to press a pedal with my foot to alert Ken the projectionist that I was ready – the pedal would make a light come on near him, which was his signal to run the film. I would dash into the frame of the screen and hide there, then the film would appear, with me in it. One of them featured me walking into the movie, snatching a ball off two basketball players. I'd run out of the picture and across the stage in front of the screen. Then up the steps, past some of the band, and onto the top of the screen, which was a box about fifteen feet deep. I would start bouncing the basketball, the two players on the film would look above them, as if they could hear me doing it. Another had me hitting tennis balls with a baseball bat – someone else behind the screen would throw tennis balls into the audience as I did.

It sounds primitive, because it was, and it took hours and hours of rehearsal to time it right, because there was no such thing as synching the film in those days. But it must have been effective for its time, because I swear people still mention it to me today: 'I was at your gig in 1988 – how did you do that thing with the basketball?' I didn't realize until we were well into the tour that I'd come full circle. I was at an airport with the crew, waiting for a delayed flight, killing time by doing that thing where everyone has to say what the first record they bought or the first gig they went to was. When I mentioned seeing Camel in Manchester, Ken the projectionist suddenly leapt up. 'Was it the one with the film of the geese? I did that!' It's odd how weird connections like that keep cropping up: Simon Merry, who's been my drummer and musical director for the past few years, says that the first artist he ever saw live was . . . me, at the NEC in Birmingham, back in 1988.

We started in the UK in December, then headed into Europe in the New Year: Sweden, Switzerland, France, Belgium, Austria, Denmark. After the show in Copenhagen, I was back at the hotel when my manager Tony walked in with Lene, the girl from the record company. I had no idea she was going to be there. I'd heard she didn't work for the label any more, and her name wasn't on the guest list. She'd apparently decided to pop into the gig on a whim on the way back from an aerobics class – she knew everyone in the music business in Copenhagen, including the people who ran the door at the venue, so they just let her in without a ticket – and had bumped into Tony, who'd invited her back to say hello. She told me she'd tried to ring me after I'd given her my number the year before, but the hotel switchboard wouldn't put her through. *Oh, for God's sake.* They were under strict instructions not to put through to my room anyone who didn't know the pseudonym I was booked in under. And I'd forgotten to tell her about the pseudonym. I'd probably still been reeling from the disappointment of finding out she had a boyfriend. *Amazing. Well done, Rick.*

There didn't seem to be any mention of her boyfriend tonight, but it was impossible to talk to her properly at the hotel. There were too many people around, including a security guard we'd employed. He was called Big Dave, he was 6 foot 4, and even if you didn't know he used to be a bare-knuckle fighter, you'd have got the idea that he was something like that simply by looking at him. Big Dave took his job of keeping an eye on me very seriously indeed. Lene thought the idea that I had a security guard was hilarious: there's a thing in Denmark called *jante*, like a national characteristic, that involves modesty, not getting too big for your boots or showing off, and having Big Dave was not part of that. She suggested we do the same thing we'd done the last time I was in Copenhagen – just peel off from everyone else and go for a drink together – but the last time I was in Copenhagen, Big Dave hadn't been with me. We attempted to head quietly to the exit, but not quietly enough. Before we'd reached the door, Big Dave was in front of it. 'Is he … coming with us?' Lene frowned. It definitely looked as if he was. In truth, I couldn't quite work out how to tell a 6 foot 4 former bare-knuckle fighter to bugger off and mind his own business in a way that wouldn't result in him taking offence, and I really didn't want to think about what might happen if Big Dave took offence.

When I said I thought so, Lene seemed to reconsider her plan. 'Do you know what? This is too weird, and I have to get up for work in the morning,' she said, and left. *Oh, for fuck's sake.*

I slumped back down in my chair. Tony suddenly materialized next to me and tapped me on the shoulder. 'Everything all right, Rick?'

I nodded unconvincingly.

'Don't worry.' He smiled and handed me a bit of paper. 'I got her number. And her address.' And then he headed to the bar.

And so began Rick Astley's attempt to get into *The Guinness Book of Records* for running up the largest hotel telephone bills in human history. I think I might have rung her that night, as soon as I thought she'd have got back home from the hotel. Certainly, I rang her every day for the rest of the tour: no matter where I was in Europe, we talked for at least an hour every day. I wrote her letters. It was strange, but that was really how we got to know each other properly, long-distance. I managed to talk her into getting the train down to Hamburg, where I was playing at a big venue called Congress Centrum. After the show, we went out to dinner, then sat up in the hotel bar until 2 a.m., by which time there was no one else there. I said I thought I should go to bed. Lene said she thought she should go to bed too. It might have been a moment, had it not been disturbed by a loud noise coming from a plant pot in the corner. We both looked over, in time to see Big Dave appear from behind it. Bloody hell, he'd been there all along. Lene and I burst out laughing and went off to our separate rooms.

She told me she was going on a skiing holiday with friends in Italy and asked me if I wanted to join her. It was possible; I was playing in Italy at the same time, and I'd have a few days off before going to Spain. But it was also impossible: if I injured myself on the slopes, and it affected any of the following dates, the tour insurance wouldn't cover it. It would cost us a fortune. I was sick of always doing what people told me to, though, so I told Tops I was going anyway. He seemed doubtful, but said OK, as long as he came along. And, by the way, he was bringing Big Dave to keep an eye on me. Him again.

So Lene came down to meet us in Milan. She came to the gig that night and it was one of the best of the European tour. The band and I were really on it, partly because the audience were amazing. It was one of the bigger gigs we had done, thousands of people singing along. I was beginning to feel a real change in who I was as an artist: I could do this and do it well. The next day, the four of us – Tops, Big Dave, Lene and I – drove to Sauze d'Oulx, a little village in the Alps, close to the border with France. Lene's friends looked a little startled when they saw me on the first day. I don't think she'd mentioned who I was – she'd told them she was going to pick up a friend, not a friend who happened to be a famous pop star with a bodyguard in tow. Then again, Lene looked a little startled when she saw me, which had nothing to do with who I was, and everything to do with what I was wearing. God knows why – insecurity? – but I'd fully equipped myself for the holiday with an expensive all-in-one ski suit in lime green, and dressing yourself completely in lime green is quite a bold move if you have red hair, particularly if you're doing something that you shouldn't be doing and need to keep it low-key. As it was, I could only have attracted more attention if I'd turned up in Sauze d'Oulx carrying a karaoke machine and a microphone and started singing 'Never Gonna Give You Up' at the top of my voice, something that became clear when we stopped for lunch. We didn't bother going to a restaurant – we just bought some nice bread and cheese and I think some wine and sat in the snow. First a group of kids approached us asking for an autograph – no problem, of course. Then two Italian nuns walked over. They held out their Bibles. I thought they wanted a donation or something, but no: they wanted me to sign them.

By then, we'd managed to lose Tops and Big Dave. It was brilliant. Lene had discovered that neither of them had much experience skiing and had booked them both into a beginner's class without asking them first. We left them there, falling over on the nursery slope. I waved as we got on the ski lift.

It was a fantastic day. I felt almost intoxicated by Lene's company. She was so fearless and confident, nothing about the weird world I now lived in seemed to faze her, whether it was the presence of Big Dave or an autograph-seeking nun. All the things I saw as a problem didn't bother her at all. She didn't care that I was famous, or about any of the crap that came with it. She seemed to treat everybody exactly the same. Maybe it was something to do with being Danish – the old *jante* thing again – or maybe it was something to do with her upbringing: from what she'd told me, her mum and dad seemed very stable, they ran a family business, they travelled a lot, they'd filled her with self-belief and optimism and a sense of adventure. Or maybe it was because she'd worked in the music industry for years and had dealt with much bigger stars than me. She knew what it was like when Whitney Houston walked into a room, so she wasn't going to be surprised by what happened around me.

Whatever it was, it was heady. And perhaps it was contagious. On the second day, I finally had a word with Tops about maybe getting Big Dave to dial down his dedication to the job of keeping an eye on me, so Lene and I went out to dinner together. We didn't book anywhere, we just wandered into this little restaurant in the village. There wasn't a menu, they simply brought you stuff – an aperitif, a bottle of wine, whatever food was in season. We talked and talked and talked and then slipped back to the hotel together.

The next morning, I was getting ready to head off to Spain for the final dates of the tour, when Lene told me she couldn't see me any more. She knew about Debbie and didn't want to get involved with someone who had a girlfriend. She wanted us to try to have a relationship, but she didn't want to try under those kinds of circumstances. I guess I had been so in the moment and loving every minute, I was obviously in denial. The fact was that I was cheating on Debbie and I knew Lene was right. I flew to Barcelona with a lot on my mind. What was I going to do? Or, rather, how the hell was I going to do it? I'd tried to break up with Debbie before, and it simply hadn't worked: we would both end up in tears, I'd have to fly somewhere the next morning and I'd be thinking,

Well, I can't leave her like this, and the whole idea of breaking up would be forgotten.

*

I flew back to England after the last date of the tour, in Madrid. When I got back to the house in Mere, it was empty. Debbie, ironically, was on a skiing holiday, with my brother Mike and his girlfriend Kay: they'd always got on well. She must have packed the dog off to her parents' house or something. I wandered through the rooms. They weren't even properly decorated or furnished, because I'd hardly ever been there. I had probably only slept in the house seven or eight nights since we bought it. What the fuck was I doing here?

I felt as if there were two voices inside my head. One of them was telling me not to be an idiot. We'd recently bought a house together. We'd been together since we were teenagers. I'd randomly met this woman in Copenhagen, hadn't seen her for fourteen months, then gone skiing with her for a couple of days and spent one night with her, in between playing in front of 12,000 people . . . it sounded like a story from another world when you thought about it like that. Was I even thinking straight? The other voice was screaming at me that this – the house, Debbie, all of it – wasn't what I wanted. What if we stayed together and Debbie got pregnant and we had a kid, when I knew that wasn't what I wanted? And I was besotted with Lene – there was a reason she'd been kind of permanently lodged somewhere in my head ever since we'd met, and the more I got to know her, the stronger I felt about her. Sometimes you're lucky enough to just know when you meet someone. Of course, if you looked at it rationally, nothing was certain with Lene. But so what? It felt like I had a chance at the life I thought I wanted. I had to grab at that, surely, rather than stick with a life I knew wasn't right.

But that still left the question of what I was going to do, how I was going to tell Debbie. What if I waited for her to come home, tried to finish with her and the same thing happened that always happened? What if she got home and I didn't have the bottle to actually tell her?

So I did something I've felt ashamed about ever since. I wrote her a letter and left it in the house. I can't remember what it said – to be honest, writing it felt like having an out-of-body experience or something, as if it wasn't really happening to me, or I couldn't quite believe I was doing it. I never heard from Debbie again. I know she stayed on in the house for a little while, then threw a party when she left, because she invited Mike and Kay and they told me. I'm pretty sure the house got a bit trashed in the process, but it needed redecorating anyway. I think she moved back in with her mum and dad after that.

It still bothers me that I ended it that way – it was weak, and it was disrespectful, and I should have dealt with it better, but I was twenty-two years old. I'm sure it was hard for her, particularly because I was in the public eye: it's different breaking up with someone who you're going to keep seeing on TV or hearing on the radio. I could see how she might perceive it as if I'd won the lottery and become a famous pop star, then ditched her, although it wasn't really like that; there was just a gap between us that was getting bigger and bigger, and I couldn't cover the distance any more. Even decades later, when I started making music again, and the whole

Rickrolling thing happened, there was occasionally a tiny thought at the back of my mind: *Fucking hell, what if Debbie sees this?* Do people ask her about it? 'Didn't you used to go out with him?' Does it dredge up a load of memories that bother her, or is she fine with it? I've got no idea, because I've got no idea where she is or what she's doing. I've sometimes thought about trying to look her up on Facebook or whatever, but I can't imagine where to start and the chances are she's married now and her surname's probably different. She never went to the press, never said anything about me in public, which is testament to the kind of person she was. The way the tabloids were and are, I'm pretty fucking sure they must have tried to get her to talk. But she didn't. I am so grateful to her that she didn't go to the press and I still feel that she is the one who handled everything with integrity and maturity, not me.

When I'd finished writing the letter, I got on the phone and booked a flight and a hotel. Then I called Lene's number and left a message for her. She wasn't back from Italy yet. My suitcase was still by the door – I hadn't unpacked – so I picked it up and headed to the airport and flew to Copenhagen.

The next evening, there was a knock at my hotel room door. It was Lene. She looked horrified when I told her what I'd done. She thought it was cowardly, shitty behaviour that didn't say a lot for my character or, she seemed to be implying, my potential as a boyfriend. She had a point, and I didn't have much in the way of excuses.

Then she suggested that I move out of the hotel and into her flat while I was there. It was March 1989, thirty-five years ago. Lene and I have been together ever since.

Chapter Ten

There is one thing I didn't mention about my flight to Denmark. I hadn't told anyone I was going, and I didn't tell anyone where I was once I got there: not my family, not my managers, not Tops, not the record label and not anybody from PWL. I suppose I didn't tell my family because it seemed too hard to explain. They didn't know anything at all about Lene, I'd never mentioned her to them and I was ashamed of how I'd ended things with Debbie. And I didn't tell anyone else because . . . well, I didn't think it was any of their business. So I just went. I vanished. In the middle of a world tour – admittedly, I had a couple of weeks off before I went to Japan, but still.

It was completely out of character – ordinarily, I did what I was told – but then again, maybe it wasn't. Perhaps I was developing a new character. I wasn't proud about how I'd broken up with Debbie, but now that I had, it felt like a weight had been lifted off me. And I'd wrestled with it enough to know that Lene was the person I absolutely wanted to be with, and that suddenly seemed vastly more important than my career. There was a voice in the back of my head going: 'It doesn't have to be about this. You've met someone, and if your career ends tomorrow, it doesn't actually matter. You've been lucky. You've made a bit of money. And it's not the priority any more.' I'm really glad that voice started speaking up. I think everyone who ever gets up on a stage does it because there's something within them that's a bit broken or missing; they want an audience to make them feel better, to love them, and that was definitely true of me. But sooner or later, you realize that ain't going to do it; you need something – or someone – else. And if you haven't got that, that realization can literally kill you.

So I spent a week holed up in Lene's flat in Frederiksberg. It was a bit like a weird dream – hang on, I seem to be in *Denmark*, living with someone I've spent hardly any time with – but I have to say, it was a really lovely dream. Lene hadn't been exaggerating: her flat was quite small. The shower was in the kitchen. The living room was filled with her record collection, which was enormous. That's what I did in the daytime, when she was out at work – go through her record collection, playing stuff. I couldn't really go out, because I didn't want anyone to spot me. Besides, it was interesting: you can tell a lot about someone from their record collection. In this case, I could tell she knew a lot more about music than I did.

After a few days, I was jolted by the thought that the record company or my managers might be pestering my relatives, asking about my whereabouts: what if my family thought something terrible had happened to me? So I called my sister Jayne and told her that I couldn't say where I was, but I was OK, in fact I was really good. The news must have got back to her about Debbie, because she started asking questions, but I said I'd explain everything when I got back, that I'd just run away for a bit, and to tell everyone not to worry about me, I was fine. Then I went back to flicking through Lene's record collection and waiting for her to come home.

We got into a kind of routine. Lene would get up, go to work, I'd mooch about a bit, then she'd come back for lunch, and I'd make her an omelette. It's something Lene occasionally brings up today: 'I remember when you used to make me an omelette every day – you haven't made me an omelette in years.' (Note to self: buy eggs, make omelette.)

When she came back in the evenings, we'd walk down the main road in Frederiksberg, get food from an Italian takeaway and take it back to the flat. I think we went out for dinner once, to her friends Michael and Henrietta's flat. They'd been on the skiing trip with us, they'd seen the autograph-hunting nuns, so they knew what was going on.

It was sort of blissful. It just felt *right*: the two of us, going our own way. It seemed uncomplicated and natural to both of us. But it had to end eventually: Japan was looming, then Australia. I was excited about going, I was enjoying playing live again, but it felt weird to be leaving. Our relationship was only just starting and I was vanishing for a month, to the other side of the world. When Lene mentioned she was getting bored with her job – the Danish record label she was working for had lost a lot of its big foreign artists, and the stuff she was left dealing with wasn't really her thing – that was all the incentive I needed to try to convince her to jack it in and come with me. 'Fuck it, let's be pirates! Let's travel the high seas!' I thought that sounded romantic, but she looked at me like I was nuts, or at least a new boyfriend who was suddenly proving a little too full-on. She patiently explained that what she meant by that was that she was thinking of diversifying, maybe getting into music videos rather than promotion, and that piracy – even metaphorical piracy – wasn't a career option.

Before I left to rejoin the tour, we went travelling in the south of France. We didn't have any plans: we'd just rock up at hotels and ask if they had a room for the night. It felt like freedom – for the previous couple of years, there had *always* been a plan or an itinerary, somewhere I knew I had to be, even if I was on holiday. I felt as if I was abandoning everything I was supposed to be doing or should be doing, and just doing what I wanted. I got a bit demob-happy. One night, after dinner, we went to a club and I asked the DJ to play two songs. The first was 'Never Too Much' by Luther Vandross, and as it was playing I sang it to Lene on the dancefloor, which I thought was romantic. The second was 'This Charming Man' by The Smiths, which wasn't particularly romantic, but I sang that to her too, this time with actions: I grabbed a bunch of flowers out of a vase on a table next to the dancefloor and started swinging them around like Morrissey. I was sort of relishing the feeling of not giving a shit. I was never that big in France, so I felt a bit anonymous there.

I flew back to London alone, met the rest of the band and crew, and recommenced my hotel phone bill world record attempt in Japan and Australia. The tour was great. In Nagoya, the promoters took us out for the most bizarre meal I've ever eaten. There were geishas there, not to serve you, but actually to lift the food off the plate with chopsticks and put it into your mouth. I managed to get the message across that this made me incredibly uncomfortable without causing offence, but even when I succeeded in convincing them to let me feed myself, the food they brought was a bit alarming. There was a clear soup with something in it that had tentacles and was visibly still attempting to swim about. There was a fish that came out on a skewer, and that was still alive too. They'd cut chunks of its flesh off and reattached them to its body without killing it. The thing would literally be watching you while you ate it. I tactfully declined. You know, I'm all for fresh food, but there's a point where food's maybe too fresh for its own good.

When I was in Australia, Lene told me there was a change of plan. She'd decided she definitely wanted to work in videos and film, as a producer. She'd been rejected for a course at the National Film School in Denmark, but had quit her job anyway – producing was what she wanted to pursue – so she was at a loose end. It seemed that she was interested in becoming a pirate, at least for a bit – a pirate internship, if you like. I was going to America to do some pre-tour promo and she could fly out to LA to meet me. She had friends out there she could spend time with while I was busy doing interviews, then she would join the tour. We had a bit of downtime in between, and I thought it might be a good idea to go on holiday for a few days. We could go to Bermuda, come back relaxed and refreshed, ready to hit the road.

It didn't quite work out like that. Bermuda was definitely quite relaxing, until the hurricane hit it. The hotel staff starting banging on the door of our bungalow at 5 a.m., screaming that we had to evacuate immediately – we were told to leave all our belongings behind and go to the main building, where it was safer. I somehow got it into my head that it was vitally important that we both wore a belt – my idea was that, when the hurricane hit, I would tie the belts together and attach us to something. I don't know where I got that idea from – my vast experience of hurricanes from growing up in the notorious tornado alley of Newton-le-Willows, presumably – but I was very shouty and insistent about the whole belt thing. I think it was just blind panic.

The scene in the main building didn't do much to calm my nerves. There were people there who'd clearly decided that the thing you should definitely do when a hurricane's approaching is to immediately get as pissed as you possibly can: they were drinking neat rum at 6 a.m. Some of them were the hotel staff, which didn't instil a lot of confidence. I'm not making this up, there was someone in there playing an acoustic guitar and singing, like the stewardess in *Airplane*! It was bedlam inside but worse outside. If you looked out of the window you couldn't see anything except a wall of dark grey, and palm trees bending over so far they looked like they were going to touch the ground. I was absolutely terrified. I couldn't even find anything to tie my belt to.

It went on all day. Eventually, someone suggested the worst of it was over – we'd apparently got off lightly – and we staggered back to our bungalow. It's hard to remember when you actually fall in love with someone, but maybe when you've been through a hurricane together you realize how much someone means to you. I've been in love with Lene ever since. We've been through a few metaphorical hurricanes over the years, but maybe relationships need that; maybe we need shaking up to realize what we have and what's important.

The next morning, the swimming pool was full of furniture and palm trees. Most of the beach now seemed to be in the tennis courts: they were buried beneath a metre and a half of sand. And the beach itself was covered in massive bones. It turned out there was a graveyard for horses nearby – no, I didn't know horses had graveyards either – and the hurricane had deposited most of its contents on the beach.

*

Suitably refreshed after our relaxing holiday of extreme weather conditions and dead horses, we flew to JFK as the tour was starting in Poughkeepsie. There was no transport there to meet us, and I couldn't get hold of Tops – this was before mobile phones – so we had to get a yellow cab. It was 88 miles away, and the traffic getting out of New York was incredible – it took us nearly two and a half hours and the price made the cost of calling Copenhagen from Adelaide on a hotel phone look like pocket money. Being a pirate was costing me a fortune. Never mind. We arrived at the hotel, and there was a sign in the lobby, welcoming Rick Astley, and Todd Rundgren. It turned out he was playing that night, in the venue near the hotel, where we were scheduled to set up the next day for rehearsals. Lene was really excited. It turned out that she loved Todd Rundgren's prog-rock band Utopia so much that, a few years before she met me, she and a friend drove for hours across America to see them – so we got tickets. I only lasted a few songs. Todd and his band were incredible musicians, but if you don't know the music it's hard to listen to a whole gig, especially when you are knackered. So I left Lene to it. Years later, Mark King from Level 42 – a huge fan of Utopia – managed to get me into Todd Rundgren just by lending me a load of CDs to play in the car. That's always annoyed Lene: 'Oh, you weren't interested when *I* said he was good, but Mark King tells you he's great and you believe *him*.' (Todd Rundgren, omelettes – it's weird the things that become a bone of contention between couples.)

One thing I had noticed during the gig was that the venue had quite a low ceiling. Just how low became apparent the next morning when our stage set and equipment had been loaded in. If I stood on one of the platforms I was supposed to stand on when I sang, my head touched the lights, and in those days stage lights were really hot. So my first world tour debuted in America with me belting out 'Together Forever' and 'Whenever You Need Somebody' bent forward, like the Hunchback of Notre-Dame in a blazer.

Things could clearly only get better, and they did. The American tour was incredible. We did two nights at Radio City Music Hall in New York, which felt like a big deal, so I flew my brothers and sister and their partners over for the gigs. Mike came along to one of the soundchecks, realized how boring soundchecks were, decided to head back to the hotel and got mobbed by fans outside the venue: 'Rick! Rick!' He was about to tell them he wasn't me, but then he thought it was funnier to play along. He ended up signing a load of their albums and having his picture taken with them. It was hilarious: you're a big enough fan to stand outside the venue all day, but you're not a big enough fan to recognize that my brother isn't me? I mean, there's definitely a family resemblance, but we don't really look that alike.

Even the worst show we played had a happy ending. For some reason, we were booked to play at the Tennessee State Fair. We seemed to be the only band playing that wasn't wearing cowboy hats. The stage was huge and the crowd was tiny; they would have all fitted on the stage. Worse, the stage was in the middle of a horse-racing track, so not only were there about 300 people sitting on bleachers that could have accommodated thousands, they were miles away from the stage. On the other side of the bleachers, the actual state fair was happening. There were fairground rides and livestock shows and monster truck rallies and pig races, all of which were clearly more of a draw than me. I didn't want to go on, but Tops talked me into it. I was finding America difficult to understand; it's one country but it's very disjointed, in music, politics, culture.

Tops said I should treat it like a rehearsal. At the end of the show, there was a massive firework display, which, given that hardly anyone was watching it, was a total waste of gunpowder.

I was still pretty miserable the next night, when we went out for dinner in Nashville. We ate at a place called the Stockyard, which Tops said was supposed to be the best meat restaurant in the world. They had a house band, who were incredible musicians. The singer was this absolutely enormous guy with a beard and a cowboy hat, much older than me. He spotted me and pointed me out to the rest of the band. They stopped what they were playing dead and launched straight into 'It Would Take a Strong, Strong Man'. It sounded *amazing*. Then they got me up on stage and I sang 'Never Gonna Give You Up' and 'Together Forever' with them. People were going nuts. It was fantastic, the complete opposite of the night before.

The tour ended in LA, at the Universal Amphitheatre. It was an unbelievable night, but it felt as if I was drawing a line under something. Before the show began, I asked one of the crew to get me as big a piece of white board as they could find, some black paint and a brush. They came back with a thing that must have been about 7x8 feet, and I painted the words FOR SALE on it in massive letters. At the end of the show, I carried it on stage and left it there. It was sort of intended to make the audience and road crew laugh, a joke about the set that we'd dragged around the world for seven or eight months now being no use to anyone else. It had been built specifically for us, so clearly you couldn't flog it. But it was saying something else as well: whatever that was, it's over, and if anybody wants it, they can come and get it, I don't need it any more. I didn't mean only the tour. I meant everything that had happened in those few years.

When we got back to Britain, Lene got a job as a runner for a video director. I thought that was brilliant. In Denmark, she'd had a company car and a decent salary, but she was happy to jack it all in and start again, at the bottom, because she really wanted to do something different. Everything seemed to be changing for me too. My management contract with Tony and Dave had run out, so I asked Tops to manage me instead. He instructed the lawyers to get me out of my deal with PWL, and contact BMG and see if they wanted to carry on with me if I wasn't working with Stock Aitken Waterman. It was a gamble, and there was no guarantee that they would. After all, all my biggest successes were with SAW. I definitely had their badge sewn on my blazer, if you like. But BMG didn't see it that way. I'd sold a lot of records in America, where no one knew or cared who the songwriters and producers were; the US audience definitely wasn't buying them because they were the latest SAW production. So they bought Pete out of his contract, and that was that. I've no idea how much they paid him. It was a really sad way for that relationship to end – we'd gone from sharing a flat to selling millions of records to this – but, frankly, the relationship had ended long before the lawyers got involved. I think Pete genuinely believed I'd gone mad. The way he thought about music meant he simply didn't see what the problem was at all – you're successful, you're doing well, why would you want a say in your own career?

It was good that BMG thought I had a chance without Pete and Mike and Matt, but it was still a daunting prospect. SAW was all I'd known. But thinking like that was daft – it wasn't as if they were the only producers in the world, and most of the music I absolutely loved sounded nothing like SAW, whether it was The Smiths, or New Order, or Luther Vandross. In truth, the fact that I loved all kinds of different music turned out to be a problem: when BMG asked me what I wanted to do next, how I wanted to sound, I wasn't sure what was right for me. I knew what I *didn't* want to sound like, but not what I did. I knew I wanted to make pop music – I wasn't suddenly going to go free jazz or industrial rock – just pop music that wasn't quite as twee as some of the stuff I'd been doing, but that was about it. They appointed an A&R guy called John Lloyd to look after me. He was lovely, but I think he was almost as out of his depth as I was: he'd been handed this huge artist who didn't really have a plan, and he'd been told to deliver a hit album.

At one point, it was mooted that I should write with Carole Bayer Sager and her then-husband, who happened to be Burt Bacharach. The story was that they were looking for young artists to collaborate with, and my name came up. Tops, John Lloyd and I went for a meeting at their house in Bel Air. It was astonishing, like something out of a movie. A maid – she was actually wearing a maid's uniform, which up until then I hadn't thought anyone did in real life – opened the door and showed us to a room. The sofas in it were the size of tour buses. There was a little anteroom just off it that you could see into: every surface in it was covered with Grammys and Oscars and other awards.

Carole arrived and seemed very nice – she looked like a cross between Elizabeth Taylor and Joan Collins – but it was hard to keep your attention on her when Burt Bacharach appeared. That was partly because he was Burt Bacharach, and partly because he turned up wearing a huge white bathrobe, holding a glass. Whatever was in the glass was even more intriguing than the bathrobe. It was a kind of fluorescent green. The concept of green juices or wheatgrass smoothies had yet to reach the UK, so I had no idea what it was. I couldn't stop staring at the glass: its contents seemed to be glowing, although perhaps that was just the LA light.

The minute Burt arrived in the room, there was a very odd, strained atmosphere – he and Carole got divorced the following year – and he didn't say much. He just sat on one of the enormous sofas, in his dressing gown, drinking his fluorescent green aperitif. I stared at it some more, then we left.

I did go back and tried writing a couple of songs with Carole, but it didn't work out – I was way too intimidated to bring any useful ideas to the table – although years later, I sang with Burt Bacharach and chatted to him backstage. He was a lovely man. It was a lot easier to talk to him when he wasn't wearing a bathrobe and drinking liquid Kryptonite.

But if that particular meeting didn't work out, I did have some ideas for the album. When the label asked me if there was anyone I wanted to write with, I suggested Mark King. I'd been a fan of Level 42 for years, ever since my brother John brought their first album home. In fact, I loved that album so much that I made a nine-tile recreation of its cover in O-Level pottery, although I kept that to myself when I went to the Isle of Wight to work with Mark. Honestly, I was a bit shy around him, but it really meant a lot to me that he'd agreed – I truly kind of idolized him – and the songs we wrote sounded pretty good. He's an amazing musician, a phenomenal drummer and guitarist as well as a bass player so incredible that, when I first heard Level 42, I thought they had *two* bass players.

And when BMG asked if there were any albums I liked the sound of, I mentioned *Strange Kind of Love*, the second album by a Scottish band called Love and Money. They were a kind of rock–soul hybrid, and I've got no idea why they weren't bigger than they were. It turned out *Strange Kind of Love* was produced by an American guy called Gary Katz, who was famous for working with Steely Dan. So we went to America to meet him, then flew back to LA with the songs I'd written with Mark King and a few tunes I'd written on my own.

The sessions were in A&M Studios, where 'We Are the World' was recorded. John Lennon had made albums there, and so had Joni Mitchell, Carole King, The Police, all sorts of legends. Gary Katz had assembled a band made up entirely of superhero musicians: LA session guys who'd played on everything. The bass player, Chuck Rainey, had worked with Aretha Franklin, Quincy Jones and every jazz legend you could think of. The guitarist was called Michael Landau – he'd played with Joni Mitchell and Pink Floyd and on *Bad* by Michael Jackson. And the drummer was Jeff Porcaro. Jeff Porcaro! If I start listing all the legendary artists he'd worked with, it would take up the rest of this book, but let's just say he was considered to be literally the greatest drummer in the world. I couldn't have conjured up a situation that sounded more different from working with Matt and Mike in the Hit Factory if I'd tried.

And yet . . . something about the session felt weirdly familiar. The band came in, listened to the demos, made some notes, then went into the studio and played the songs exactly the same: literally the only thing they changed was that Chuck Rainey didn't slap the bass with his thumb the way Mark King did – he played it with his fingers. *Well, of* course *they did, Rick, you idiot. They're session musicians, they're there to do a job* – 'some pop thing', as I overheard Michael Landau say to a friend on the phone in the control room. They're not going to sit there deconstructing the demos and working out new ways to play everything. I might have expected the producer to do that, but clearly Gary Katz wasn't the kind of producer who starts suggesting you move the middle eight, or switch the guitar to an acoustic, or maybe change that chord there, or make the solo a little shorter. He was the kind of producer who saw his job as getting everything set up, everyone in the right place, with the right equipment, then letting everyone get on with it while he works out where he's having dinner – he was particularly keen on the lobster at the Palm Restaurant on Flower Street. That approach is probably fine if you're working with Steely Dan, those two auteur geniuses who have a very clear idea of exactly how they want everything to be, but it's not so great if you're working with a twenty-three-year-old from Newton-le-Willows who's really not used to being in charge and completely intimidated by his surroundings. As it was, the whole thing felt like an incredibly expensive exercise in painting by numbers. It wasn't that different from working with Mike and Matt: 'Here you are, it goes like this, take it or leave it.'

We all sat in the control room and listened to the tracks. They sounded great. Of course they sounded great: they were recorded in A&M Studios by the guy who produced *The Nightfly* by Donald Fagen – an album that sounds so perfect they use it to test out hi-fi systems and studio speakers and sound systems at gigs – and they've got Jeff-fricking-Porcaro playing the drums on them. But I didn't want a technically perfect copy of the demo. As one song was playing, I spoke up. 'Is there any way we could maybe change the drums in the middle eight? Just go from the hi-hat to the ride cymbal or something? It needs a bit of a lift there.'

Everyone looked at me. *Oh God.* Then Jeff Porcaro, God love him, stood up. 'The kid's right,' he agreed. 'The kid's right. Let's take it again.' And they all trooped into the studio and did another take.

He was probably only saying it to make me feel better, but I could have hugged him. I wandered into the studio as they were finishing up and he beckoned me over and asked if I played the drums. Well, er, no, not like you play the drums, but I was the drummer in a band when I was younger. He smiled and nodded towards his drum kit. 'Jump on, then.'

So I got to play Jeff Porcaro's drums, while he chatted to me about drumming, how he always played wearing riding boots. It was like a dream come true. It was the best thing about the LA sessions. We didn't even use the stuff we'd recorded there. When we got back to England, we realized the demos somehow sounded better: the tracks we'd recorded in LA were technically perfect, but they'd lost some of the feel in the originals. It wasn't Gary Katz's fault – it was just a mismatch between producer and artist that didn't work at all. You know, who goes from working with SAW to working with Steely Dan's producer? It's too big a leap, no matter how great the Love and Money album sounded to me. But I'll tell you what: he was right about the lobster at the Palm Restaurant.

Work on my new album stumbled on. I started writing songs with Rob Fisher from Climie Fisher, which went really well. We came up with 'Cry for Help', which ended up being the first single. We got a song from Michael McDonald – not that I think for a minute that Michael McDonald wrote a song and went, 'Get that to Rick Astley'; it was available and I loved it. And we ended up with Elton John playing piano on a couple of tracks. I'd met him in LA, and he'd taken Lene and me out to dinner, then offered to play on my next album without being asked. I couldn't believe it, but that's Elton: he's just incredibly enthusiastic about new music, whether it's his own or someone else's. In the end the album was produced by Gary Stevenson, who produced the first two Go West albums. I loved those records and Pete Cox is a great singer and sounds amazing on them. I felt we needed somebody to make the most of my voice and, after talking to Gary about how we would make the record, he suggested that I should co-produce it with him. We recorded most of the album on the Isle of Man at Gary's studio.

The result was a pretty decent album, but, in retrospect, I wish the label had pushed me a bit more. That's not Gary's fault. He's a great producer and still a great friend but he had to try to make the transition from the SAW sound to something new for me, while I was trying to find out what I wanted to sound like. I wish they'd got hold of a load of shit-hot pop producers and tried them out, to see how it worked. If someone had told me iconic American R&B songwriting duo Jam and Lewis had a song for me, I'd have cycled to America to hear it. I can't blame them for simply letting me do what I wanted – not having a say was one of the reasons it had all gone wrong with SAW – but I needed a little more guidance.

I called the album *Free*, a nod to the fact that I was free to do any kind of album I wanted to. I chose the first single and I was really nervous when it was released. 'Cry for Help' might not have been an industrial rock or free jazz track, but it was different enough from the songs that had made me famous to make me worried. It was a ballad, with a choir on it. There were real musicians playing on it; the guy who drummed on it, Vinnie Colaiuta, had played with Frank Zappa, for God's sake. I didn't even look the same: I'd grown my hair long. I was in a minivan with Tops, going round UK radio stations doing promo, when we found out the single had made the Top 10. The relief was incredible. I simply thought: *Thank God for that, there are some people out there who still want to hear me sing.* It started really picking up radio play in America, so much that I got an award for 2 million plays on what they call Adult Contemporary Radio. It ended up going to No. 7 in America, and hung around on the radio for ages – it felt like a much bigger moment there for me than most of the singles off my previous album. We got asked to perform at the World Music Awards in Monte Carlo, which was a thoroughly bizarre couple of days. David Hasselhoff was presenting, and the bill was just bonkers: Nana Mouskouri next to Technotronic, Samantha Fox, Cliff Richard, Grace Jones and Ringo Starr. And Status Quo, who it turned out had the hotel room above me and Lene.

We were standing out on the balcony, and we could hear this music coming from somewhere. We looked up, and I swear to God, on the balcony above us, there was Rick Parfitt and Francis Rossi, with their guitars strapped on them, doing the whole Status Quo twelve-bar blues thing – dur-dur-DUR-du-dur-dur-DUR – as if they were on stage, rather than outside a hotel room, staring out at the sea.

At the ceremony itself, I was just about to go on stage when in the wings I saw Ursula Andress and Britt Ekland, staring at each other in fits of laughter. They seemed to be, and there's no polite way of saying this, comparing their bosoms. I have no idea why: maybe they'd both had surgery. If they had, the doctors had done a brilliant job – they both looked incredible – but the sight of two legendary sex symbols pointing at each other's breasts and laughing is quite distracting when you're readying yourself to give a live performance.

I met Ursula the next morning, as we were leaving the hotel. We were just getting in our hire car, when she appeared at the top of the stairs and shouted at us: 'Darlings! Darlings! I need to get to the airport!' When we said she could come with us, she nodded, clapped her hands, and six bellboys appeared behind her, each one of them staggering under the weight of dozens of suitcases. We pointed out that there was no way we could fit all her luggage in the car without everyone else getting out, including the driver, so off she went to seek alternative transport.

So for a few weeks, I thought we'd done it – the single was selling, we were on the radio and TV. And then everything started to go wrong. The MD of RCA was fired, the new MD fired everyone who'd worked with the old MD and suddenly, with all the upheaval, the record company seemed to be unravelling.

We put out another single, 'Move Right Out': it was another song I'd co-written with Rob Fisher, like 'Cry for Help'. It didn't even make the Top 40 in Britain or America. Maybe people just didn't like it – it wasn't some barnstorming stop-you-dead-in-your-tracks single – but it felt as if there were other problems. My brother Mike went round a load of record shops in Wigan, Warrington and St Helens, and told me that none of them had a copy of the single to sell him. Clearly the distribution was in a bit of a mess. I'd thought I wasn't bothered by commercial success – I'd had enough of it already, I was thoroughly sick of being tabloid fodder – and I'd thought I would be happy if I was allowed to make music, selling enough that the record label would green-light a follow-up, and a follow-up to the follow-up, but this was a weird feeling to adjust to. My debut single had been huge, so I'd never really known anything other than success: I always joke that I put out 'Never Gonna Give You Up' and it was all downhill from there. The stupid thing is, whenever you read about an artist who's been around for a long time, an Elton John or a Paul McCartney or whoever, they've always had setbacks, albums that didn't click, singles that flopped. I'm sure it was disappointing, but they didn't automatically assume their career was over when it happened. But I'd come from that SAW world, where you were a certain kind of pop star, and the worth of what you did was measured by its commercial success. It was all or nothing: you were either having hits or you were in the bin.

Suddenly, you could feel the momentum slipping away. If the single wasn't a hit in the UK, then radio stations and TV shows in Europe didn't really want to know. The album, *Free*, did all right – it went gold in Britain, and sold a million albums worldwide – but the third single, 'Never Knew Love', just died, despite a video that involved me literally swinging on a trapeze. I spent a morning learning how to do it at a circus school in Islington. It was incredibly hard, even though I only had to swing on the thing three times – it killed my arms and took the skin off my hands.

I was pretty nervous when we came to actually shoot the video at Gerry Cottle's circus on Ealing Common, so Tops climbed up the ladder to the trapeze to reassure me. That didn't help much, largely because when Tops got to the top of the ladder, he went white and audibly muttered, 'Fucking hell, that's higher than I thought.' Then I couldn't grab hold of the trapeze when it swung towards me, because there was a spotlight shining in my eyes.

To add another layer of weirdness to proceedings, the TV presenter Jeremy Beadle suddenly walked into the big top unannounced and started poking around the place: he happened to live nearby and he loved circuses, so he just decided to wander over and take a look at what was going on. The end result looked pretty good, but no one actually saw it because, by then, no TV shows were interested. The single got to No. 70.

We were supposed to go on tour again in America, and I allowed myself to be talked out of it after the rehearsals had started. I don't know what happened, whether promoters had started telling Tops we should leave it, or whether Tops thought it wasn't going to work, and was worried about the effect that would have on me. He'd seen me get really upset at the Tennessee State Fair, when nobody turned up, so maybe he thought, *If we go, and nobody comes, it'll crush him, let's skip it*. It wasn't his fault and he had my best interests at heart, but in retrospect, I think I should have gone and done it, and lived through it. I think I'm pretty good live – put me in a pub, put me anywhere, and I'm good. I think part of the problem was that I couldn't fill the kind of big venues I'd played on the first tour, but that would have been fine. It would have been a bit weird playing small theatres a couple of years after selling out Radio City Music Hall two nights in a row, but I wouldn't have minded trying to rebuild things that way. Instead, we decided to leave it, and just kind of called it a day on *Free*.

*

There was a lot of other stuff going on in my life at that time. For one thing, we had bought a farmhouse in the Cotswolds. The decision was partly prompted by the fact that Lene had found out she was pregnant. It wasn't planned or anything; it simply happened. I was excited, but I had a bit of trepidation as well. I was twenty-five and turned twenty-six the day after Emilie was born, on 5 February 1992. That wasn't young to have kids where I was from – people I knew in Newton had got married and started families when they were twenty or twenty-one – but I felt younger than I was: I really hadn't done a lot of growing up since I'd left school, because my daily life had been completely consumed by my career. Plus, I was worried about what kind of dad I'd be. My whole experience of parenting was coloured by my upbringing: my mum and dad had not had the best of times, so who was to say that I wouldn't be a disaster area too? I definitely had a bit of my dad's temper; nothing like as bad as him, but I could still go from zero to sixty in seconds if I got angry.

The house in the Cotswolds needed a lot of work doing to it, but we moved in anyway and did it up gradually: a new kitchen, new bathrooms, everything. It had a few acres of land, and a barn that had been converted into a ballroom at some point in the 1920s, with a proper floated wooden floor. I thought I could convert it into a studio, but then, I wasn't sure what the future held for me in music. I'd had an album that didn't really work in the way I'd hoped it would. Did that mean I was done? And if I was done, did I need a studio? And more importantly, if I was done, did I have enough money to support us for the foreseeable future?

Moving to the Cotswolds felt a bit like running away: you know, 'Former pop star buys big house in the countryside', all those cliches. In truth, I didn't mind the idea of running away, forgetting about everything and just concentrating on being a dad, maybe giving myself time to think about where I now was in the world. But beyond being twenty-six and having a new baby, I couldn't come up with any answers.

Chapter Eleven

The question of where my career was going next – if it was going anywhere at all – was answered for me. We hadn't been in the new house in the Cotswolds that long when BMG got in touch. They told us that Madonna had made a new film, called *Body of Evidence*, and they were looking for people to write songs for the soundtrack. I didn't really understand why Madonna wasn't getting involved with the soundtrack for her own film, but maybe she didn't want the public to confuse Madonna the singer with Madonna the serious actor. Or maybe Madonna had already realized that *Body of Evidence* was going to be one of the all-time great cinematic turkeys, a huge critical and commercial flop, and didn't want her music associated with it.

We, of course, had no idea. They didn't tell us anything about the film beyond the fact that it starred Madonna and Willem Dafoe. We didn't know what it was about. We had no idea that it was an erotic thriller and we certainly didn't know that it was so bad that audiences apparently started laughing during the sex scenes and cheered when Madonna's character was killed off, neither of which they were supposed to do. It's actually really hard to write a song for a film you know nothing about, but in this case, perhaps it was for the best.

So, Rob Fisher and I wrote a few songs, one of which was called 'Hopelessly'. We knocked together a demo and the record company loved it. Then we heard that the film-makers loved it too and they wanted it to be in the movie. God knows why. 'Hopelessly' does sound quite cinematic, like something you'd hear as the credits roll, which I suppose was our big idea. But it's also a really romantic ballad, which doesn't fit with a film about a woman who killed her husband – apparently by shagging him to death while he was on cocaine – and features Madonna engaging in a sadomasochistic relationship with Willem Dafoe that involves her dripping hot wax onto his penis.

But we weren't to know that at this point. All we knew was that the *Body of Evidence* people liked it, and they needed a finished version fast. The film soundtrack was being overseen by a guy called Ron Fair – he later became a big record producer and worked with Christina Aguilera and the Black Eyed Peas – and he was coming over to Britain in two weeks to oversee the recording session. We asked Gary Stevenson to produce it. Even though *Free* hadn't turned into the commercial success that everyone wanted it to be, I was still proud of the track 'Cry for Help', which I'd worked on with Gary and Rob. And besides, Ron Fair had worked on

Go West's album as an A&R – a job which basically means guiding the project to completion, overseeing the choice of songs and the recording and working as a liaison between the artist and the record company – so Gary already knew him.

When Ron arrived in the UK, we had Metropolis Studios in Chiswick booked for the recording. It all went very well. Ron Fair was a genuinely nice guy. He pointed out that if it was going to be a single, we'd need another track for the B-side, and asked me if I had anything. I told him I had a song I'd written on my own called 'Body and Soul'. It was a bit of a cliched title, but he thought it would do. We discovered that Ron was a great pianist and got him to play on it. He did a fantastic solo on the electric piano.

The record company loved the results, and they told us that the film people in America did too. Then BMG asked if we had any more songs. They thought it would be good if we had an album. Their logic was that 'Hopelessly' was almost a guaranteed hit, because it was going to be in the new Madonna film and no matter how that turned out, it was going to get a lot of publicity just because it had Madonna in it: they wanted an album to capitalize on its sure-fire success.

So we started frantically assembling an album: there were some songs I'd put together myself, some I'd done with Rob and some I'd written with Dave West. Dave was Gary Stevenson's programmer and right-hand man. He's a super-talented guy and, again, we are still friends today. I wrote some more with Lisa Stansfield and the two guys she'd written all her hits with, Ian Devaney and Andy Morris. Lisa, Ian and Andy had been in a band in the eighties called Blue Zone, and Lisa and Ian eventually ended up getting married.

Gary and I produced the new album at his new home studio in Oxfordshire. The record label left us to it, which probably wasn't the best idea, because Gary's a muso and I'm secretly a bit of a muso too. I've never really stopped being the kid in FBI who spent hours watching *The Tube*, studying every instrument that every musician on the show was playing. So there were a lot of six-hour-long conversations about equipment or the exact sound of the hi-hats.

But the album got done. For want of a better title we called it *Body and Soul* too, and BMG were really excited. It was a total change of mood from a couple of years previously, when you couldn't even find a copy of my new single in any record shops. There was a new team there, a new managing director, and Take That had recently broken really big for the label, so there was a great sense of confidence in the offices: we know how to make pop music truly successful, and Rick Astley's back. It was infectious, at least until the phone call came from the film people in America, telling us there had been a major rethink of the *Body of Evidence* soundtrack. They'd decided they weren't going to put songs in the film any more, they were simply going to go with an orchestral score. I've no idea why. If they gave a reason, no one ever told me.

That phone call changed everything. Suddenly, the record label were stuck with an album that no one really wanted, that hadn't really been A&R'd and that no longer had a reason to exist. What were they going to do? As far as I could see, their big idea was to ignore it. It was as if a memo had been sent round the offices: 'If Rick Astley comes into the building, remember to look out of the window and hope he doesn't notice you.' Still, they threw a big expensive launch party for the album, at Quaglino's, a restaurant that had been famous in the 1930s and 1940s, which had reopened not long before and had become so fashionable that it was a running joke in *Absolutely Fabulous*: Edwina and Patsy were always going for 'a light lunch at Quag's'. I stood in Quag's, drinking champagne, feeling about as unfashionable as you could get. Maybe I was being paranoid, but I kind of sensed that people were looking at me thinking, *That guy's the past – why are they spending all this money trying to save his career? What's the point?*

The worst thing was, they were right. Everything about *Body and Soul* was, to use a technical term, a total fucking disaster. We shot two videos for potential singles in America, and they were so catastrophic we didn't use them. The shoot was hilariously bad: I had a spot on my chin, I looked like a bag of spanners, and was required to roll around on a beach, kissing a girl who had absolutely enormous boobs, the latest and perhaps the greatest in a long line of completely inappropriate love interests in my videos. The whole thing was excruciating. We reshot the videos, but it didn't make any difference. You could tell the record label didn't think the singles had a chance by the way they padded the B-sides out with my old hits – 'When I Fall in Love', 'Whenever You Need Somebody', 'Cry for Help' – as though that might be an incentive for people to buy them. It clearly wasn't. The first single, 'The Ones You Love', scraped into the bottom end of the Top 50 in the UK and didn't make the American charts at all. When the album came out, it just died – it didn't get anywhere near the charts. I did an interview in an office at BMG and found myself idly looking at the shelves behind the journalist as I talked. They were covered in rows of cassette singles. One of them was mine of 'Hopelessly', which had come out as the second single. Someone had taken a marker pen and crossed out the last two letters of the title, so the spine of the cassette said: 'RICK ASTLEY – HOPELESS'. Yeah, I thought, that just about sums things up.

There was a handful of good moments. I loved going around Europe with a couple of keyboard players and some backing singers and doing a few songs at radio stations. It felt good to be performing live.

But really, I knew the whole enterprise was complete bollocks. We'd rushed into the studio to make an album because someone on a whim had said we were going to get a song in a film, then someone on a whim had decided we weren't, and we were left with a total mess. I don't think the *Body and Soul* album is a bad record at all, Gary always makes things sound great, but without real direction and momentum at a record label it's pointless, Hopeless. It was depressing to the point that it really started affecting me. I'd never been hugely keen on travelling by plane, ever since we'd gone up in that light aircraft when I was a kid, and my brother Mike had convinced me we were going to crash. Now, my fear of flying became a real issue. I tried going to a hypnotherapist, but it didn't work. I was still increasingly terrified of getting on a plane.

I suspect it wasn't a fear of flying so much as a fear of having to go to another radio station or TV show and pretend everything was going great when it clearly wasn't. I simply wanted the record label to write the whole thing off as a mistake and knock it on the head. But record companies don't think like that: they've spent a load of money on making an album, so they want to keep the promotion going, in case there's a chance of something suddenly working. It sometimes happens. Look at Robbie Williams: his first solo album was dying until they released 'Angels' as the fourth single, and then it went totally nuts, the album started to sell millions.

And, in absolute fairness to the record company, there were some signs my album wasn't completely finished, at least in America. 'Hopelessly' started picking up a lot of radio play over there, on what they call 'adult contemporary' stations, which is a kind of polite way of saying easy listening. Whatever you called them, the adult contemporary stations had an effect. 'Hopelessly' began climbing the US singles chart. We were booked to appear on a late-night talk show in New York, which was a big deal. It looked like we had a chance.

The days leading up to my New York trip were not fun. Tops had started to work round my fear of flying by getting me to travel in Europe by train. But you couldn't get a train back to Britain. We flew back home from Germany and the flight was awful: loads of turbulence. It probably wasn't that bad, but it was terrible for me, given the state of mind I was in. I remember thinking: *If I get through this flight in one piece, I'm never getting on a fucking plane again.* Back in the UK, I went to another hypnotherapist, then travelled down to Bournemouth for a BMG conference. M People were performing live – they were massive at that point, one hit single after another, more evidence that the label really knew what they were doing when it came to selling pop music. I wasn't playing. It felt as if I was only there for the sake of it, which seemed to be the reason I'd done a lot of things recently, including releasing my last album.

The next day, Tops picked me up in the car. There was a driver taking us to Heathrow to fly to New York for the big TV show. We were heading up the M4 when I started to panic: 'Tops, I can't get on the plane. I won't make it. The plane won't make it. If we get on that plane, we're going to die. I can't do it.'

Tops glanced at me. 'Are you sure?' he asked.

I started to cry. 'I can't do it. I can't get on the plane.'

He nodded. 'I'm not going to try to make you, Rick.'

Maybe he should have done – plenty of managers would – but I was so grateful that he didn't. My relationship with Tops wasn't like that. We'd become so close since we'd been thrown together at PWL that there was a kind of paternal aspect to it; in a way, he was like a surrogate dad to me. He really cared about me – I don't think it's an exaggeration to say we loved each other, and still do – and Tops was more interested in making sure I was OK than in making me do things I didn't want to do. I think he knew that if I carried on, it was going to totally fuck me up, I was going to become genuinely ill, and he was desperate to stop that happening.

We turned off at the next junction and drove back home. Concorde took off without us on it. Tops called the record label in America and told them we weren't coming, that I wasn't comfortable flying. They were really understanding and said they'd sort it out. I was upset – I hated letting people down – but I was also relieved. I'd simply had enough. Not only of flying – I'd had enough of the whole thing. I realized the sense of relief outweighed any feelings of guilt. And I didn't have to do this any more. I knew how much money I had in the bank, and it was more than enough for me, Lene and Emilie to live off, very comfortably, for the foreseeable future. You never knew, maybe it would be topped up with some royalties if they did a Greatest Hits album or something, but even if it wasn't, we had plenty.

You remember when I was back in Newton, singing with FBI, I said what I really wanted was a sense of stability? It's not the most rock-and-roll ambition to have – let's face it, it's probably not what was driving Guns N' Roses or Led Zeppelin – but it was true: that was really what I wanted. And I'd done it. I had a home and a family, and enough money that I wasn't going to have to lie awake at night wondering how to pay the bills or the mortgage. And if I'd achieved what I wanted to achieve, what was the point of making myself miserable, even sending myself crazy, trying to get people interested in an album they clearly weren't interested in? And it really was miserable, flogging yourself to death, knowing that no one was that bothered. You could sense it when you turned up at a radio station or TV show: they were always polite and professional, but the feeling of 'Oh God, is he here again?' was hard to miss. It was clear this was over, that I'd be better off walking away.

I told Tops I was done. Not just with the trip to America, or with promoting *Body and Soul*: done permanently. I said he should talk to our lawyer and ask BMG if I could get out of my contract. Frankly, I think the label were more relieved than anything else. The deal we'd done with them when I split from Stock Aitken Waterman was a really good one. I got big advances for every album I made for them, so if

I'd made another they would have had to pay me a massive chunk of money. It didn't make sense, throwing more cash at someone who wasn't having hits any more. They certainly didn't come up with an alternative plan – there was no sense that they wanted me to leave it for a year, then see how I was feeling, and maybe try making another album – but nor did they ask for a percentage or an override royalty if I did make another album for someone else. They wanted to knock it on the head, shake hands and leave it at that. I gave Tops a chunk of money as severance pay. I knew he'd say no if I offered it to him, so I paid it into his bank.

And that was that. My pop career was over. I was twenty-seven years old.

There's a kind of myth about what we might as well call my retirement. Good old Rick Astley, such a down-to-earth bloke, he walked away from his career and happily got on with leading a quiet life. It's a lovely idea, and because I've never talked much about what really happened, people think that's what happened. But it wasn't like that – at least, not at first.

On the surface, I was hugely relieved to be shot of the whole thing. I felt as if I'd been let off the hook: *Thank fuck for that, I can just get on with being a dad for a while.* Underneath that, though, I was miserable about the whole situation. One of the things I think I inherited from my dad was his depressive side. He wasn't down all the time, but there were times when he'd clearly slipped into a really dark place. I remember him looking out of the Portakabin window one day, saying, 'I shouldn't have done this, I've let you all down, I shouldn't have done this,' over and over again. He had these sayings that we got used to hearing when we were kids, but when I thought about them later, they were all incredibly sad, all saying the same thing: *I don't want to be here.* As well as 'Open the gates and let me out', he would say 'All I ask is a tall ship and a star to steer her by'. I discovered that one was from a poem by John Masefield called 'Sea Fever': it's about escaping your life, getting away. Of course, being my dad, he'd be entirely lost in melancholy one minute, then the next he'd completely snap out of it – he'd go straight from pleading for a tall ship and star to steer her by to announcing he'd just bought another horse.

That underlying sadness sort of seeped into me: for someone who's been incredibly lucky in their life, I'm a terrible pessimist about things. I have a tendency to always look on the dark side of life, and, as much as I was glad to be out of it, the way my career had ended had really knocked my self-belief.

In fact, the way I felt in 1994, my whole career looked like it had been an awful mistake. There was part of me that wished I'd stayed in FBI and taken my chances making the music I wanted to make. I felt embarrassed about the whole SAW thing, how quickly it had turned from something that I thought was pretty great – this mad, seat-of-the-pants enterprise that made records like 'You Spin Me Round' and 'Say I'm Your Number One' – into this crappy, tacky manufactured-pop machine that didn't seem to care about the quality of what it produced: it quite literally wasn't what I'd signed up to.

I knew they were capable of doing great things, but they'd ended up being something people took the piss out of, *and I completely understood why.* If I hadn't been one of their artists, I'd have taken the piss out of them too. I didn't want to be associated with them, and yet I was, irrevocably. It felt as if you were never going to hear the name Rick Astley without the SAW names attached to it, the same way no one at school heard the name Rick Astley without automatically thinking 'that kid who lives in a Portakabin'. It was mortifying.

And then, I'd got what I wanted: I was more involved with making my own music, and it had turned into a complete shit-show. The worst thing about it was that it had looked like it was going to succeed: I'd had a Top 10 single around the world, people were talking about me in a different way, and I'd thought I'd done it. I'd had a glimpse of being what I always wanted to be, which was a singer and musician who could do it for themselves, and then the rug had been completely pulled out from underneath me.

In a weird way, it would have been better if 'Cry for Help' had been a flop as well, if the immediate reaction had been, 'No thanks, we're not interested in you without SAW, go away.' That would have been easier to understand and easier to bear. Instead, it had been: 'We love this song, it's great, you're going to get an award for a million plays on American radio, and you'll still be hearing it supermarkets in twenty-five years' time . . . oh, hang on, we're not interested now – fuck off.' It was just confusing and frustrating and depressing. I felt defeated, and it turned me into a total pain in the arse.

I was a nightmare to live with. Lene had really grabbed life by the scruff of the neck, which is her all over. She'd been accepted on a course by a film school in New York, employed a nanny and took herself and Emilie off there for six months while I was working on *Body and Soul*; then she'd come back and started working as a director's assistant, making concert films and music videos. It was all really taking off for her. I, on the other hand, didn't really know how to fill my days. I hadn't been very comfortable with fame, but I didn't know what to do with myself after I was famous. I sort of mooched around, went out for a lot of meals, spent hours looking at expensive furniture in the Conran Shop. There are obviously far worse ways to pass your time, but it wasn't hugely fulfilling. The temper I'd also inherited from my dad began to flare up more often, maybe because I'd been angry about lots of things during my career – the way SAW had been, the fact that I never seemed to have time to do anything – and I'd bottled it up.

Whatever the reason, it was never a pretty sight. I wouldn't scream and shout in front of Emilie, but I'd do it when I thought no one could hear. I'd clench my fist and punch the palm of my other hand as hard as I could, over and over again, until I was just standing there with both my hands in agony. And occasionally I would take myself off into the garden and smash something up, exactly the way my dad did. In a weird way, it made me understand his behaviour a bit better. I suppose it's about control: you feel like your life is out of your control, so you control *something* to the point of obliterating it out of existence. Still, understandable or not, it's a bit of a twatty thing to do.

I gradually retreated into myself. If Lene invited people over to the house for dinner, I'd decide I wasn't interested at the last minute and would stay up in the bedroom – stupid stuff like that. I suppose it was depression. People have suggested I was having a breakdown, but I'm not sure about that: I think in my head having a breakdown is associated with being in a white medical smock, medicated, in an institution somewhere, which I definitely wasn't. Whatever it was, Lene got sick of constantly making excuses for me. It wasn't how she wanted to live. Things started to get tense between us.

We'd decided to move back to London. It made sense, because Lene's work was there and we wanted Emilie to go to a school in Richmond where one of Lene's best friends' kids were. We looked around it on an open day and couldn't believe how great it was. That was where we bought a house. It needed a lot of work doing to it, and in true Horace style, I decided not to get a building company involved, that I'd do some of the work myself. I really threw myself into it. I had a little team of people helping me. There was a guy called Andrew Frampton who'd played keyboards for me when I was promoting *Body and Soul* around radio stations in Europe. He was in a band called Frampton Hill with his brother Dan and a drummer, Simon Hill. Tops had introduced them to Pete Waterman, who was going to sign them to his new label, Coliseum. They were at a loose end, waiting for things to happen, so I recruited them as my building team. We spent weeks ripping wallpaper off walls, tearing out rotten wood, knocking things down. We used to sleep on the top floor in sleeping bags. I really enjoyed doing it, but there was no getting around the fact that I was essentially running away from the problems at home. I spent so much time at the new house that it was almost as if Lene and I had separated. She and Emilie had left the house in the Cotswolds and were renting a place in Fulham.

One day when I actually was there, rather than in a sleeping bag in the middle of a load of rubble, Lene told me she'd got talking to a woman at the gym that morning. She was called Rosa Lee, which I thought made her sound like someone with a headscarf and a crystal ball and an interest in reading tea leaves. But she was a therapist, an American woman much older than us, and Lene had been fascinated by her – fascinated enough to book a session with her. She came back from that session with her mind blown; she said she'd experienced a lot of emotions that she'd been bottling up, or didn't even know she'd had. She suggested I should go too.

I would never have gone if Lene hadn't instigated it, but even that first session was totally life-changing. It didn't always feel as if I was in therapy, more like talking to a very wise, older woman. She wouldn't let you off the hook about anything: if you talked around an issue, or made excuses, or kept saying, 'The reason I'm upset is because of this,' she'd go, 'Well, is it really? Are you sure you're not just doing this because . . .' and lead you down this path until you realized what was really going on inside. It made me understand a lot of stuff – about my background, about my success, about my lack of self-worth. I realized that I'd lived my life with a set of beliefs and prejudices and fears that were founded in coming from a small town in the North-West in a certain era, with a certain kind of upbringing, and that a lot of negative aspects of my behaviour that were rooted in the way I'd grown up were weirdly amplified by being really famous for a bit: feeling self-conscious, feeling embarrassed, feeling that people were prejudiced against me because of where I was from, being afraid of being abandoned, being constantly worried about what was coming next. More than anything, I realized that I overthink things, because I'd had to overthink everything when I was a kid.

I always had to try to work out what mood my dad was in, what he was going to say or do; I had to try to work out how my mum was going to react to things, how she was going to behave. I've got a feeling that overthinking things isn't that different to going mad: when I see mentally unwell people in the street, I sometimes feel that's what they're doing, over-thinking out loud. Whether that's true or not, it's definitely not a very healthy trait.

The therapy helped me switch the overthinking off, and to see things in a different way, a bit more detached from my upbringing. Honestly, I don't like going on about those therapy sessions because they were a privilege. I had the time and money to delve really deep into myself – we did couples therapy, group therapy, and I went on my own a lot, every day for a few weeks – and most people don't have that option. But it really sorted me and Lene out. It didn't fix anything exactly, but it gave me the tools to deal with stuff better – it ultimately took away some of the fear I felt. Gradually, Lene and I managed to close the gap between us and get back onto something like an even keel.

And so, life got slowly better. We moved into the house in Richmond, and Emilie started school. It was a bit nuts, there were a lot of really famous people's kids there. It was weird seeing Mick Jagger and Jerry Hall at a parents' evening, or finding yourself trying to remember the code that let you into the playground to pick up your kids with Ade Edmond-son, or lining up for the dads' race on sports day and realizing that you're running against Daley Thompson (we made him start miles behind everyone else and he still totally flattened us all). But the main thing that struck me about Emilie's school wasn't the celebrity offspring, but that the teachers really seemed to care about the pupils. I loved that and wished everyone had the chance to be educated somewhere like that.

And I adored being around as she was growing up – having the time to pick her up from school or watch *The Simpsons* with her when she got home, or just laze around on the sofa with her – mundane stuff that doesn't seem so mundane once your kids have grown up and left home. There was a line in an episode of *Modern Family* where they ask Jay, the grandad, what the most important job is for him within his family. He keeps thinking about it for ages and eventually says, 'Just showing up. Just being there.' That truly hit home for me because it was something that I was able to do. Far more than the music I made, that seemed to be the point of everything that had happened to me in the eighties: it had bought me the ability to do those things with Emilie.

We had a wonderful, quiet life. In a way, I suppose I wanted to protect Emilie from my past, from the career I'd had. I wanted her to feel she was growing up in a normal household, and that we did normal things – two things I'd never felt growing up. I didn't want her to feel odd or strange. We had a nice house, in a nice area of London, but it wasn't ostentatious, it wasn't some mad ex-pop star's house, and nor was it a Portakabin. We didn't have a mad ex-popstar's car either – or a pony and trap, for that matter – we had a Volvo estate.

It's strange that when you've really got time on your hands, it doesn't feel as if you have: it just flies past. You look at the calendar and realize it's a Friday and that another week has gone by without you noticing. Lene's career as a video producer really took off – ironically, she ended up working with Madonna on the video for 'Hung Up' – and then she graduated into feature films. I sort of dabbled in things. I went into business with an old school friend who was a hairdresser: I bought a property in Chelsea, and rented it out to him as a salon, although it didn't really work out. We took a lot of holidays. I hardly ever got recognized, but on the rare occasions I did, it was quite nice: maybe they'd squeeze you into a restaurant that was fully booked, or upgrade you to a suite at a hotel. Nobody felt the urge to tell me I was a wanker any more.

I also kept my hand in with music, more or less. I had a vague idea that I might become a professional songwriter for hire: quite a few ex-pop stars seemed to be doing that, people like Cathy Dennis, who I'd met when I was doing promotion in America in the early nineties. I'd bought a mixing desk when we had the house in the Cotswolds, and had moved it down to Fulham, but that clearly wasn't working out – it had just sat there, taking up most of the living room. So I started out with a room in a rehearsal studio in Shepherd's Bush where I set up a load of equipment, then I decided to build myself a studio in Parson's Green, about half an hour from where we lived in Richmond. Lene always says I spent more time there playing computer games than I did writing songs, but I did pursue a few different things.

There was a project that came up with a Japanese group who wanted their songs translated into English, which I worked on with Andrew Frampton. I went off to a few songwriting boot camps. One was run by Chris Difford from Squeeze, at a massive house down in Devon. There were all sorts of people there – Nik Kershaw, and Joey Tempest from Europe. You went down for breakfast in the morning and your name was on a board next to someone else's and the two of you had to go and write a song together that day. It was really fun and energizing, even if nothing really came out of it for me. You'd hear something a young guy who specialized in writing hits for country artists did that day and it would completely blow you away. The other was in a castle in France – a medieval one, with a moat and turrets – that belonged to Miles Copeland, the former manager of The Police. He'd apparently bought it because his wife liked painting in the region, the way anyone else might have encouraged her hobby by buying her a new easel. I probably took that one a bit less seriously than I should have done. There was a lot of nice French wine and cognac on offer, which didn't help much. But one song came out of it that got recorded – 'Mission Statement', which I co-wrote with Fish, the former vocalist of Marillion, and which he released on his album *Raingods with Zippos*. I've no idea what Fish's fans made of him co-writing a song with Rick Astley, but if nothing else, it's completely different from anything else I've done: it sounds a bit like 'Radar Love' by Golden Earring.

I lacked the self-confidence to push myself as a songwriter. The only other time something I wrote was released, it was by One True Voice, a boy band who won *Popstars: The Rivals*. Or rather jointly won it: the other winners were Girls Aloud, the idea being that the two winning bands would compete for the Christmas No. 1 spot. Pete Waterman was mentoring them and asked me to get involved. In the years since I'd left SAW, I'd managed to repair my relationship with all of them, although they'd fallen out with each other, over money. I knew a lot of people who'd worked with Pete on Steps and I'd visited Mike and Matt in their new studio and had a cup of tea with them. I guess the fact that I was prepared to work with Pete again says something about how I'd managed to deal with what I'd seen as the stigma of being associated with SAW in the years since I'd retired from being a performer, but why Pete asked me, I'll never know. It was a really high-profile thing; he should have gone to one of the biggest songwriters in Britain. I suppose the problem was that someone who was one of the biggest songwriters in Britain would have wanted to produce the thing themselves, and Pete wanted control of that.

I tried writing a couple of songs with one of the guys in One True Voice, to be included on their forthcoming debut album. Bless him, he wanted to take their music in a more rock direction, so I spent quite a lot of the session gently trying to suggest that that wasn't going to fly with Pete Waterman. For a single, I gave Pete a song I'd co-written with my friend Kevin Hughes, called 'Shakespeare's Way with Words'. We'd done a demo that was definitely very pop but trying to be a little bit cooler than usual – it had a really funky rhythm and pizzicato strings on it, a sound that was big on hip American R&B records at the time. Certainly, it was a bit cooler than the track that came out. Pete just totally . . . Pete Waterman-ed it. By the time he'd finished with it, it sounded like Steps. He'd literally removed every single thing that Kev and I thought was interesting about the demo.

Meanwhile, Girls Aloud were working with this amazing songwriting and production team called Xenomania, who came up with these completely great ideas, really exciting and original: drum and bass beats with rockabilly guitar over the top of them for their debut single, 'Sound of the Underground'; a punky pop song with a riff that sounded like 'My Sharona' by The Knack for its follow-up, 'No Good Advice'. It was meant to be a contest, but it was no contest at all. One True Voice ended up splitting up a few weeks after the song was released. They never even made a debut album.

So my career as a songwriter for hire wasn't exactly a glittering success. I simply didn't have the ruthlessness, if you like, to make it work. It's no good going around and telling people, 'Oh, I've written a couple of songs, I think they're OK.' You're supposed to burst into their offices and go, 'These are the greatest songs that you will ever hear and without them your artist will fail.' I wasn't really cut out to do that. I enjoyed writing them, but I assumed that no one would really want to know what I'd come up with, because I'd written them. I thought that once they heard my name, no record label would let me through the front door. After the way things had ended with my career, I figured that people would think that having Rick Astley attached to a project would jinx it. For all the good that therapy did me, I definitely still had some insecurities about my past.

But the songwriting did have one unexpected side effect. I made up a CD of my songs, which I passed around to a few people. One of them was Chrissie Harwood, a friend of Lene and mine who worked in the international department at BMG. She had a meeting with a German A&R about a potential project and played him a couple of my songs. The German A&R liked them but wondered why I didn't record them myself. He got in touch with me via Chrissie and asked if we could set up a meeting. I told him I didn't really want to. He insisted: it would only be a conversation, no pressure to do anything. So I ended up in the offices of Polydor in Germany, discussing making an album.

To say I was wary of the idea is putting it mildly. But I eventually agreed, with some caveats. I didn't want the album to come out anywhere other than Germany, particularly not in the UK. I saw it as a way of quietly dipping my toe into the water of being a performer again, not a comeback. The last thing I wanted was a British record company getting involved and turning it into a bigger deal than I wanted it to be: I didn't like the idea of a UK label's promotional department suddenly booking me onto a load of TV shows, who'd only want me on for curiosity's sake. I thought that if everything turned out great, and the album was successful in Germany and I enjoyed doing it, then that would be fantastic, we could see how things went from there. But if it wasn't, and I found the whole experience another nightmare, then I could pull the plug a lot more quickly and easily if it was only released in one country.

In a sense that's what happened. The album, *Keep It Turned On*, was OK. I co-wrote a lot of the tracks with Chris Braide, whom I'd met at one of those songwriting boot camps, and who went on to work with all sorts of people: Sia, Nicki Minaj, Britney Spears. Some of the songs were pretty good, but some of them weren't good enough. It wasn't a huge hit, but it wasn't a total flop either. I did a bit of radio and TV in Germany with a couple of guys miming drums and keyboards, and in fact it was quite a good laugh. I didn't really take it seriously, or rather, I didn't think the chances of it turning into something big were particularly high. It would have been nice if it had, but I maintained a healthy degree of scepticism about the whole thing: the likelihood of having a successful pop career once in your life is incredibly slim; the likelihood of having a successful pop career for a second time, after an eight-year break, is even smaller. And when it became clear the album wasn't going to be a huge hit, I just politely said, 'thanks very much' to everyone involved in it and quietly walked away. No harm done. I don't even think the release of *Keep It Turned On* even registered in Britain.

It was good for me, in a way. The whole experience definitely wasn't a nightmare – I certainly hadn't hated it the way I'd hated trying to promote *Body and Soul* back in the early nineties. And, whatever the outcome, it was interesting that someone at a major record label had been so eager to work with me, or at least, had looked at me and, rather than immediately backing away, had thought: *You never know, you know, it might happen for this guy again.* I mean, it really hadn't, but it was still interesting that someone felt it might, despite everything. It was the thought that counted. And, the following year, BMG in the UK included a couple of the *Keep It Tuned On* tracks on a Greatest Hits album. I had no idea what kind of reception a Rick Astley Greatest Hits album would get – I didn't know whether anyone really remembered or cared about the music I'd released in the eighties any more. It sold 150,000 copies and went gold. That was interesting too.

Chapter Twelve

Tops had started his own record label, or more exactly, Tops had co-founded a sub-label within RCA with Andrew Frampton and two other guys, an A&R called Paul Lisberg and Steve Kipner, an Australian songwriter with an incredible track record – he'd co-written 'Physical' for Olivia Newton-John and 'Genie in a Bottle' for Christina Aguilera, and he worked with everyone from Rod Stewart to Dolly Parton. They called the label Phonogenic and their first signing was Natasha Bedingfield. They set up a little showcase gig for her at the Half Moon in Putney, and I said I'd go along.

In the audience, I started talking to Simon Moran, a concert promoter who'd also come along to take a look at Tops and Co.'s new signing. I'd heard of Simon before. Of course I had – everyone in the British music industry knows who Simon Moran is. 'Concert promoter' is slightly underplaying it: he owns SJM, one of the biggest gig-promotion companies in

Britain, and he's the director of the Academy Music Group, which owns Brixton Academy and Shepherd's Bush Empire, among other venues. He's the man who got Take That to re-form and promoted their Progress tour, which at the time was the biggest-grossing tour in British history. He also owns Warrington Wolves rugby league club.

Within a few minutes of being introduced to him, it was pretty obvious why Simon was so successful. He's a really lovely guy. He's also very persuasive. He asked what I was up to and I told him not much. The thing in Germany had been fine, but it hadn't exactly instilled me with a great desire to carry on. It fizzled out, and I sort of fizzled out with it. He asked why I wasn't singing, and I gave him the standard answer I gave everyone when they asked that: it had been fun, but I felt those days were over; I'd moved on. Simon thought that was daft; he thought that I should go out and play gigs. I said I wasn't sure. He apparently was: he said it was madness that I wasn't doing it. He told me we should have another chat about it.

The other chat was much like the first one. Whatever objections I raised, Simon had an answer. I didn't have a band. Simon insisted it would be straightforward to put a band together – all I really had to do was turn up and sing. I told him I didn't know what kind of venues I should play. He told me to leave that to him, he'd book a few small venues. Why not do it? It wouldn't cost me anything. I told him I didn't have anything to sing; at that stage, I didn't really want to do my old hits. He told me to think of something. I mentioned my dad singing old Frank Sinatra songs around the house. Great, he said – sing them. I guess it wasn't an idea that seemed completely out of the blue, because I'd had a hit with 'When I Fall in Love' back in the eighties.

So that's how I ended up, a little unexpectedly, singing 'Fly Me to the Moon' at a club in Dublin. It was the first time I'd set foot on a live stage for fifteen years, and the first time my daughter Emilie ever saw me perform. Despite my best efforts to shield her from my pop career – which, on a couple of occasions, had extended to quickly changing the station when 'Never Gonna Give You Up' came on the radio in the car – she'd found out about her dad's past when a dinner lady at school had produced an old fan magazine from the eighties and shown it to her. She took it all in her stride, and I think the fact that she was at a school with a load of really famous people's children might have helped – to be honest, if your classmate's dad is Mick Jagger, the fact that your dad is Rick Astley definitely has a hint of 'so what?' about it.

I'd had my doubts about the tour, but I really loved it. The band that was put together was fantastic: a stand-up bass player, a drummer who played with brushes rather than sticks, piano, guitar, sax and trumpet. The venues we played were small, places like Ronnie Scott's jazz club in London and The Stables in Milton Keynes. My old PWL friend Mike Duffy was back in England for a while from Australia, so I got him to come along with me – I wanted us to spend some time together, so we could catch up. I decided we should have a stage set, even though there was no budget. I thought the music we were playing was quite cosy and old-fashioned-sounding, and I came up with the idea of making the stage look like your gran's house. I got Duffy to go out and buy a couple of ancient standard lamps from junk shops, and one of those old electric fires with the fake coal effect. I brought an old couch we had hanging around in our kitchen. The road crew didn't like the idea at all – 'Legally, Rick, you can't have that on stage. It's not been safety tested' – but I thought it looked great, and I liked the idea of singing to an audience while sitting on a couch from my house.

*

My mum came along to the show in Manchester, and she really enjoyed it. Our relationship was still pretty strained. All the time I'd been famous, she'd only ever seemed to be able to relate to me as Rick Astley, pop star, someone to sign autographs and say hello to her friends' kids. I didn't mind doing that at all; I just wanted her to see that I was also her son, but that didn't really seem to register fully with her. The pane of glass between her and the rest of us was still there. When I made some money, I'd bought her a house in Newton, but I'd bought it in my name, rather than hers. To no one's great surprise, her marriage to Bob the bus driver hadn't lasted five minutes. I wanted her to be comfortable and tried to help her financially but she never wanted money. It was hard even to treat her to things as she always said that she didn't need anything and that I should 'save my money'. In the later years of her life she restarted her relationship with Trevor, the chap who loved his motorbikes. They seemed happy and I was very pleased for them.

She seemed content enough in the house – she loved decorating it – but there wasn't any real bond between us. I'd hoped that becoming a grandma would change things – some people who aren't great at being actual parents really thrive in that role – but it didn't at all. She seemed either baffled by, or uninterested in Emilie. It wasn't personal; she was exactly the same with all her other grandkids. There was some kind of barrier between her and them too. It made me incredibly sad: she was my mum and yet we'd never been close, there wasn't that connection. She just didn't seem to get any pleasure out of the things that gave me pleasure, no matter how much I tried. I took her to Paris in the late nineties, thinking, *Right, I'm going to take her on holiday and really spoil her.* It was exhausting: it felt as if she was digging her heels in to be contrary and refusing to enjoy herself. My main memory is taking her to the Louvre, and her complaining because they didn't have any sausage rolls in the cafe.

I suppose my dad should have been at the show too, given that it was him who had introduced me to the songs I was singing, but by then things had completely broken down between us. We'd stayed in touch, and he'd occasionally come to visit us; he preferred it when we lived in the Cotswolds, because he didn't like London at all. Once, when he'd been ill, we even went on holiday together, to a little summer house outside Copenhagen where Lene and I used to take Emilie when we went over to visit her family – but it was hard work, because you never knew which version of Dad you were going to get on the end of the phone, or at the end of a long journey back up North.

He could be great. When Jayne and Barry had a son, Robert, Dad really took to him. He attached a child's car seat to the pony and trap and used to take him on drives around Newton. Watching them trot along together, with my dad's old brass-band tapes blaring out as usual, I could see him the way my friends must have seen him: good old Ozzy, this charming eccentric guy, doing things his way, totally not bound by the kind of boring rules in the way everyone else's dad seemed to be.

Then something would happen to remind you that this wasn't the whole story. Dad could be every bit as much of a nightmare to deal with as he had been when I was a kid. He was always falling out with one or the other of his children. Sometimes it went on for months or years at a time, and it was always over nothing. It was as if he was actively trying to find reasons not to be happy.

My turn came a few years after Emilie was born. Completely out of nowhere, he sent me a letter. It was really vicious and unpleasant, making all kinds of crazy accusations. It was like a poison pen letter, but it wasn't anonymous; it was signed by my dad. I had no idea what he was talking about – it basically seemed to be a long-distance version of one of his inexplicable rages. I wondered if he'd had a few drinks before he wrote it, but, whatever the reason, some of the stuff he was saying was incredibly hurtful and malicious. If he wanted to get a rise out of me, he succeeded. I'd simply had enough. I really do think he was unwell, unable to control the way he was, but I'd been dealing with it for nearly thirty years, and I couldn't deal with it any more. There didn't seem to be any point in confronting him about it – my dad never changed his mind about anything, you were wasting your time trying – so I simply cut him off. I never spoke to my dad again. When I told Jayne and my brothers about the letter, they laughed; what he was saying was so mad, so completely ungrounded in any kind of reality that you had to either laugh about it or cry, and none of us were going to do that. But the weird thing was, none of them ever tried to talk me out of it, none of them thought I was overreacting or doing something I would regret. They knew what he was like.

*

We ended up doing a second tour of bigger venues, which meant dragging the couch from our kitchen onto the stage of the Shepherd's Bush Empire. Somewhere along the way, someone from BMG must have come along to one of the shows, because they asked me to do an album. Robbie Williams had recently had a huge hit with *Swing When You're Winning*, and the Great American Songbook had suddenly become hip once more. Tops had started managing my career again – or as much of a career as I had to manage – and we talked over the idea. We thought it might be a good idea to make the album in America; after all, that's where the music I was performing came from. The name of producer Peter Collins came up. Tops knew him from years back: they had both worked with Pete Waterman in the days before Stock Aitken Waterman. He'd done all sorts since then – Alice Cooper, Rush, Nik Kershaw, you name it – and he was based in Nashville, so he could put a great band together really easily: you can't walk into a bar in Nashville without hearing a musician talented enough to be a superstar. It all sounded great. We booked a studio in LA.

A couple of days before we were due to leave, we were in the car park at Sony-BMG when the managing director, Rob Stringer, drove past us in his Range Rover. He slowed down, wound the window down and said hello. He asked about the album we were going to make: we were going to America to make a covers record, right? We said we were. 'Well, whatever you do,' he said cheerfully, 'don't make a swing record!' And then he drove off.

Tops and I looked at each other. The boss of the record label telling us not to make a swing album clearly constituted quite a serious problem, given that we were literally going to America to make a swing album in forty-eight hours' time. I suppose what he meant was that a lot of people had started thinking along the same lines in the wake of Robbie Williams's success with *Swing When You're Winning*: Rod Stewart was recording a series of Great American Songbook albums, Westlife were doing a tribute to the Rat Pack, the finalists on *Pop Idol* had done a big-band album, plus there was a new wave of smooth jazz singers like Michael Bublé and Jamie Cullum, and the market was getting overcrowded. He had a point, although it would have been nice if someone at the label had made it a bit earlier on.

We flew to LA anyway, and ended up recording a kind of mish-mash of covers. In the studio, people just threw out names of classic songs and we recorded them, so you ended up with an album with some songs that fitted the original brief mixed up with some Burt Bacharach tunes and sixties and seventies easy-listening hits like 'And I Love You So'. It sounded great in the studio, but a bit less great when you actually listened to the record, I'm not sure why. We called it *Portrait*, and it was OK, but not the type of thing that was going to make anyone grab their friends and go, 'Oh my God, have you heard Rick Astley's covers album?' It kind of slipped out – the record label didn't do much to promote it and neither did I – but it still managed to get in the Top 30.

In the aftermath of *Portrait*, I got an offer to go to Japan to play a sort of nostalgia concert with a bunch of other eighties artists. I wasn't sure about it at all, but someone else was. Or rather, two other people were: Lene and Emilie. I should add that it wasn't out of any great desire on their part to see me on stage again; they just wanted to go to Japan. The money was really good, and it seemed like virtually no effort. There was a great band and they were a lot of fun, but it was effectively like a giant karaoke night. All I had to do was sing a few songs. But that wasn't really the point. The point was that my wife and daughter basically cornered me in the kitchen one morning and demanded I do it. So I agreed.

There was a special detour on that particular trip that I haven't mentioned yet. On the way to Japan, we had to stop off in LA because Lene had been nominated for an Oscar. While I'd been tinkering with making albums and playing live, her career in film had really grown. She'd moved from working in pop videos to making short films and she eventually moved on to producing feature films, with a director called Sean Ellis. The film that got nominated was called *Cashback*. It starred Sean Biggerstaff and Emilia Fox and was about a student working the nightshift in a supermarket who can stop time. Some of it was shot at our house, and one of the scenes there involved the main character recalling how, as a boy, he had seen a Swedish student naked. My main memory of that is unexpectedly encountering both the film crew and the glamour model who was playing the naked Swedish student in our kitchen. It's somewhat awkward, trying to make a cup of tea when there's a young blonde girl you've never met before on the other side of the kitchen island, who's clearly got nothing on under her dressing gown. I decided to go to a cafe instead.

Anyway, *Cashback* won a load of awards at film festivals in Europe and America, but a nomination for Best Short Film at the Oscars was the big one. We flew to LA en route to Japan. I got my tux on. Lene bought a vintage Bill Blass dress and borrowed these incredibly expensive diamond earrings from a famous LA jeweller's. She had her make-up done in the hotel room. She looked stunning. We went in a limo and did the red carpet outside the old Chinese Theatre on the Hollywood Walk of Fame. It was fantastic: I was completely anonymous, no one noticed me at all. Then we sat down for the ceremony. What you don't realize – or rather, what *I* didn't realize – is how long the bloody Oscars ceremony is. We were sat there for four hours. Lene's film didn't win, which was disappointing, but simply being nominated for an Oscar is something to be incredibly proud of. What was a problem was my stomach. I thought I was a little peckish when we got there, but by a couple of hours in, I was starving. And we were only halfway through. I think the fact we were jet-lagged made it worse. If I didn't do something about it soon, the sound of my stomach rumbling was going to drown out George Clooney's acceptance speech. Eventually, I sneaked out and found a bar somewhere in the building. So that's my main memory of the Oscars: pleading with a bloke behind a bar for something to eat: 'Hello, mate, my wife's been nominated for an Oscar – have you got any crisps I can take back in with me?'

Afterwards, we did the all the parties: Elton John's AIDS Foundation one, the lot. It was fantastic. In fact, it was weirdly like being in a film. We got back to the Sunset Marquis, started chatting to someone at the bar, then ended up going out to another party with them. I remember standing there at 4 a.m. with a glass of really nice wine, thinking, *Oh God, I've got to fly to Japan to sing 'Never Gonna Give You Up' tomorrow.*

I arrived in Japan in a bit of a state. I'd made the plane, but I'd had a few drinks at the airport and popped a sleeping pill after take-off to deal with my fear of flying. If the Japanese promoter was surprised to see the famously clean-cut eighties pop star Rick Astley stumbling through the arrivals gate in a haze of tranquilizers and alcohol, he was good enough not to mention it as he steered me to the bullet train to Osaka.

I'm not going to say I didn't spend the gigs feeling a bit confused. Hang on, first I was at home, then I was at the Oscars, trying to get a packet of crisps, now I appear to be on stage in Japan singing a load of songs I haven't sung for twenty years – if I look down and I'm not wearing any trousers, this is definitely a weird dream. But the shows were fantastic. Confused or not, I really enjoyed myself. And by the reserved standards of Japan, the crowd were going absolutely nuts. It's one thing hearing that a Greatest Hits album has sold well, another thing entirely watching a big audience react like that to your old songs. You could truly see the amount of joy those songs were bringing, or had brought in the past. Whatever anybody else said about them, whatever anybody else thought about them, they were songs that clearly meant something to the people in the audience – perhaps they'd been their favourite tracks to dance to when they were younger, or they'd soundtracked their first kiss, or they'd been on the radio all the time when they'd met their partner.

I came offstage in Tokyo and Tops was standing in the wings. I was pretty elated. 'They actually really liked me!' I said, as if it hadn't previously occurred to me that anyone did.

Tops rolled his eyes. 'Of course they fucking like you,' he sighed.

We had a great family holiday in Japan. I'd been there before, but it was all new to Lene and Emilie, and it felt as if we were having a fantastic adventure in one of the most amazing countries on earth, staying in traditional inns, or *ryokans*, being shown around temples and palaces that had been designed so the floors squeaked to alert the occupants to the presence of ninja assassins. I kept thinking about the shows I'd just played. Stupid as this sounds, it had never dawned on me that you could simply turn up and sing and people would love it. The sort of elation you get from seeing people loving what you do, without any of the complications that seemed to come with my success in the eighties – the tabloids, the situation at PWL, the criticism, the overwork, the creeping feeling that I wasn't really in control of my own life – was quite addictive.

When we got back home, other offers for similar events started to come in. It turned out there was a huge market for eighties revival shows: across the UK and Europe, in South-East Asia and South America and South Africa. I started saying yes to them. Emilie was older now, so I didn't need to be around as much, being a dad. I could deal with the flying, more or less, by having a few drinks. I've tried hypnotherapy several times, but it didn't stick, so I just sort of happy myself with alcohol – a few Chardonnays or gin and tonics – before I get on board. If I'm either a bit tipsy or asleep during the flight, I'm basically OK. It's probably not the medically recommended way of managing a fear of flying, but it works for me.

I'm not going to lie, the money was definitely part of the incentive: we weren't broke by any stretch of the imagination, but we'd lived a really nice life on the money I'd earned in the late eighties for the best part of twenty years, and I liked the idea of replenishing the coffers so that we could continue to live a really nice life. But I wouldn't have done it if I didn't love those eighties revival shows.

People sometimes look down on them as nostalgia events, but you could say that of anyone you go and see live in order to hear their old hits, whether it's Fleetwood Mac or the Stone Roses or the Rolling Stones; if they play anything new, people go and get a beer, because they're there largely for reasons of nostalgia. Everything about them was great. I got to go to places I'd never been to at the height of my career, places I genuinely had no idea I'd been huge. That was how I ended up on stage with Manilla's leading Rick Astley impersonator. I loved the band that backed me up, we got on really well. I loved having a laugh with the other artists. I used to serve Bananarama with a couple of gin and tonics at the side of the stage – like I'd once served them cups of tea when they turned up at the SAW studios – or just sit on a flight case at the back of the stage watching Mark King, thinking about how my teenage self would have freaked out at the thought of watching Mark King from Level 42 doing his thing up close. The audiences were huge, the indoor events were always in arenas, tens of thousands of people turned up to the big weekend-long events – it was a proper festival.

In contrast to everything I'd done in the eighties, there was no pressure about these events; they were simply fun. I didn't have a new album to sell, or even a record label; my contract with BMG had ended. There was no worrying about how the new material would go down, no thought in the back of your mind about whether or not it was good enough to get this TV slot or that radio playlist, because I didn't have any new material. There was no arguing about running order, or who went on before who: the length of your set and where you were on the bill was dictated by the number of hits you'd had, simple as that. It wasn't like a gig of your own, where the success or the failure of the evening is firmly on your shoulders. No one played for longer than forty minutes or an hour; some people only did a couple of songs.

There was something incredibly unpretentious about it. Everyone knew why they were there and why the audience were there. You never saw anyone screaming at the musicians who were on stage because they'd not played a song exactly how it was on the record. Of course you took it seriously, but it was ultimately a bit of a grin. You did your hits and then you got offstage and drove yourself home. If you weren't top of the bill, and the event was somewhere relatively nearby, you could be sitting in your living room with a glass of wine before the gig had even ended. Honestly, I can't think of a single bad word to say about them.

We started getting offers to headline shows and do private

gigs, which meant getting a longer set together, but that was fine. We threw in a couple of tracks from my first album and a couple of cover versions. I love singing cover versions. It got to the stage where those kinds of gigs were effectively my job, and I was very happy with that – far happier than I'd ever been when I was selling millions of records.

And then something really, really weird happened.

The Macy's Thanksgiving Day Parade is a proper American institution. It's been going on for nearly a hundred years. It's been televised live across the country every year since 1953, a three-hour riot of marching bands, floats, cheerleaders, clown cars, police motorcycle units and giant balloons that are either stunning or slightly terrifying, depending on how you feel about looking up and seeing a 68-foot inflatable Ronald McDonald looming across the sky. Really huge stars appear in it: over the years, everyone from Ginger Rogers and Shirley Temple to Diana Ross and Dolly Parton has turned up. In 2008, there was Miley Cyrus, James Taylor, Lang Lang and Andy Williams, eighty years old and still belting out 'It's the Most Wonderful Time of the Year'. And me, although I didn't see much of the parade. I spent it hidden inside a giant cartoon house on the *Foster's Home for Imaginary Friends* float, as it drove down Broadway, in between a giant Buzz Lightyear balloon and the Mike Miller Spirit of America Dance Stars. *Foster's Home for Imaginary Friends* is a Cartoon Network show about . . . well, about children's imaginary friends. It features a chicken called Coco that has a kind of palm tree on its head, and a blue bollard-shaped thing called Bloo. The float stopped outside Macy's, the characters from the cartoon sang a song called 'Best Friend', then I suddenly burst out and sang a couple of verses of 'Never Gonna Give You Up'. The announcer described me as 'internet phenom Rick Astley'.

Sometimes, a career in pop music goes more or less according to plan. You release a song you know is good, and with a bit of luck it becomes a hit. You play a gig armed with a load of hits the audience loves and it goes down well. Other times, it throws up situations that are completely inexplicable, such as finding yourself on a float outside Macy's on a freezing cold Thursday morning in November, fifteen years after you last got anywhere near the American charts, miming one of your old hits in the company of a giant cartoon cat called Bloppypants. As the float drives off, you wave to the cheering crowd and you look at Bloppypants and, like the guy in the Talking Heads song, you ask yourself: *Well, how did I get here?*

The truth is I don't really know. The whole thing with the Macy's Thanksgiving Day Parade and *Foster's Home for Imaginary Friends* and Bloppypants was the climax of a series of events, but I truly have no idea how that series of events started. The first I knew was one morning when we were on holiday on the Amalfi Coast. I checked my emails and saw one from my friend Andrew. The email had a link in it: I can't remember what Andrew said the link was, but it definitely wasn't the video for 'Never Gonna Give You Up', and yet that was what appeared when I clicked on it. I sent him an email back, asking what it was all about. He then sent me a different link, but, when I clicked on it, it took me to the video of 'Never Gonna Give You Up' again. I sent another email, asking Andrew if he might consider stopping sending me links to the video of my debut single and saying they were something else. The email back had another link it. Click. Once again, there I was: outside the youth club in Shepherd's Bush, insisting I was no stranger to love.

Eventually, I rang Andrew in LA and asked what the hell he thought he was playing at. He seemed to think it was hilarious – 'I Rickrolled Rick Astley!' I told him I didn't get it, and he seemed genuinely shocked. 'Have you not heard about Rickrolling?'

He explained it to me: people were posting links on message boards and in emails, claiming they were to something exciting, but when you clicked on it . . . well, you know. He said it had already happened a lot to him. Andrew's very hot on technology and music, how the former affects the other. He thought it was a big deal. I wasn't really sure what to make of it. I guess I could have been hugely offended by it – one way of looking at the joke was that it promised something thrilling and delivered this naff old video instead – but I didn't think it was really mean-spirited in that way. I liked the fact that a lot of the people doing it seemed to be too young to remember 'Never Gonna Give You Up' the first time around. I guess that meant the song was reaching a different audience. Ultimately, it was just a laugh, a daft joke on the internet. I didn't think much more about it.

But it didn't go away. It got bigger and bigger and bigger. The YouTube figures for the 'Never Gonna Give You Up' video went through the roof. Eighteen million Americans were supposed to have been Rickrolled by 2008, although how they worked that figure out I've got no idea. It started turning up at sports games in America. Protesters outside the headquarters of the Scientology movement chanted the song. Politicians started making references to it: at one point, when Barack Obama was president, the White House – the actual fricking White House – Rickrolled people on Twitter.

Sometimes it seemed stupid. As a result of the attention caused by Rickrolling, I got nominated as the Best Act Ever at the MTV European Video Awards. Then it turned out that I'd won, apparently as the result of a public vote. I didn't go. I mean, it was funny, but I wasn't going to stand there and behave as if I actually deserved it. It would have been embarrassing. U2 had been nominated, and I knew at least one person from U2 was going to be there: Paul McCartney had won the Ultimate Legend Award, and Bono was presenting it to him. There was no way I was going to get on stage in front of Bono and pretend I was a better artist than him, or Green Day, or any of the other nominees. It was a joke, and I wasn't annoyed about it at all, but I didn't need to be part of the joke physically. Besides, Rickrolling was the kind of thing that could turn really negative – people could get sick of it, particularly if you seemed to be milking it for all it was worth. It was best to just let it run its own course. In the end, Perez Hilton accepted the award on my behalf, which I thought made a kind of sense: it's an internet phenomenon and so was he.

Still, you couldn't deny the effect that Rickrolling had on that song. It took a single from three decades ago and made it part of the modern landscape. The video's now had 1 billion views on YouTube, and it's been streamed on Spotify 800 million times, which is insane, and I'm really grateful for it. We're now sort of used to old songs suddenly becoming ubiquitous because they've gone viral for one reason or another – things like Kate Bush's 'Running Up That Hill' or 'Murder on the Dancefloor' by Sophie Ellis-Bextor – and, in a way, Rickrolling was one of the first times that happened. The song started getting used on movie soundtracks; you could see its effect in the audiences at shows, or in the crowd that turned up to see me if I played a festival, and even the fact that I got booked to play at certain festivals. On stage in America one night, I looked out at the front row and saw a line of teenagers, wearing T-shirts that spelled out NEVER GONNA GIVE YOU UP, a few letters at a time. They could hardly have been born when I retired from music, let alone when I was actually happening. I got the band to stop playing and started talking to them: 'What are you guys doing here? Did all your mums get sick and give you their tickets or something? Were you meaning to go and see Slipknot? Did you get dropped off at the wrong gig and think, "Well, we're here now, we might as well make the best of it"?'

I don't know how my career would have turned out without Rickrolling, but it would be stupid to say that it hasn't ultimately done me a lot of good. Pop music is a pretty ageist world and there's something really nice about kids discovering something for themselves, deciding whether they like it or not without worrying about how cool or uncool it's deemed to be, or what audience it's supposed to attract. And occasionally, something came up attached to Rickrolling that I thought sounded like a good idea. The Macy's Thanksgiving Day Parade was like that – they asked, I mentioned it to a few friends in America and they all freaked out, telling me what a big deal it was and that I absolutely had to do it.

I also did an advert for a car insurance company in America that was hilarious. It was a perfect recreation of the original video, with me at the end, complaining about Rickrolling still being a thing and a QR code that appeared onscreen: if you pointed your phone at it, it didn't take you to information about car insurance.

And that's the weirdest aspect of Rickrolling. It is still a thing. I assumed people would get sick of it after a few years, but no. That song just seems to have become an aspect of everyday twenty-first-century life. As an artist, you couldn't wish for any more than that, no matter how it happens. Fourteen years after the whole thing started, Greta Thunberg interrupted a speech she was making at a climate-change benefit show and began singing it. Around the same time, I was doing a Reddit chat with fans, when someone posted that they had a photo of us together, taken backstage when he was twelve. I thought that sounded really sweet, so I clicked on the link. I'm sure I don't need to tell you what happened next.

Chapter Thirteen

A couple of weeks before the Macy's Thanksgiving Day Parade, I'd been asked to take part in a benefit show at the rugby club in Warrington. A man called Garry Newlove had been murdered by a group of teenagers in the town, and his widow, Helen, wanted to set up a charity in his memory to provide opportunities for kids in the town. One of the ideas was to start a community radio station, and she wanted people with a connection to the area to take part, so she asked me and the comedian Peter Kay. There were only a few hundred people there but, like the apparently innocuous email from Andrew that alerted me to Rickrolling, it turned out to be the start of another very unlikely chain of events for me.

Peter was a huge star. He was supposed to be the compère, but whenever he tried to take a seat, he got mithered by people in the audience. So he ended up sitting on the stage throughout the whole thing. We sang 'Never Gonna Give You Up' together at the end, and he asked me if I'd do a guest appearance on his new TV show. It was a parody of TV talent shows, and Peter got a very Peter Kay-ish selection of people involved – he had Paul McCartney and the Cheeky Girls – and talked them into doing some fairly incredible things: Paul McCartney had to sing the theme tune of *Blankety Blank*. I got off fairly lightly, duetting a version of 'Something's Gotten Hold of My Heart' with one of the talent show's acts.

After that, Peter asked if I would be the opening act when he played a residency at the Manchester Evening News Arena: he was doing twenty nights there, calling it the Tour That Doesn't Tour Tour, the idea being that he wouldn't have to travel far, he could go home to Bolton and be with his family at the end of each show. But then demand for tickets was so crazy that he changed its name to the Tour That Doesn't Tour Tour – Now on Tour, added shows around the UK, and asked if I'd be the support act in London as well.

There was one condition: I couldn't tell anyone what I was doing. He wanted it to totally wrongfoot the audience on the first night – they would just walk in expecting to see a comedy show, they'd hear Peter's voice come over the sound system – 'Ladies and gentlemen . . .' – and I'd come on with my band. It sounded quite risky, but I remembered Elton John's guitarist Davey Johnstone telling me that, in the 1970s, they'd toured America with Billy Connolly as their support act. Admittedly, Billy Connolly later said he went down with Elton's audience 'like a fart in a spacesuit', but at least there was a precedent.

It went remarkably well. We did a medley of Manchester songs when we played in Manchester, which was hilarious – we had to segue from 'There Is a Light That Never Goes Out' by The Smiths into 'Back for Good' by Take That. We even slipped a new song into the set, a thing I'd written with Andrew Frampton called 'Lights Out'. It sounded completely different to the stuff people associated with me – it's quite arena rock, sort of like me and Andrew pretending to be Take That pretending to be Coldplay pretending to be U2 – but it got a really good reaction. We started seeing people sharing videos of it on social media. Sometimes, there was a bit of 'I didn't think I liked Rick Astley but . . .' attached, which was interesting: blokes saying they'd have gone to the bar when they realized I was the support act, but their wife forced them to sit through my set and they ended up enjoying the one new song I played.

And then Peter's tour became such a big deal – it ended up as the biggest-selling comedy tour in history – that the fact I was supporting him began attracting attention. Radio 2 started playing 'Lights Out'. It got on their A-list, the list of songs that the station's guaranteed to play a certain number of times every day, for seven weeks. Unwittingly becoming an internet meme and supporting a stand-up comedian on tour is definitely an odd way to reactivate a pop career, but it felt like something was happening. It's incredibly hard to get a new song on the radio, and I'd done it without really trying. I didn't even have a record deal.

And it didn't look like I was going to get one. I'd recorded a load of other songs at home, a whole album's worth of material, which sometimes turns up online called *My Red Book*

– trust me, I'm even more astounded than you are about the fact that there are people who collect Rick Astley bootlegs, but they seem to exist. Yet when Tops took the songs to a record label he thought would be interested, they didn't want to know. I don't mean they didn't like them; I mean they literally didn't want to know. The guy he spoke to said he wouldn't even listen to them. We tried putting out another track, 'Superman', ourselves, but without the Peter Kay connection making it newsworthy, it didn't really work. When we took it to radio, they started asking questions. 'What label's putting it out?' There isn't one. 'What's the plan for promotion?' There isn't one of those either. We'd effectively turned up at Radio 2 with a song on a CD and asked them to play it, and it doesn't really work like that. Tops thought about doing something with the tracks on his own label, Phonogenic. But I don't think he felt it would work. Phonogenic had a lot of young artists, like Natasha Bedingfield and The Script. I was older, I used to sound like this, now I sound like this – where did I fit in?

I went out on tour again, this time playing standing venues – I'd always played arenas or festivals or small seated clubs, never the kind of places where people spilled beer on you when they bumped into you – and it was great. I got to play my new songs to an audience, and insisted on doing a raffle midway through each show, giving away bottles of Brut aftershave, stupid things like that. In fact, I wanted to do a meat raffle, but it turns out running a meat raffle in the middle of a gig isn't allowed, in case you were thinking of doing one.

Still, it was hard not to think I'd come to a dead end, that if I wanted to do new music, it probably wasn't going to happen with Tops managing me. I sometimes wondered if he didn't push things enough, out of concern for me, because in the eighties he'd seen how sensitive I could be about things going wrong: 'Oh, if we do an album and it doesn't work, it'll knock him back, he'll feel embarrassed, he won't even want to do the eighties revival shows any more because he'll think people are laughing at him.' I could totally understand why he thought that – I had been like that back then, but I had been really young, and becoming famous when you're twenty-one doesn't give you a lot of space to grow up in. But now I was almost fifty, I'd had time off, I'd been a dad – Emilie was nearly an adult by now. I still had insecurities, of course, but I was a lot more grounded than I had been. Besides, what was another flop album? Depending on your definition of 'flop', I'd had somewhere between two and four of those already.

So I went to see Tops a few days before Christmas and told him I thought we should stop working together. It was a really hard thing to do emotionally, because we'd been through so much. He had always fought my corner, always looked out for my best interests; we'd shared some incredible times together, and some completely miserable ones. I ended up crying as I told him.

I knew it was the right thing to do, though. Unlike the time in the early nineties when I'd retired, I didn't feel as if I was leaving him in the lurch – he had his label. And it didn't really impact on our friendship. When Lene and I finally got married, after twenty-something years together, Tops was my best man. We did it on a whim, because Emilie asked one day: 'When are you two going to get married?' I made her get on the computer and check the available dates at the local registry office: they had one on a Saturday in a couple of weeks. I called Tops and asked what he was doing that day. Believe it or not, he stopped by on the way to judge a ju-jitsu competition in Birmingham. I thought that was a lovely thing. Not the ju-jitsu competition; him being there as my best man. It was all very low-key: we had the wedding, with Emilie and Tops and his wife Lesley, and Lene's best friend Tine; then we went out for lunch in Richmond, then Lene and I went to the cinema. We meant to have a big party at some point afterwards. That was ten years ago, and we still haven't got around to it yet.

In fairness, Lene and I have never got around to throwing that big post-wedding party because we've been incredibly busy. After Tops and I broke up, he started forwarding me the emails he would have dealt with as my manager. I remember looking at them that Christmas, while we were on holiday in Denmark, thinking: *What do I do with these?* They were offers from promoters and things like that. I didn't think it felt right to answer them myself, so I asked Lene if she'd help out. She replied to the emails, checked the contracts, booked the gigs, then asked me what I was going to do next. I told her I didn't really know – I was just happy doing the eighties revival shows. I said if she had any suggestions, I'd be pleased to hear them.

The thing about Lene is that she's kind of fearless; she simply makes things happen. Nothing seemed to faze her, whether it was turning up in England and talking herself into a job at a record company, or completely switching her career up and working in films. She had no hang-ups about the idea of me releasing new material. Maybe that was because she wasn't working at a record label and hearing the kind of negativity that floated around anything that didn't fit into their standard way of doing things: this artist is older than thirty, it's over, we'll never get it on radio, we're never going to get this to work, forget about it. She simply went for it. She contacted our friend Giles Martin and asked him if he knew anyone who could recommend some songs I could sing that would be suitable for my voice. He put her in touch with a publisher who sent her a bunch of tracks by different writers. She picked two of them, both by Chris Stapleton, who at that stage wasn't Chris Stapleton the multiple-Grammy-winning country superstar: he was Chris Stapleton, the jobbing Nashville songwriter. She suggested I record them, so I did, in the little studio I'd built at home. I loved the songs, but Chris's vocal delivery was so amazing, it was really hard to sing them myself. Still, Lene played the results to a couple of guys who worked for BMG in Germany, and they were really enthusiastic. They liked the songs and thought my voice sounded good. They wanted to know what our plan was.

We didn't have one. Lene suggested getting more jobbing songwriters involved, but I felt quite spurred on to write some more songs myself – perhaps that had been her plan all along. I started picking at it gradually, jotting things down, coming up with ideas, beavering away in my home studio, playing everything myself: drums, piano, guitars, the lot. I'm not the greatest musician in the world, but I really liked the way it sounded – there was a naturalness to it that was the opposite of getting a load of crack session musicians in. It was hard work, but in another way, it was easy. There was no real pressure. There was no record company breathing down my neck, no one worrying what the first single was going to be. I'd sometimes play a song or two to friends who were visiting and ask them what they thought, usually after everyone had had a couple of drinks. In fact, I did it so often to our friends Kevin and Jacqui that I started calling them my red wine A&Rs. And I didn't put any pressure on myself. I wanted the songs to be as good as possible, but beyond that, I wasn't bothered. I wasn't desperate to be more famous or to get back to where I had been in the eighties. I was perfectly happy doing the eighties shows. Besides, I'd found another creative outlet.

Perhaps 'creative outlet' is a bit strong for The Luddites, though. It was basically a bunch of forty-something men making a racket. It all started with a garden party that my friend Graham Stack was invited to. Graham's a songwriter and producer – he co-wrote 'On a Night Like This' for Kylie, among a load of other hits – although for years his main gig has been as the musical director of *The X Factor* and *The X Factor USA*, and *Britain's Got Talent* and *America's Got Talent*. I'd met him after I'd decided to bring my career to an end and was dabbling with the idea of becoming a professional songwriter. We tried writing some songs together in his little studio. The songs never came to anything, but we lived nearby and we always kept in touch. He told me a neighbour of his was moving to France, and he wanted to put a band together to play at his leaving party in his back garden. He asked me if I'd play drums and sing and I said yes. He said he'd find a bass player, and at our first rehearsal, in walked another neighbour of mine, Simon Mattacks. He didn't know I was going to be there; Graham had just told him he had a drummer who could sing a bit. Simon had said he could sing too, but when he saw me sitting behind the drum kit with my microphone, he suggested it was probably best if he left the vocals to me. We jammed through a set of punk songs – 'Should I Stay or Should I Go' by The Clash, stuff by the Sex Pistols – and things like The White Stripes' 'Seven Nation Army', The Hives' 'Hate to Say I Told You So' and 'Song 2' by Blur. We called ourselves The Luddites because there was absolutely no technology involved: if we couldn't jam through a song on guitar, bass and drums, we threw it out. It was just brilliant, a total riot. We couldn't work out why more people don't form an amateur punk band, but that's middle-aged men for you.

We played at the garden party and didn't want to stop, so we decided to do a charity gig at the local cricket club. We did it in fancy dress – we came on in orange boiler suits, like prisoners, chained together with plastic chains – and we supported ourselves: we called ourselves Cottage Pie and did acoustic, folky songs, sporting beards and white smocks. It was a hoot. More people heard about it, so we ended up playing a thousand-capacity theatre in Kingston called the Rose. Then Simon Moran got wind of it and booked us into the Shepherd's Bush Empire as a charity gig for the Nordoff–Robbins foundation. Chris Evans heard about it and mentioned it on his radio show and we nearly sold it out. It's ridiculous, but it's so much fun. Everyone who's ever seen The Luddites seems to have loved it – although perhaps not as much as The Luddites did – with the exception of one lady who saw us in Kingston and sent an email complaining afterwards: 'I thought I was coming to see Rick Astley and instead, I was met with this abusive, loud horrible music, with this foul-mouthed singer on the drums, who used disgusting language.' Erm, yeah: that *was* Rick Astley.

So I had my eighties gigs, and I had The Luddites to satisfy my baser urges. I was completely content. It also slowly became apparent that I was making a new Rick Astley album in the spare room off the kitchen. And, for the first time in my entire career, I was making exactly the album I wanted to – it had only taken me twenty-nine years to do that. The songs I was writing felt different, more personal. I certainly didn't sit down with the intention of writing something about my relationship with my dad and how I thought music had saved me, but the words sort of fell out of me, and that was 'Keep Singing'. That kept happening: I'd start writing something and realize I was writing about my past, or my tendency to bleak moods, or my career, how thankful I was to have survived being a successful pop star without too much damage.

Frankly, I didn't have any great ambitions for it. I liked the idea of doing something, aged fifty, that showed what I was capable of – not to anyone else, just to myself – which is why we ended up calling the album *50*. But everyone I played it to seemed to like it, even the people I hadn't given a couple of glasses of Malbec to first. Simon Moran thought it was great. We played some songs to BMG and they said they loved them. I was so lucky to be back with BMG; the team in the UK were amazing and showed a lot of faith in the record and me. I was also very lucky to have Lene as my manager.

I know how hard it is for women in the music industry

sometimes and I know that Lene felt she had to prove herself even more because she was my wife. I can tell you, without bias or favour, that without Lene, *50* would not have happened the way it did and you would not be reading this autobiography. She drove the whole thing, partly out of love but I also think partly because she thought the music and I deserved a shot.

Lene also put a team of independent people together to work on the promotion for the album. We asked a guy called Richard Perry, who did radio promotion, to come and have a listen. I liked the idea of him working on the album, because the first job he'd ever taken the reins on in promotion was getting 'Never Gonna Give You Up' out to radio stations. We had always had a hug and laughed about still being 'here' whenever we bumped into each other. Lene went to chat to him about the idea of getting involved and played him a couple of things. She has very good instincts about people and thought he was the right person for the job. He seemed a little surprised when the album began. I think he'd maybe turned up for old times' sake, not really expecting to have much interest in the music. When the album finished, he told me he thought he could get six tracks from it on the radio. I thought he was just being nice – being a radio plugger is all about convincing people, you have to have the gift of the gab, and Rich has definitely had that. He got six tracks from it on the radio.

Then radio shows and TV programmes wanted me to do interviews. I was genuinely astonished they wanted me in the building – there's a huge difference between getting Rick Astley on your show to talk about playing at an eighties festival and getting Rick Astley on to talk about his new album, just as there's a huge difference between playing a few new songs in among the big hits and expecting people to buy a whole album of new songs. They might love the music you made thirty years ago to death, but there's no guarantee whatsoever that it means they're going to feel the same about the music you're making now.

But they did genuinely seem interested. It probably didn't hurt that there was a kind of underdog story attached to it: this guy from the eighties who's been written off, or walked away, making an album at home, entirely off his own bat, and people liking it. The record label told me that *50* looked set to become a Top 10 album on pre-release orders alone. Bloody hell: the last time I'd had a Top 10 album, Margaret Thatcher had been prime minister and – if you want another indicator of how times had changed – Stock Aitken Waterman were the biggest thing in pop. Then the prediction of how it was going to do went from Top 10 to Top 3. Then it became a race for No. 1 that week, between me and Tom Odell. I've got be honest: I felt horrible. I really like Tom Odell – he's a fantastic songwriter. And while I obviously wanted a No. 1 album, I didn't like the idea of keeping a young artist like Tom Odell off the top of the charts. You know, I've had my fifteen minutes early on in my career, I already know what it feels like to have a No. 1 album, I can always sit back in my easy chair with my slippers on and relive that moment. Snatching it away from some guy in his twenties on his second album simply felt wrong.

It would have been easier if my sales had totally annihilated his, if I could have gone, 'Well, look, I sold 100,000 more than you,' but it was a proper knife-edge battle. One day Tom was doing better than me, the next, I was doing better than him. I started wishing there were two No. 1s: one for established artists and one for new artists. Exactly the same thing happened a few years later, with my album *Are We There Yet?*, which ended up locked in a battle for No. 1 with a young rapper called Ren. If anything, that was worse – he'd never even got in the charts before, his album was self-released, and he had a rare debilitating illness that meant he was too ill to promote it. What's more, I thought that what he was doing was truly original and brave: his music wasn't really like anything I'd ever heard before. I ended up posting a video on my social media telling my fans they should give him a listen, and another video when he did make No. 1 congratulating him.

In the end, though, *50* got to No. 1. I can't lie, it felt amazing. I'd finally made an album I was really proud of. I'd done it all myself. And it had gone to No. 1. If somebody had told me even a couple of years before that that was going to happen, I would have laughed at them. I was a lot more comfortable with being Rick Astley than I once had been, but the idea of releasing an album of my own songs, that I'd played every instrument on and produced myself, then watching it go to the top of the charts, would have been completely mad to me. Just after it was announced, I was at the studios of Magic FM, where I'd started presenting a little radio show on a Sunday afternoon. I enjoyed doing the show, I got to interview people who were real heroes of mine, like Stewart Copeland from The Police. When I came out of the studio where I'd been recording my show, the whole staff of the

company that owned Magic had lined up along the big stair-
well in the middle of the building. They started applauding
as I walked down, and they didn't stop until I'd left. I found
it incredibly moving. Because of the way things had worked
out with SAW – the backlash, the people shouting 'wanker'
in the street – I always basically assume that people think
I'm a bit of a twat, or, at best, a loveably naff figure, a charming reminder of an old era in pop. The idea that people were
impressed by what I'd done, the songs I'd written and what
they'd achieved, was kind of a new sensation, and it caught
me off-guard.

More importantly, *50* kept selling. It wasn't only die-
hard Rick Astley fans buying it; word had clearly got round
about it. Maybe the word that had got round was a bit like
the social media comments when I played 'Lights Out' at
the Peter Kay shows: 'I didn't think I liked Rick Astley, but
this is nothing like the music he's famous for – give it a
listen.' By the end of the month, it had gone platinum. I've
got a tendency towards self-deprecation and an inclination
to look on the gloomy side of things – you've probably
noticed – but even I was forced to admit that this was an
achievement. So was the fact that BMG told me, after its
release, that they started getting managers of older artists
coming for meetings and saying 'We want to do a Rick
Astley', or asking which producers and songwriters were
involved in *50*, so they could employ them on their next
album, not realizing that I'd done the whole thing myself.
They started signing more 'heritage' artists and doing really
well with them. I'm not for a minute suggesting that was
down to me or Lene, but the success of *50* was definitely

a signpost, showing people that it could be done, however improbable it seemed.

Whenever I started to get used to my new success, something would happen that made me go: *No, hang on, this is actually pretty fucking weird.* We were in Japan, playing at the Summer Sonic Festival, when our translator mentioned that he'd heard that the Foo Fighters were playing my music in their dressing room. I'm sorry: *What?* I'd heard about them doing a kind of Rickroll thing when the Westboro Baptist Church picketed one of their shows in Kansas City: there were a load of people standing outside the venue holding up homophobic signs, so the Foo Fighters drove past on a flatbed truck blaring out 'Never Gonna Give You Up', with one of their roadies – a huge tattooed guy – dancing in a pair of skimpy rainbow budgie-smugglers. 'Nothing says love like a little Rick Astley in your life,' Dave Grohl told the audience afterwards, and I was flattered and delighted: I'm a huge Foo Fighters fan. But it was one thing them using my music to troll a load of homophobic arseholes, another thing to be listening to it backstage at a festival.

Lene and I were on our way to see the Foo Fighters when the translator told me about their backstage soundtrack. I'd played earlier in the day and they were headlining. The Foo Fighters had said that any other artists on the bill who wanted to were welcome to watch their set from the side of the stage, which I thought was pretty cool. There was a big crowd of people there. We stood behind a barrier, with the rest of my band, having a few beers while getting a fantastic view of the show. At one point, in the middle of playing a song, their guitarist, Chris Shiflett, walked over and, spotting a friend in the crowd at the side of the stage, gave him a hug and walked away, still playing. I thought that was pretty cool as well.

A couple of songs later, we noticed Dave Grohl walking towards us, clearly intending on doing the same thing. I moved out of the way so that he could spot whoever it was he wanted to say hello to. He moved in the same direction that I did. I moved in the opposite direction, keen to get out of his line of vision. Dave Grohl moved in the opposite direction too. Shit. Now he was standing right in front of me. He stopped playing his guitar and reached his arms out to give me a hug. 'Hey,' he said. 'How you doin'? I'm Dave.'

'I know,' I said. 'I'm Rick.'

'I know,' he said, and walked off.

I looked at Lene and shrugged. *That's really sweet*, I thought: *Dave Grohl's just walked over to introduce himself in the middle of a song. What a lovely guy.*

About fifteen minutes later, a roadie came over to us. Holding a microphone, he moved the barrier between us and the stage. 'Dave wants you out front,' he said.

This time I looked at Lene with a panicked expression – *What the fuck is this about?* But I was so jet-lagged – and, frankly, tipsy – that I followed him, rather than asking him what was going on. I could hear Dave Grohl talking to the crowd, introducing me as 'our new best friend, Rick Astley'. My immediate thought was that he was going to talk about the Westboro Baptist Church and the Rickrolling thing. I was wrong. Dave Grohl gave me another hug and said, 'We're going to play "Never Gonna Give You Up", but it's going to sound like "Smells Like Teen Spirit".' The presence of the microphone in my hand indicated that I was going to be singing.

Well, OK, here goes nothing. I thought I'd better say something to the audience. Caught up in the moment, I screamed, 'COME ON YOU MOTHERFUCKERS!' There was a thud from the drum kit: Taylor Hawkins was heaving with laughter. They launched into their version of the song, which did indeed sound remarkably like 'Smells Like Teen Spirit'. It was completely bizarre and hugely enjoyable: really, really fun.

'Thank you!' I yelled at the end. 'That was fucking nuts!'

'Fookin' noots,' said Dave Grohl, in what was, I assumed, his impersonation of a Lancashire accent.

Afterwards, we piled into the band's buses and went to a party. Dave Grohl and I ended up chatting about drumming – it turned out his daughter was learning drums by playing along with AC/DC's *Highway to Hell*, like I had. He mentioned that there had been a famous festival in the 1970s called the California Jam – Deep Purple, Black Sabbath and Aerosmith had played there – the Foo Fighters were resurrecting it, and Queens of the Stone Age were performing as well. 'Hey!' he said. 'You should play there too!'

I nodded and thought: *Yeah, you've had a few. This has been a lovely evening, and an unforgettable moment in my career, but the conversation now appears to have tipped into the realm of drunken madness.* We left with a hug, and I didn't think any more about it, until a couple of months later when Lene got an email asking if I was still coming to perform with the Foo Fighters at the California Jam. Of course we went. I sang the version of 'Never Gonna Give You Up' that sounded like 'Smells Like Teen Spirit'. Dave Grohl told the audience that I was a 'badass motherfucker'.

The whole thing was, once again, fucking nuts, and I said so as I left the stage.

'Noots,' Dave Grohl agreed.

*

I'd heard from Jayne and my brothers that my dad wasn't well. He'd moved to a flat in North Wales, and he was still as difficult as ever. If I'd ever had a phone call from one of them saying, 'You'll never guess, recently he's turned into a different guy, he's desperate to speak to you,' then I probably would have gone to see him, but that wasn't the case. He just carried on being himself – he was on a path he couldn't deviate from emotionally. Instead, his behaviour was becoming erratic in a different way. One day, he turned up on my brother Mike's doorstep. Without any warning, he'd got in a taxi and told the driver to take him there. Mike lived outside Wigan, in a place called Appley Bridge. It was 90 miles from where my dad lived. Eventually, he moved into a home.

I was on tour in Spain when Jayne rang me to say that Dad had been taken really ill and they didn't think he was going to last another twenty-four hours. It was strange, I wasn't even really upset about it. It made me thoughtful, but my overriding feeling was 'what a shame': what could have been, what the possibilities were, how none of that had worked out. I supposed I'd already mourned my dad long before he died, when our relationship had finally broken down.

I prepared myself for the news that he'd died, but in fact he lasted months after that phone call. Again, I wondered if that was a sign, that, against the odds, I had a chance to go and see him. I thought about it a lot, and then decided not to. I didn't want to see him twenty-five years later as a decrepit old man. I had memories of my dad, nice memories, and I wanted to keep hold of them. I've talked about the super-negative side of him in this book, because I want to be honest, but I don't dwell on them in my everyday life. I just put them down to him being ill, in the same way that if someone was physically ill, you wouldn't base all your memories around their illness – you'd try to cling on to the other things about them, the good bits.

When he eventually died, I didn't feel in pain about it – as I said, I'd mourned him a long time ago, and I knew his death was only a matter of time. For a few months, I'd thought, *Well, it could be any day now*, and then one day it was. There wasn't a funeral. Jayne had talked about it with all of us: the home he was in had an option simply to have someone quietly cremated and then give you their ashes, and that's what we decided to do. Jayne kept Dad's ashes until all of us could get together for a kind of memorial.

Weirdly, we ended up having a memorial for my dad and a memorial for my mum on the same day. Mum had been ill for a long time; the last time I saw her, she had lost a lot of weight and looked really unwell, although she was still living in her house, looking after herself. Her death was from old age, really, maybe speeded up a little by a fall she'd had at home. I'd talked about buying her somewhere else to live, an assisted-living place, but she didn't want to leave her house. Not long after we thought we'd convinced her to move – and my sister Jayne had started looking at places for her – she went into hospital and never really came out. I was going to go and see her, but Jayne said she wouldn't know who I was.

I decided not to go; I didn't want to see her like that. I absolutely would have gone if she had known that I was there, but, as it was, the only reason to go was for my own benefit, and I didn't see what benefit there would be, seeing her in that sort of zombie state, where they're just keeping you alive for the sake of keeping you alive.

And, if I was being really, brutally truthful, I really wasn't sure how close I was to my mum anyway. I wasn't certain about anything with my mum. Frankly, she was a complete mystery to me – I simply didn't understand her, I couldn't get how her brain worked. I always kept in touch, although she never seemed particularly interested in talking to me and always sounded as if she wanted to get off the phone, which was depressing. I felt that I was only doing it because I thought I should. I tried to get her an iPad, to keep in contact with her kids and their families better, but I couldn't sell the idea. I told her it would be easy to use, and all of us would be able to send photos of her grandkids on it, but she just wasn't interested: 'They're only photos,' she said. I mean, what kind of grandparent doesn't want to see photos of their grandkids?

I've got happy memories of her – everything from watching old films with her when I was kid, to much later on, when I got her to come on stage with me at Haydock Park and play the piano when we did 'When I Fall in Love'. She was great – Mum was a brilliant pianist – and what's more she really bossed the band around in rehearsals, which I thought was hilarious. But the truth is that I felt I didn't really know her, even though I'd known her all my life. I never really understood what the problem was – maybe it was linked to losing a child when she was young, or maybe it had something to do with the unhappiness of her marriage to my dad – but there definitely was a problem there, and it was never fixed.

After she died, I went back up North. There's a place called Horwich, a town between Bolton and Chorley, and Mum's family had had a little cottage there when she was a girl, by the reservoir. She always loved it there, so my sister and brothers and I scattered her ashes in a stream nearby. Then we drove down to the cottage Dad had bought and never moved into near Clitheroe, and found a pub nearby. I asked the barman for five whiskies. He recognized me and asked me for a selfie. I said yes – he wasn't to know that I was in the middle of giving my dad a send-off, and I wouldn't have dreamed of telling him – and me and my brothers and sister laughed about it afterwards. But being asked for a selfie when you're on your way to scatter your dad's ashes felt a perfect symbol of how daft and meaningless fame is, how you can never get away from it, even when it's completely inappropriate. It's a strange thing. You owe your fans everything, really; they've given you the life you have, and the gratitude you have towards them is huge. But on the other hand, there's no escape from it, you can't switch it off when you want to, and that can be exhausting.

We took Dad's ashes to a river nearby. We drank our whiskies and I recited his favourite poem, 'Sea Fever' by John Masefield: 'I must go down to the seas again, to the lonely sea and sky / And all I ask is a tall ship and a star to sail her by.' I read the whole thing, even though I don't think Dad actually knew all the words; he'd just said the line about the tall ship and the star a lot, like a personal motto, maybe a reference to a freedom he wanted but never really had. When I reached the last line – 'a quiet sleep and a sweet dream when the long trick's over' – we poured the fifth whisky, my dad's, into the river.

It was a peculiar atmosphere. We were all crying, but kind of laughing at the same time. I think that's how we've always dealt with my dad, and the memory of him – with humour. For all his faults, he was a hilarious character. Whenever we talk about him we end up howling with laughter about him, and our upbringing and how fucking nuts it was. Perhaps the politest way to describe it is 'colourful'. What it wasn't was boring, and in a weird way, I've come to appreciate that. I'd prefer it if I hadn't inherited some aspects of my dad's temper, and his ability to slip into a dark mood, but there are things I inherited from my dad that I think are good. I want to do things for myself. If I find myself immersed in some huge DIY project that's got on top of me, that I realize too late I should probably have paid someone else to do, I know why I've done it: it's my dad's genes rearing their head again. I often send my sister or one of my brothers a text that says, 'Oh God, I've gone full Horace again.' They know exactly what I mean.

If I had the ability to change anything about my life, it would be my parents. I don't think they actively set out to be bad parents – who does? – but they weren't built to cope with it. I'd prefer to have been brought up by two more normal people, because my actual parents were so peculiar that I've been known to suggest they were a couple of aliens who fell to earth after their spaceship disintegrated over Newton-le-Willows. They had no idea of how to get back, so they tried to make the best of it and fit in, without much success.

But then I wonder what my life would have been like if

my parents had been normal. You don't know, do you? Would I have got so involved in music if I hadn't been desperate to get away from them and make a life of my own? I have no idea. And if I hadn't been involved in music, would I have been as happy as I am? In fact, if I hadn't been involved in music, then I wouldn't have met Lene, and we wouldn't have had Emilie, and they're the two most important things in my life . . . You can go on and on for ever, thinking like that, and I sometimes do. But it always comes back to the same thing: now, at least, I have a fantastic life. So perhaps it's best that I can't swap anything about the way I got there.

Chapter Fourteen

There was a knock on the door of my dressing room at *Top of the Pops*. It was February 1989, and I was on the show singing the title track of my second album, *Hold Me in Your Arms*. It was the last single I released with PWL. I'd already made the decision to leave, but I was still – just about – a Stock Aitken Waterman artist.

That made the request from my visitor when I opened the door all the more surprising. It was someone I didn't recognize, who said they were working with Morrissey. Morrissey was, apparently, wondering if he could come to my dressing room so he could have a photograph taken with me. What? I knew Morrissey was on the show as well – I'd watched him doing a run-through of his new single, 'The Last of the Famous International Playboys', but I'd done it from a very discreet distance. Generally speaking, indie musicians like Morrissey were not big Rick Astley fans. They thought I was a total twat, a mindless puppet sent out to do the evil bidding of Pete Waterman, who was intent on destroying everything they liked about music: a band called The Wonderstuff even had a song called 'Astley in the Noose'. So I really didn't think Morrissey would want to know I was a huge fan of his. He was a fairly mysterious character – he still is – but the one thing everyone knew for sure about him was that he had a very sharp tongue; he was always wishing death on people he didn't like in interviews, things like that. I didn't fancy being on the receiving end of that.

And now there was someone at the door telling me he wanted a photograph with me. Was this a joke? Why would Morrissey want that? Was he taking the piss? Did he want to come to my dressing room so he could tell me how awful he thought I was? I supposed there was only one way to find out, so I said of course he could.

It wasn't exactly a great meeting of minds. Morrissey seemed quite shy and I was absolutely baffled as to what was going on, but he seemed perfectly nice: quiet, but friendly enough. I told him I was a fan, but I left out some of the gory details – I decided not to mention having stalked his former bass player around Manchester. He didn't explain why he wanted a photo, but we had our picture taken together – a Polaroid, sitting on a sofa, both grinning at the camera. And that was that: he was in and out of there in five minutes.

I never thought about it much again – it was just another peculiar meeting from the years I was a big pop star, like the one with Ozzy Osbourne. I was waiting in the bar of the Sunset Marquis in LA for a car to pick me up, and a very distinctive Brummie accent shouted out, 'Hey! You're that

What's-his-name kid, aren't you?' It was Ozzy – who looked as if he'd had a few – beckoning me over to the table where he was sitting with his wife Sharon, and an ever-growing collection of empty glasses. He started asking me if I was going on tour, and told me if I was, to give him a call: 'You'll need musicians,' he said, nodding, 'and I've worked with the greatest musicians in the world – I'll put you in touch.'

I was about to thank him, when Sharon suddenly leaned over and gave him a slap across the head. 'Don't be so stupid, Ozzy!' she snapped. 'He doesn't want any of your long-haired, tattooed monsters playing for him! He's a nice young boy! Leave him alone!'

You just file these things away somewhere in a mental box labelled 'My Weird Life': Ozzy Osbourne offered to help me put a band together and then his wife thumped him and told him to shut up; Morrissey wanted a Polaroid with me at *Top of the Pops*. But the Morrissey photo turned up again, years later: he used it as the cover of a re-release of 'The Last of the Famous International Playboys', when David Bowie's estate wouldn't let him use a photo of them together. It was funny, I'd forgotten that Morrissey and I had near-identical haircuts at the time – we were at completely different ends of the musical spectrum and yet we almost looked as if we could be in a band together. When the *NME* asked me about it, I told them how much I loved The Smiths and said that I'd like to do a gig in Manchester where I only played songs by them. Then I realized how ridiculous that sounded and added that if I did, people would probably throw up or smash the venue in up in disgust.

And then I met the indie band Blossoms at the reopening

of the Manchester Arena. In 2017, a terrorist had blown himself up at an Ariana Grande concert there, killing twenty-two people: kids who'd gone to see a pop show, parents who were waiting to pick them up, staff at the venue. There was a plan to build a memorial to those who died, and the venue reopened with a benefit concert to raise funds. Many of the artists who played were local: Blossoms come from Stockport, The Courteeners and Noel Gallagher come from the city itself, and Newton's only about 20 miles away. Peter Kay appeared as well. He used to work as an usher at the Arena, as he's always keen to remind people. I was once performing there, as part of an eighties tour and, in the middle of a song, the audience started going nuts for no reason at all as far as I could see. Peter, who must have been at the gig, had come on stage behind me, without warning, dressed in one of the yellow jackets that the ushers wear, and was wandering around, as if he was inspecting the stage or something.

The Arena reopening gig was a fantastic night. It was a real honour to be asked. It was incredibly emotional, of course, but it was also really good fun. When I was doing the eighties shows, I'd got into the habit of graffitiing my own dressing-room sign: I'd write underneath my name so that instead of saying RICK ASTLEY it now said RICK ASTLEY IS A TIT. It had become a kind of running joke at those gigs. It was a daft, piss-taking thing to do to kill the time backstage. I did it to my dressing-room sign at the Manchester Arena and didn't think any more about it until I saw Noel Gallagher's security guy quietly ripping down the sign with my name on it – presumably in case I saw it and became offended – and I had to go and sheepishly tell them that I'd graffitied it myself.

Later, Noel Gallagher told me he'd had a bollocking from the guy: he'd burst into his dressing room and accused him of bullying other acts on the bill. When he said he didn't know what they were talking about, they said someone had written an abusive message on Rick Astley's dressing-room door and they assumed it was him; Noel's always been known for his forthright opinions about other artists.

There was a bit of a party in Noel's dressing room after the show and I got chatting to Blossoms. They told me they'd started their own podcast, just them sitting in Stockport, talking about whatever was on their minds, sometimes with a special guest, and they asked me if I wanted to come on: you had to pick your five favourite songs from Manchester. I chose New Order's 'Blue Monday', 'Supersonic' by Oasis, 'Ever Fallen in Love' by Buzzcocks, 'Love Will Tear Us Apart' by Joy Division and 'Please, Please, Please Let Me Get What I Want' by The Smiths. The guys in Blossoms loved The Smiths too, and we ended up talking about how unlikely it was that The Smiths would ever re-form, or that Morrissey or Johnny Marr would ever do a gig where they only performed Smiths songs. I told them about seeing a Smiths tribute band called The Smyths at the Half Moon pub in Putney, and how I thought it was a shame that they were only playing to 200 people – they were really good – and how amazing it would be to hear a set of Smiths songs at a bigger show. And that somehow ended up with an invitation to come to their rehearsal room in Stockport and . . . work up a set of Smiths songs for a gig, with Blossoms playing and me singing.

After that meeting, I got back in touch with Blossoms and said that if they were having second thoughts, it was fine with me. I knew it would be a controversial thing to do, as Smiths fans are very precious about the band and their music. Any backlash from it didn't matter to me at all – you know, I'm in my fifties, I've got a really established career; people can say whatever they want about me and it's not a problem, I'm past worrying – but I felt quite protective of Blossoms: they were having hit albums and selling out tours, but they were still a young band, and a young alternative band at that. I didn't want to get them involved in anything that was injurious to their reputation. But no, they definitely wanted to do it.

Here's the first thing I learned at the rehearsals: Smiths songs are bloody difficult to perform. Everyone knows that Johnny Marr is an astonishing guitarist, and that Smiths songs have these amazingly intricate and inventive guitar parts – he's just one guy, and yet he sounds like five guitarists playing at once. But it's more than that. The Smiths' rhythm section – Andy Rourke and Mike Joyce – were incredible. Their songs have really unusual structures; they're not merely verse-chorus-verse, they're all over the place. And I know every word to every Smiths song, and, like every Smiths fan, think I can do a pretty good Morrissey impersonation after a couple of drinks, but his lyrics are really, really hard to sing properly. They're complex and they're clever and every word matters: something like Cemetery Gates is ridiculous. The line about the sun doing salutations to the dawn – you try singing that and not sounding like you're busking it. We occasionally took to having a quick drink in the rehearsal studio before trying something particularly tricky, and that definitely seemed to help.

To announce the gigs, I sang a couple of Smiths songs

with Blossoms as an encore at their show at the Forum in London. We were going to do two nights, one in London and one in Manchester. The reaction was as mad as I expected it to be. Lene and I sat in bed the morning tickets went on sale, killing ourselves laughing at the responses on social media, both good and bad. If you were old enough to remember the late eighties, the idea of Rick Astley singing Smiths songs was quite a difficult thing to conjure with. A few people were really upset, they thought it was sacrilege, and I totally got that. And at least they expressed it in a funny way: 'Has someone been stealing ideas from Alan Partridge?'; 'What next? Shakin' Stevens and The Charlatans perform the songs of The Fall?'

Most people, though, seemed to be really happy for precisely the reasons I was: they wanted to see the songs live and got that it was a homage, not a joke. The gigs were fantastic, really joyous, a celebration, the whole audience singing along. We unexpectedly got the seal of approval from Morrissey. His nephew came to the gig in Manchester, met us backstage for a drink afterwards and told us he thought it was a nice thing to do, and the next day, Morrissey posted a photo his nephew had taken at the gig and put a message on his website thanking us, with the headline, 'If there's something you'd like to try – Astley, Astley, Astley', which I thought was fantastic.

The shows with Blossoms were amazing, and I loved that we ended up becoming good friends who hang out together – the age gap between me and the band members didn't seem to matter at all. And the fact that we did them in the first place – had some crazy idea and went 'sod it, let's do it' – was evidence of a change in how I thought about my career. I'd spent most of the late eighties doing what I was told. As an artist I'd been fitted in a box, and I was supposed to keep within that box. It was very successful, I'm incredibly grateful for that success, and I had some unbelievable experiences, but, I've got to be honest: it hadn't been fun.

Somewhere between the eighties revival shows, doing The Luddites and releasing *50*, I'd worked out that you could enjoy yourself, and you could do what you wanted to do. I made the follow-up to *50*, *Beautiful Life*, in exactly the same way – only me, playing everything, in the studio that's off our kitchen – and when that was a Top 10 hit too, I realized I'd got to a certain point in my career where I was just part of the wallpaper, and with that came a kind of acceptance that goes beyond what anyone used to think about you, or the artist you're supposed to be. At my shows, if I wanted to interrupt playing the hits on stage in order to get behind a drum kit and do a version of AC/DC's 'Highway to Hell', I could. What's more, the audience seemed to love it as well. If Mary Berry mentioned that she'd always wanted to play the drums when I appeared on her cooking show, I could get her on stage with us at Camp Bestival and let her bash the hell out of the kit while I sang *Beautiful Life*'s title track. And if the BBC wanted me to do their New Year's Eve concert at the Roundhouse in London, and I thought it would be fun to bring Rylan Clark on stage with me to sing a kind of homoerotic duet version of 'You Spin Me Round (Like a Record)', I can do that as well. The audiences always seem to love things like that – it's good to give them something unexpected. Sharleen Spiteri from

Texas duetted 'Ain't No Mountain High Enough' that New Year's Eve with me too and I loved it. Talented people are so easy to hang out with, whereas it's usually drama with the not-so-talented ones.

If Lene and I knocked together a video for a new single on her iPhone, that was fine, and if, during lockdown, I felt like posting a video of myself pressure-washing the wheelie bins in our garden while dancing to Dua Lipa's 'Don't Start Now', that was apparently more than fine. One minute I'd be supporting Take That or touring around America with New Kids on the Block, the next I'd be singing 'Barbarism Begins at Home' with Blossoms or performing 'The Lady Is a Tramp' and 'The Way You Look Tonight' in a bow tie, with an orchestra, at the Royal Albert Hall. It felt as if there was a real freedom to what I did now.

That's how I ended up on stage in Hamburg, with a cardboard box on my head, singing an industrial metal song called 'Paint Is My World'. It was something that Simon from The Luddites and I had written as a joke: it sounds a bit like Rammstein, but with the theme from the kids' TV show *Rainbow* in the middle of it. Simon had come on tour with me for a week around Europe, and somehow the idea of actually performing it with the band came up. We simply went for it: I can't really remember what the cardboard box had to do with it, but it must have seemed like a good idea at the time. Simon stood on stage, holding a pot plant and singing the lyrics in German. What made it even funnier was that the backing musicians who had worked with Take That on the tour where I supported them had turned up to see the show – they were playing in Hamburg the same night with

ELO. I could see them up on the balcony in the venue, look-ing completely bewildered about what was going on: 'Why's he playing a heavy metal version of the theme tune from *Rainbow* in Germany, where they don't know what *Rainbow* was? Who's the guy with the pot plant?'

It was on the same tour that we came up with a funk song called 'Cycling Through Belgium', which I performed in Brussels, riding a bike around the stage. And then there's 'Monkey Shit and Gravel Dirt', which came out of a rehearsal in Wandsworth: Our keyboard player Rob started playing a couple of chords and I began singing 'monkey shit and gravel dirt' – just nonsense words – along to them. We ended up with a kind of epic stadium rock ballad, with a massive guitar solo in the middle of it, and I decided we could play that live as well. The band thought I was joking, but I'm pleased to inform you that we've subsequently played it at some of the biggest venues in Britain. I like the idea that you come and see Rick Astley, expecting to hear 'Never Gonna Give You Up' and 'Together Forever' – which I probably should em-phasize you definitely are going to hear, by the way, in case you're reading this and reconsidering the wisdom of buying tickets for my next tour – and you end up listening to 'Mon-key Shit and Gravel Dirt'. And I also like the idea of doing things for no other reason than I can, because for a long time, I couldn't. God bless my fans, because they seem to be on board with it too.

We spent the Covid lockdown the same way as everyone else did – stuck at home, wondering when it was going to end, looking at a schedule full of cancelled gigs and festivals, either glued to the news or trying not to watch when the news became too much. It was only me and Lene at home. Emilie had moved to Denmark, where she had her own garden design business and a fiancé who'll be her husband by the time you read this. We banged pots for the NHS, but that seemed a bit of a feeble way to say thank you for everything they were doing. After it was over, we played free gigs at Wembley and at the Manchester Arena for key workers. There had always been a running joke in The Luddites that we'd play at Wembley one day, so I brought them with me to that show: KT Tunstall was opening for me and she 'rocked' 'Highway to Hell' with us.

*

One of the festival appearances that had been cancelled due to Covid was Glastonbury. I was astonished they'd asked me to play in the first place, and more astonished still when they repeated the offer after the festival returned, in 2022. I made a short documentary for the BBC about playing there, and you can see me laughing in disbelief as I get out of the car backstage. It was partly because the closest I'd been to Glastonbury in the past was dropping Emilie off outside, or watching it on TV, and you can't really get a sense of the sheer scale of the festival from either of those things: it's ridiculously big, the size of a city, complete with suburbs. But it was mostly because I was Rick fricking Astley and, however much Glastonbury had changed over the decades, and whatever the impact had been of Rickrolling and the Peter Kay shows and the success of *50* and everything else that had happened over the past ten years, it still seemed faintly ridiculous that I was there. There was definitely something incongruous about it – that was obviously why the BBC wanted to make a little documentary about it, and why so many radio and TV shows wanted me to talk about my forthcoming performance.

We spent the Friday going to see a few bands. We watched The Hives and Texas. Watching Sharleen work the stage was both amazing – Texas went down really well – and slightly daunting: it somehow brought it home that I had to get on the same stage the next day. The Foo Fighters were the surprise guests, so we went and saw them, then hung out with them again backstage. Paul McCartney was backstage too: Dave Grohl is friends with him, so we all sat around and chatted. I've met Paul McCartney a couple of times and he's lovely, just one of the guys. But it doesn't matter how many famous people you meet, there's always something about encountering an actual Beatle that makes you go 'fucking *hell*' – although not out loud, obviously.

We were playing on Saturday lunchtime, the first act of the day. By late morning, my surprise at being invited to play had turned into a different emotion entirely. I was terrified. I'd played plenty of festivals in recent years, but you can't get past the fact that Glastonbury is different: it's the biggest festival in the world, it attracts more attention, it's got something about it that sets it apart from everything else. But my nerves were rooted in feelings a bit more straightforward than that. Looking out from the wings of the Pyramid Stage a short while before I was due on, I couldn't help noticing there was absolutely nobody there waiting for me to start. *Shit*, I thought, *I've finally done it. I've pushed it too far. I've discovered where the limits of this so-called comeback are, and they're here, in an empty field in Somerset, in front of the BBC cameras that are broadcasting this thing live. What made me think that I could do this?*

I must have said something to that effect out loud, because Emilie, who was over from Denmark and steaming my suit for me backstage, told me to calm down and just enjoy myself, whatever happened. It was really good advice. If you're going to play Glastonbury, there's not a lot of point in walking on stage uncertain about what you're doing, thinking, *Hmm, not sure about his – well, we'll see how it goes.* You have to go out there absolutely raring to go, like a tiger, or, at least, your version of what a tiger is. I had to gee myself up. A pre-gig shot of Jägermeister with the band backstage helped.

But even gee'd and Jägermeister-ed up, the noise from the crowd as I walked on stage knocked me back. I have no idea how it happened, but 80,000 people seemed to have materialized out of nowhere in the space of about twenty minutes. More importantly, they seemed pleased to see me, as if Rick Astley appearing at Glastonbury was the most normal thing on earth: they didn't seem to have got the memo that SAW pop stars from the eighties weren't supposed to be there. It was incredible, and it got better and better. By the end of the set, when I did 'Never Gonna Give You Up', the crowd seemed to stretch as far as I could see. The security guards at the foot of the stage got into a line and started doing a synchronized dance routine. The whole thing felt unreal, as if I was having some kind of out-of-body experience.

The same afternoon, Blossoms and I played a Smiths set unannounced on the Woodsies Stage. It was meant to be secret – it wasn't listed in the official running order – but word had clearly got around. The crowd was so big, it spilled out of the tent: there were so many people outside, listening. Inside, it was swelteringly hot and completely euphoric: when we played 'There Is a Light That Never Goes Out', you could hardly hear the band over the audience singing along. The Pyramid Stage, the Smiths set – all of it was incredible.

The next morning, I was on the BBC again. The interviewer asked me if being a hit at Glastonbury meant I was, officially, cool. It was a good question, if you thought about it. The fact that I'd gone down so well definitely seemed to be an indication that old, long-standing notions of what was and wasn't deemed cool and acceptable didn't really hold true in the twenty-first century, and so, I suppose, did the fact that not everyone turning up to my gigs was old enough to remember my eighties hits first-hand, or the fact that a band like Blossoms were happy to work with me, or that Morrissey had given the Smiths shows the thumbs up. I definitely felt I was a bit more accepted than I had been, and playing at Glastonbury seemed to underline that, on a scale that not even I could argue with: Yeah, Rick Astley's allowed here – that's fine.

But I just shrugged. 'As big and as amazing as Glastonbury is, it still ain't going to make me cool,' I said, and then told the interviewer I didn't really care, I was loving every minute of my career these days, and I had so much going on that I didn't need to worry about being cool any more.

I genuinely meant it. There was a huge amount going on. I released *Are We There Yet?* a few months after Glastonbury. It was the third album in a row I'd made alone, at home, and

I thought it was more American-sounding than its predecessors. I'd been in the States for months with the New Kids on the Block tour before I made it and maybe that affected its tone. Fifty-six dates and 22,000 miles across America, playing places I'd never heard of, but which seemed to have huge arenas filled with New Kids on the Block fans, cities like Edinburgh in Texas, right down at the border with Mexico. I think that certainly had an impact.

One of the songs, 'Driving Me Crazy', definitely had its roots in that trip to the States: there's a line in it that goes, 'Sometimes I question why we're here / Just holding your hand takes away my fear', which came out of Lene and me getting caught in an actual tornado while we were travelling between gigs in Minneapolis and Milwaukee. It was the whole, full-on thing, like you see in disaster movies – tornado alerts blaring out of your iPhone; having to seek shelter in the storeroom of a petrol station; a guy rushing in at the last minute, completely drenched, because it had blown out all the windows in his vehicle; coming out afterwards to find the storm had turned an eighteen-wheeler truck over on its side. It was terrifying. Lene and I just sat in this storeroom, holding hands really tightly, looking into each other's eyes, and that's where that lyric comes from.

Some people thought the album's title had a kind of finality about it – 'are we there yet?' is something you say towards the end of a journey – but the only thing that was really final about it was that I'd promised myself I wasn't going to make another album that way in future. I've loved doing it. I love the fact that I can get out of bed, grab a coffee, walk straight into the studio at ten past seven in my pyjamas, pick up a guitar and have a song going by a quarter to nine or whatever, but it's incredibly time-consuming, really hard work: I mean, I'm not exactly digging ditches for a living, but you know what I mean. And I think I'd like to try something different. Then again, I'm not that keen on getting in a room with other songwriters and producers. I tried working with some quite big-name songwriters after I made *50*, and it felt as if the music became more theirs than mine. Sometimes, you get the sense they've arrived with a song basically written, and your only role is to make the odd suggestion. You play them some ideas you've got, they go, 'Great, that's fantastic,' you go and put the kettle on and, by the time you get back, your ideas have been put to one side, and you're working on the song they've prepared in advance. That's fine – I suppose it's what they're paid to do: come up with a hit – but I think I'd like to do a proper collaboration, where you share the reins 50:50 with another artist or a band. I've met a lot of people over the past five or ten years who have shown me quite a lot of respect, which is something that never really happened back in the day, so maybe it would work with one of them.

Then again, there's every chance that I'll change my mind completely and make another record at home. I'm not really sure what the future holds. Part of me would genuinely like to go to university and get a proper education. I'd like to do a degree in Classical studies: I can see myself in a tweed suit, riding a bicycle with a basket on the front of it, studying Ancient Rome. And another part of me thinks: *Rick, you idiot, what are you thinking? You haven't even got any O-Levels – you sat there eating Polos and staring out of the window, remember? Just because* Spartacus *is your favourite film and you've read a few books about history doesn't mean you can do a degree in Classical studies.* Lene and I have talked a lot about retiring to Italy. Emilie lives in Denmark, with her partner, so there's nothing really keeping us in Britain. I keep thinking we should really do that soon – we can't wait another fifteen years, because we'll be too knackered to do it then. But at the moment it's still only something we're toying with.

So, I don't know. If my career's taught me anything, it's that things never quite work out the way you think they're going to. I signed up with SAW, this production team that made records like 'You Spin Me Round' and 'Say I'm Your Number One' – cool, clubby pop music – and by the time I actually made a record with them, they were something entirely different: this ultra-commercial pop machine, the Hit Factory. They thought they were making completely disposable music for Tracey and Dave to dance to on a Friday night, but nearly forty years later, I sometimes look out at the audience when I'm singing and you can see how much those songs still mean to people. They've been through the tumble dryer of life and gone back to this music that really struck them when they were young, that makes them think of their last day at school, or the first time they kissed the person they've been married to for thirty years. It can get a bit emotional sometimes. I have to remind myself: 'Don't start doing that – you're not here to cry, you're here to sing the songs.' They weren't really supposed to mean anything, and yet they've obviously ended up meaning something.

I thought I'd be happier if I had more control over what I was doing, and I ended up quitting music entirely. I thought I'd quit music entirely, and I ended up making music again. I thought everyone felt I was a complete twat, and I ended up with people calling me a national treasure, whatever one of those is – I'm not really sure, but it's definitely an improvement on being a complete twat. I thought I was just dealing in nostalgia and I ended up at No. 1 with a new album that I wrote, played and produced myself. There's an old clip of me on YouTube being interviewed in the late eighties, very hesitantly telling the interviewers I'd like to write more of my own songs, but if you'd informed young Rick how *50* would eventually work out, I can tell you for a fact, he wouldn't have believed you. 'The thing is, Rick, you're going to end up playing Glastonbury, singing Smiths songs with an alternative rock band': the lad in the denim shirt would have assumed you were taking the mick out of him.

None of it worked out the way I thought it would, but it all worked out fine. If there's a lesson in there, it's that you can't know what's going to happen.

Unless you're singing about whether or not you're going to give someone up, you can never say never.

Acknowledgements

In the writing of this book, I've realized there would never be enough space to mention all the amazing people I have worked with. I have so many fun and special memories . . . but maybe that's for another book!

Everyone below played a part in where I am today and I wouldn't be here without all of them. So, with much love, thank you to: Simon Merry; Jay Cox; Adam Evans; Rob Taggart; Dawn Joseph; Lauren Johnson-Reynolds; Adetoun Ayoola; Andrea Grant; Tori Lucion; Samantha White; Luke Barrett; Sara Ferrero; Sam Parker; Benji Bannister; Ali Pike; Jamie Cowlin; Lewis Underwood; James Sharpe; Emma Herdman; Ellie Mead; Peter Neill; Eva Martin; Edie Dawson; Oli Crump; Matteo Cifelli; Speth Hughes; Julian Bishop; Annette Stevenson; Julian Hickman; Dave Preston; Kevin Sefton; John Pryer; Barnsley Grain; Lewis White; Tony Gittins; Reuben Warnes; Toby Plant; Bob Knight;

Jim Knight; Barnaby Dickinson; George Hogg; Malcolm Edmonstone; Marius De Vries; Steve Sidwell; John Thirkel; Phil Smith; Gloria Robakowski; Sylvia Mason James; Nat Augustin; Pam Morre; Charlie Morgan; Roland Kerriage; Harry Morgan; Anthony Clark; Les Nemes; Patrick Howley; Simon Mattacks; Graham Stack; Mark 'Scooby' Widdowson; Pete Faint; Simon Gaulding; Amy Power; Scarlett Wilde; Richard Brook; Jonathan Atkinson; John Maul; Toby Chapman; Stelios Kalisperides; Ray Fensome; Steve Power; Doug Harper; Simon Bates; Paul 'Harry' Harris; Paul Christmas; Dave Ital; Neville Malcolm; Chris Dagley; Jez Frank; Simon Thorpe; Mike Bradley; Chris Brown; Will Hopper; Peter 'Pep' Dale; Kevin 'Neddy' Needham; Phil Bond; Geoff Spencer; Chris York; Barry Dickins; Sarah Mattheson; Dan Frampton; Chris Evans; John Stevens; Victoria Newbold; Chris Organ; Mark Walker; Richard Weitz; Marc Geiger; David Levy; Francesca Blackburn; Ella Street; Ugne Sebekaite; Adela McBrine; Lucy Dickins; Kirk Sommer; Jackie and David Heartfield; Hartwig Masuch; Fred Casimir; Dominique Kulling; Alistair Norbury; Gemma Reilly Hammond; Sam Hill; Louise Hart; Dan Baxter; Holly Barringer; Warul 'Woz' Islam; Jo Power; Laura Ohnona; Andy Prevezer; Kevin McCabe; Mikkel Bjergsø; Ian Clark; Roma Madden.

I want to give an enormous thank you to all the amazing staff at SJM Concerts, BMG and WME agency for all their hard work and constant support over the years.

From the moment I met the Pan Macmillan team in the reception of WME, I had a really good feeling about our meeting. It was better than expected. Since agreeing to do the book together, the encouragement, warm guidance and excitement along the way, from the entire team, has never waned. A special thank you to Sara Cywinski, who never openly doubted me or my story, even when I did. And thank you, thank you, thank you to Lydia Ramah, Poppy North, Josie Turner, Jamie Forrest, Andy Joannou, Helen Hughes, Siobhan Hooper, Lucy Hale, Melissa Bond and Laura Marlow, plus Stuart Dwyer and the entire sales force.

Another special thank you to Simon Mattacks, for his patience and guidance in taking on the daunting task of producing my audiobook recording.

And a final very special thank you to Matilda Forbes Watson, who has brilliantly put this project together with Pan Macmillan and always made me feel totally secure.

If you are reading this and your name isn't here but should be, I'm sorry . . . Drinks on me next time x

Picture Credits

All images from author's personal collection, unless stated below.

Plate Section 1
p. 4, Bjorn Borg © Landmark Media/Alamy Stock Photo
p. 5, Rick sitting in suit © Paul Cox
p. 5, Lene and Rick at BMI Awards © Shutterstock
p. 5, Rick with Marti Pellow © Mirrorpix/Shutterstock
p. 6, 'Well Done Rick Astley' © Trinity Mirror/Mirrorpix/Alamy Stock Photo
p. 6, New York © Peter Carrette
p. 7, Rick putting up curtains © Lene Bausager
p. 7, Rick and Tops at A&M © Lene Bausager
p. 8, 1988–9 world tour stage © Lene Bausager
p. 8, mirror costume change © Lene Bausager

Plate Section 2
p. 1, Prince's Trust © Terry O'Neill
p. 1, Rick with Princess Diana © Alpha Press Photo Agency
p. 1, Rick with Prince William © Aaron Chown/Getty Images
p. 3, Are We There Yet? crew on stage © Oli Crump
p. 3, crew and band at rehearsal © Peter Neill
p. 3, KT Tunstall performance © Peter Neill
p. 4, New Kids on the Block tour © Paris Visione
p. 4, Rick with Take That © Jamie Lucas
p. 4, Rick with A-ha © Duncan Barnes
p. 4, Swinging Christmas © Kamyar Ghanbari
p. 5, Rick with Dave Grohl © Jenn Five
p. 5, The Luddites © Lene Bausager
pp. 6–7, Glastonbury images © Peter Neill
p. 8, Lene and Rick at Royal Albert Hall © Peter Neill
p. 8, new BMG © Peter Neill
p. 8, Rick with Simon Moran and Peter Kay © Lene Bausager
p. 8, Rick with Jimmy Jam and Richard Weitz © Lene Bausager